Breathe Strong, Perform Better

Alison McConnell, PhD

Human Kinetics

Library of Congress Cataloging-in-Publication Data

McConnell, Alison, 1961-
    Breathe strong, perform better / Alison McConnell.
        p. cm.
    Includes bibliographical references and index.
    ISBN-13: 978-0-7360-9169-5 (soft cover)
    ISBN-10: 0-7360-9169-6 (soft cover)
    1. Breathing exercises. 2. Muscles. I. Title.
    RA782.M33 2011
    613'.192--dc22

                                    2010051950

ISBN-10: 0-7360-9169-6 (print)
ISBN-13: 978-0-7360-9169-5 (print)

Acquisitions Editor: Peter Murphy; **Developmental Editor:** Leigh Keylock; **Managing Editor:** Laura Podeschi; **Assistant Editor:** Elizabeth Evans; **Copyeditor:** Pat Connolly; **Indexer:** Betty Frizzéll; **Permission Manager:** Martha Gullo; **Graphic Designer:** Joe Buck; **Graphic Artist:** Tara Welsch; **Cover Designer:** Keith Blomberg; **Photographer (cover):** PASCAL PAVANI/AFP/Getty Images; **Photographer (interior):** Julie Arthur; **Photo Production Manager:** Jason Allen; **Art Manager:** Kelly Hendren; **Associate Art Manager:** Alan L. Wilborn; **Illustrations:** © Human Kinetics, unless otherwise noted; **Printer:** McNaughton & Gunn

We thank The West Hants Club in Bournemouth, Dorset, UK, for assistance in providing the location for the photo shoot for this book.

Human Kinetics books are available at special discounts for bulk purchase. Special editions or book excerpts can also be created to specification. For details, contact the Special Sales Manager at Human Kinetics.

Printed in the United States of America   10   9   8   7   6   5   4   3   2   1

The paper in this book is certified under a sustainable forestry program.

Human Kinetics
Web site: www.HumanKinetics.com

United States: Human Kinetics
P.O. Box 5076
Champaign, IL 61825-5076
800-747-4457
e-mail: humank@hkusa.com

Canada: Human Kinetics
475 Devonshire Road Unit 100
Windsor, ON N8Y 2L5
800-465-7301 (in Canada only)
e-mail: info@hkcanada.com

Europe: Human Kinetics
107 Bradford Road
Stanningley
Leeds LS28 6AT, United Kingdom
+44 (0) 113 255 5665
e-mail: hk@hkeurope.com

Australia: Human Kinetics
57A Price Avenue
Lower Mitcham, South Australia 5062
08 8372 0999
e-mail: info@hkaustralia.com

New Zealand: Human Kinetics
P.O. Box 80
Torrens Park, South Australia 5062
0800 222 062
e-mail: info@hknewzealand.com

E5113

To my parents, Ian (deceased) and Audrey. If it's true that we are products of our genes and our upbringing, then this book is as much your achievement as it is mine. Thanks for giving me such a great start in life. I love you both, and I miss you, Dad—more than you could ever know.

Contents

Foreword

Although high-level performance might seem effortless to those watching, athletes and coaches know that performing at the limits of one's potential is underpinned by a great deal of hard work, dedication, and attention to detail. Winning four gold medals in consecutive Olympic Games is an achievement in which I take great pride. Obviously, I was fortunate to have the anatomy, physiology, and psychology that allowed me to excel as an oarsman, but my career was also underpinned by the expertise of a highly skilled support team and by sport science. Advances in knowledge in sport science are few and far between, but numbered among those rarities is the discovery that breathing has such a profound influence on performance that it merits specific training. Speaking as someone whose lungs were always considered in the elite range even among Olympic oarsmen, I know the benefits that this training can bring. My teammates and I spent many hours training both at sea level and at altitude, and the importance of breathing training was driven home to us day after day.

Alison McConnell is the world's leading expert on breathing training, and in sharing her expertise in *Breathe Strong, Perform Better,* she presents the most up-to-date information on the topic. This book is a wonderful example of how academic research can and should be translated into knowledge and techniques that anyone in any sport—whether a keen amateur or an aspiring Olympic medalist—can easily understand and apply in order to achieve better results.

I'm very pleased to have the opportunity to endorse Alison's work. If you want to perform better or just make exercising feel easier, I urge you to read this book. Its contents might make the difference between merely competing and truly performing to gold-medal standards.

Good luck and enjoy!
Sir Matthew Pinsent
Four-time gold medalist, 1992-2004
10-time world champion, 1991-2002

Preface

Some 20 years ago, I began to question the universally held belief (among sport scientists) that breathing did not limit exercise performance. The magnitude of this heresy cannot be overstated, and the shift in thinking that has occurred over those 20 years has been nothing short of seismic. Now, specific training of the breathing muscles is an integral part of conditioning in elite sport, and it has filtered to the grassroots level in a huge range of sport and fitness settings. So obvious is the logic of breathing muscle training—and so impressive are its outcomes—that it has become one of those "no-brainers" that so often arise with the benefit of 20/20 hindsight. Just as we now wonder how our grandparents didn't understand the importance of fluid balance during exercise, people now wonder why it's taken until the first decade of the 21st century for breathing muscles to be considered an integral part of the conditioning process.

Although huge strides have now been made, we still have a way to go, because even the most progressive and enlightened of scientists and coaches still don't *fully* appreciate how fundamentally the breathing muscles contribute to performance and movement in sports. In other words, the need for breathing to be considered as an integral part of functional movements is not widely understood. Nor should it be, because the science that underpins this is relatively new and highly specialized.

Breathe Strong, Perform Better seeks to plug this knowledge gap by giving people access to information that is normally the preserve of scientists, professional coaches, and elite athletes. The book is for anyone who wants to optimize the many benefits that arise from improving the physical performance of the breathing muscles. Whether you are an Olympic contender, a coach of high school athletes, or a fitness enthusiast who just wants to make your workouts more comfortable, this book contains something for you. The book will therefore be of interest to the following:

- Athletes and recreationally active people
- Coaches, sport scientists, and sports medicine practitioners
- Physical therapists, rehabilitation professionals, and personal trainers

Breathe Strong, Perform Better is a distillation of almost 20 years of research and practical experience of breathing training. Based on world-leading scientific research, this book describes cutting-edge applications of breathing training for a wide range of sports and fitness activities, including techniques that have been applied to athletes who were (or have become) world or Olympic champions. The book provides readers with the knowledge they need to get the best possible results from breathing training, as well as getting better results from their other training by optimizing the breathing muscle contribution to that training.

If you've never heard of breathing muscle training, your first question might be "Why would I want to train my breathing muscles?" The long answer is contained within the pages of this book, but the short answer is that whoever you are, training your breathing muscles can make any physical challenge feel easier. So whether you're participating in a 40K cycling time trial, an interval training session, or a step class, training your breathing muscles will help you breathe easier.

This book is also a response to an important development that has taken place in rehabilitation and conditioning over recent years—the rise of functional training. The application of functional training techniques to a wide range of settings has become mainstream, but it currently lacks a vital component. The missing link in functional training is the integration of breathing and the contribution of breathing muscles to functional movements. *Breathe Strong, Perform Better* provides this link, and it explains how to achieve the best results for specific sports and fitness settings. Functional breathing training will not only enhance performance, but also will reduce the risk of injury, because it enables the breathing muscles to accommodate their role in helping to stabilize the body's core more effectively.

This book is intended to answer all your questions about breathing training, whether those questions are scientific or highly applied. Your questions might include the following: What are the benefits to performance? What's the best equipment to use? How long will it take? What's the best training regimen? How do I ensure that I get results? How do I know I've improved? How does it work? How do I train functionally for my sport? In addition to answering these questions, the book contains case studies that illustrate how different athletes came to try breathing muscle training, the approach they took, and the results they achieved.

I'm often asked why I became interested in the fairly obscure subject of breathing. As is often the case with scientists, my interest originated from my own experience and my desire to understand what was happening to me and why. As a student in the early 1980s, my life was dominated by two things: my academic study of human physiology and my love of competitive sport. These two interests were not unconnected. As a mediocre rower, I was always let down by the apparent inability of my breathing to keep pace with the demands of racing (or training for that matter). One of my crewmates once commented that I sounded as though someone had taken me by the throat at 500 meters and hadn't let go. I felt severely limited by my breathing, but everything I'd been taught about the limitations to exercise performance told me that breathing was not a limiting factor to my performance (this will be explained further in chapter 1).

For some time, I accepted the common belief that breathing does not limit exercise performance. However, my personal (mostly excruciating) experience eventually propelled me on a quest to understand more about breathing, about the conditions under which it becomes limiting, and especially about how we might overcome these limitations. The rest, as the saying goes, is history. My quest for understanding has been a fascinating journey that has led me beyond exercise physiology and into territory that has broadened my horizons. Like so much of science, the journey began as a bit of a detective story, where snippets of evidence from seemingly unrelated areas were pieced together, eventually providing that final "eureka" moment when everything fell into place. This book enables you to share in what I've learned on my journey; the many tangents from my original path are reflected in the breadth of applications for breathing training that now exist (breathing muscle training is not just for mediocre, breathless rowers!). Some of these applications are medical and are beyond the scope of this book (except asthma), but the number of applications in sport has amazed even me.

Exercise scientists are arguably unique among scientists, because we are usually practitioners in what we study. Unlike, say, an astrophysicist who has no experience of going into space, exercise scientists know exactly what the challenges of sport competition are, because they have almost certainly taken part in competitive sport at some time. In other words, exercise scientists have the ability to view things from both sides of the fence. One of the most gratifying compliments that I ever received was from a coach who told me, "You have an excellent feel for the practical application of research to [elite] sport." This ability is reflected in my experience of applying the knowledge and insight I have gained as a scientist to the task of providing innovative, evidence-based advice on how to get the best results from breathing training. The book enables you to benefit from this, as well as from the feedback I've gained from the athletes, coaches, and other practitioners whom I've worked with over the past 15 years.

Breathe Strong, Perform Better is divided into two parts. The first part explains some of the science and theory of breathing, while the second part is a practical guide on how to get the most out of breathing training. Although these sections are inevitably interlinked, it is not necessary to read the science in order to benefit from the practical guidance. The theoretical section (part I) provides information on the theoretical building blocks that support the practice (part II). Accordingly, readers can dip in and out of part I based on their need and interest. For example, coaches are quite rightly suspicious of snake oil sellers who peddle potions and gadgets "guaranteed" to improve performance. Therefore, most coaches will want to review the section describing the underpinning theory and evidence of the ergogenic effect of breathing muscle training (chapter 4) before committing themselves (or their athletes) to putting it into practice.

The theoretical building blocks include aspects of the relevant anatomy and physiology of the breathing pump muscles and other muscles that are involved in breathing (chapter 1). As a part of this discussion, the rationale for specific breathing muscle training is established. This includes a description of the respiratory system as a source of exercise limitation, as well as a description of the most common chronic condition that affects athletes—asthma. The role of breathing muscles in functional movements is also explained, because this provides the rationale for functional breathing training. Consideration is also given to breathing patterns during different exercise modalities. From chapter 1, we move on to consider how breathing muscles limit training and competition (chapter 2). This information is subdivided into specific sporting contexts, providing insights into the range of benefits that can be derived in these contexts. Chapter 2 also summarizes the rationale for functional breathing training. The next chapter (chapter 3) describes how breathing muscles respond to training, thereby setting the scene for chapter 4, which describes the performance benefits of breathing muscle training in a range of sports.

The practical section of *Breathe Strong, Perform Better* (part II) begins by guiding readers through generic aspects of the most widely used form of breathing training—that is, inspiratory resistance training. In chapter 5, the general principles of training are considered, as well as different methods of training (resistance versus endurance) and proprietary equipment. Chapter 6 describes foundation training and provides guidance on principles such as posture and breathing technique. This chapter also provides a step-by-step guide to getting started with foundation training. Finally, chapters 7 to 10 introduce some functional training techniques, each taking a sport-specific approach. These chapters are supplemented by case studies and narratives from users that contain helpful tips for optimal results. The insights from these elements will help you see how creatively inspiratory muscle training (IMT) can be applied. In chapter 11, the specific exercises listed in chapters 7 through 10 are described in step-by-step detail.

My aim in writing this book has been to provide readers with the knowledge, insight, and confidence to tailor breathing muscle training creatively to the specific needs of their own applications. If, as a result, I have made myself obsolete as an expert on breathing training, then as the saying goes, "my work here is done."

Acknowledgments

There are so many people who have contributed directly and indirectly to *Breathe Strong, Perform Better*. These include the academic colleagues and PhD students with whom I have worked over the years, as well as the scientists whose research provided the insights that have shaped my thinking. You are too numerous to mention individually, but you know who you are, and you have all made some contribution to the development of the ideas that have led to this book.

I'm also eternally grateful to Professor Mike Caine and Claire Hodson. In 1996, they joined me on my perilous journey to create an innovative product that people could use to train their breathing. Without Mike and Claire's faith and talent, the POWERbreathe might never have seen the light of day, let alone commercial success. The insights on which *Breathe Strong, Perform Better* are founded were made possible by the collective contribution that all three of us made to the creation of POWERbreathe. Thank you both.

To the thousands of customers (especially the "early adopters") who put their trust in POWERbreathe, I also say thank you. Your belief that breathing training would deliver what we claimed is much appreciated, and your feedback has helped to shape the evolution of an entirely new way of improving performance.

Over the years, I have worked with many coaches and athletes, and their knowledge and insights have inevitably helped to shape the contents of this book. However, in the preparation of exercises contained within *Breathe Strong, Perform Better*, I owe a particular debt of gratitude to the coaches who shared their ideas and gave me specific feedback on my own. They are Jack Ade, Dan Boothby, Dan Bullock, Eddie Fletcher, Paul Gamble, and Arthur Horne. Cheers, guys!

I am also very grateful to my long-suffering photography models, Ryan Moore and Maxine Craig, who withstood the many hours of shooting with good humor, not to mention phenomenal local muscle endurance. I am also enormously grateful to my photographer, Julie Arthur, who joined me on a steep learning curve; it was challenging, but we got there in the end! Thanks also to Paul Davies for his help with post-production. My gratitude also goes to the West Hants Club in my hometown of Bournemouth in Dorset, England, and in particular to Mark Daley for the use of the club's facilities for the photography and to HaB International Ltd. for donating the breathing muscle trainers that were used (www.powerbreath .com). The principals at HaB—Harry and Anne—also deserve a special mention. Thanks for all your support over the years; I've loved working with you guys, and long may it continue.

This is my first book, and thanks to the expert team at Human Kinetics, it has been a relatively painless gestation. In particular, I'd like to thank Dr. John Dickinson for suggesting that I write the book, Peter Murphy for taking over the reins from John, Leigh Keylock for her really excellent and insightful editorial input on the first draft, and Laura Podeschi, who guided me through the final furlong with charm and efficiency.

I'm also grateful and honored that Sir Matthew Pinsent agreed to write the foreword for *Breathe Strong, Perform Better*. Matt is one of my sporting heroes, but he also personifies what the combination of innate physiology, dedication, and sheer hard work can achieve. You're a legend!

Last, but by no means least, I want to thank my partner, Mel, who has put up with the highs and lows of committing the past 20 years of my professional life to print. I couldn't have done it without you (or the lovely latte and biscotti that fuelled my typing).

The Science of Breathing

art I of *Breathe Strong, Perform Better* consists of four chapters that provide the theoretical building blocks for the practical guidance on breathing muscle training that is provided in part II. Reading part I is not essential in order to put the guidance in part II into practice; however, part I contains information that will help empower you with the knowledge to use part II as a source of creative inspiration (no pun intended), rather than a recipe book that must be followed to the letter.

Chapter 1 provides an overview of breathing during exercise and introduces the many muscles (obvious and less obvious) that are involved in this most essential of processes. The chapter also introduces some lesser-known functions of the breathing muscles, such as core stabilization. The role of the breathing muscles in functional movements is also explained, because this provides the rationale for functional breathing training. Chapter 2 examines how breathing limits exercise performance at a fundamental level, and it considers some specific limitations induced by various sports. The adaptations induced in breathing muscles in response to specific breathing training are described in chapter 3. This leads on to chapter 4, which contains a description of the physiological and functional benefits of breathing muscle training.

Chapter

1

Breathing During Exercise

Breathing signifies both the start and the end of our lives, and it is the most fundamental of physiological processes. Because breathing occurs automatically, it only enters our consciousness when it fails to keep pace with our needs. When this happens, human beings experience one of the most frightening sensations they encounter in life—the feeling of being out of breath, of not being able to breathe enough, or worse still, of suffocation. Only under these circumstances are we reminded of how important breathing is and how alarming it can be not to be able to breathe enough. Although this book does not promise to banish this sensation from your life completely, the book will provide the tools to minimize its intensity, as well as its impact on your activities. Furthermore, *Breathe Strong, Perform Better* recognizes, for the first time, the pivotal role that the breathing (or respiratory) muscles have as stabilizers, postural controllers, and prime movers of the trunk during sport activities.

Most people find the whole area of breathing completely mystifying and have no notion of how breathing is brought about, how it responds to exercise, how and why these responses differ at different exercise intensities, or how the lungs themselves respond to training. When it comes to the involvement of the breathing muscles in nonrespiratory actions such as core stabilization, knowledge is even more limited. The lack of knowledge is a direct reflection of the lack of information that is available on the subject to the average person. This chapter provides an introduction to respiratory physiology. In addition, the chapter explores a few of the myths about breathing that are misleading and unhelpful to people who want to benefit from improvement in their breathing.

AN INTRODUCTION TO BREATHING

The reason that we need to breathe is obvious, but the actual processes underlying the act of breathing are a mystery to the majority of people. For example, most people think of breathing as simply serving the role of supplying oxygen, but there is more to breathing than just oxygen supply, especially during heavy exercise. In

How Breathing Helps to Delay Fatigue

Muscles can liberate energy from stored substrates using two types of metabolic pathways: those requiring oxygen (aerobic) and those not requiring oxygen (anaerobic). Aerobic pathways are more efficient and result in the production of harmless carbon dioxide and water, but they liberate energy slowly. In contrast, anaerobic pathways are less efficient, result in the production of harmful lactic acid (also known as lactate), and liberate energy much faster. Lactic acid has been linked to the onset of muscle fatigue, because it leads to acidification of the muscle fibers, which interferes with the normal process of contraction. Muscles are able to use aerobic pathways for low- to moderate-intensity exercise; however, these pathways liberate energy too slowly to meet the requirements of high-intensity exercise, so anaerobic pathways must be used to supplement energy liberation. The accumulation of lactic acid from anaerobic metabolism is the reason that high-intensity exercise cannot be sustained for more than a few minutes. Without the body's ability to slow down the acidification of muscle using a process called buffering, people would be able to sustain high-intensity exercise for an even shorter period. Buffering neutralizes the acid component of lactic acid (the hydrogen ion [H^+]) by pairing it with an alkali, a process that slows down the acidification of the muscle and delays fatigue. Where does the alkali come from? The alkali is liberated and then combined with the H^+ by the removal of carbon dioxide from the blood by hyperventilation. The need to buffer lactic acid is the reason that breathing increases steeply at the so-called lactate threshold. This is how breathing helps to delay fatigue.

fact, the supply of oxygen becomes a secondary objective of breathing during heavy exercise, when the emphasis of its role switches to getting rid of the by-product of exercise, carbon dioxide. This latter role of breathing is vital to delaying fatigue during heavy exercise (see How Breathing Helps to Delay Fatigue). Just like a car engine, human beings use oxygen to burn carbon-based fuels (carbohydrate and fat) in order to release energy. The end result of this chemical reaction is the production of carbon dioxide and water. The process of managing the by-products of metabolism is discussed in more detail later in this chapter.

At the most fundamental level, breathing is the simple act of moving air in and out of the lungs, and the purpose of breathing is the exchange of oxygen and carbon dioxide between the air around us and the small blood vessels (capillaries) within the lungs. Once combined with the blood inside the capillaries, the oxygen can be transported to every cell in the body. As mentioned, oxygen is used by cells to release energy from the body's energy stores, and carbon dioxide is one of the by-products of this process (as it is in the combustion of coal or oil). During exercise, the rate at which this process takes place must increase, which means that breathing must also increase to keep pace with demand. Failure to do so results in changes that lead to breathlessness, increased effort perception, and premature fatigue.

Structure of the Breathing System

The breathing system is illustrated in figure 1.1 and is made up of all the structures that guide air into the lungs (nose, mouth, and airways), plus the lungs themselves and the structures that surround the lungs (thoracic cavity, including the rib cage). The right lung comprises three lobes, while the left has two, which allows space for the heart to nestle between the left lobes, sloping toward the left. The weight of both adult lungs is between 1.5 and 2.2 pounds (0.7 and 1.0 kg) when weighed at autopsy; however, in life, they probably weigh twice this amount, because the blood vessels within the lungs (pulmonary circulation) will be filled with about 0.9 liters of blood (weighing about 2.1 pounds [0.95 kg]). In other words, the adult human has about 4.4 pounds (2 kg) of lungs hanging inside the rib cage.

The tubes that guide the air from the outside world into the lungs are known as airways. The airways branch a total of 23 times, creating a treelike structure that ends in the air sacs (alveoli) where the exchange of oxygen and carbon dioxide takes place. Air enters via the nose and mouth; then it travels into the pharynx (throat), through the glottis, and down the trachea. Next, the air travels into the right and left (primary) bronchi, and then through the branching structure of the remaining airways to the alveoli. The alveoli are collections of air sacs, similar to a bunch of grapes, which are surrounded by a dense network of tiny blood vessels called capillaries (think of a bunch of grapes inside a net shopping bag—see figure 1.1). The

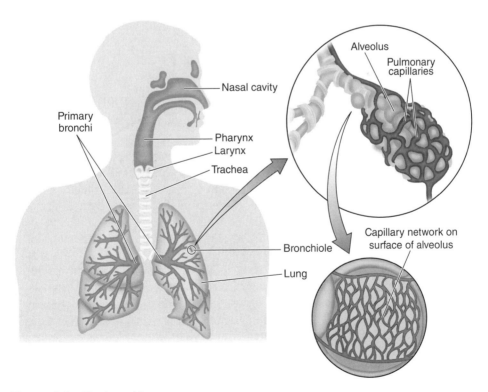

Figure 1.1 The breathing system.

regions of the lung without alveoli (including the airways) are known as the conducting zone, while the regions with alveoli are known as the respiratory zone—that is, the zone where oxygen and carbon dioxide are exchanged. An important feature of the conducting airways is that the larger airways, such as the trachea (windpipe), are reinforced with cartilage rings that help prevent collapse, whereas the walls of smaller airways contain small rings of muscle that, when contracted, narrow the airways. Normally, these tiny muscles would be relaxed, and the airways open, but in people with asthma, the muscles contract in response to specific triggers, leading to airway narrowing and obstruction of airflow. Exercise is one of the most common triggers of airway narrowing in people with asthma, and exercise-induced asthma is discussed in more detail later in this chapter.

The branching structure of the lungs is an impressive work of evolution that has resulted in adult human lungs having a combined surface area of about 646 square feet (60 m²), which is about the same as a singles badminton court and about 40 times the area of the skin. Why the need for such a huge area? Like so much

Why Breathing Doesn't Limit Oxygen Transport

The transport of oxygen to the working muscles involves four stages:

1. Alveolar ventilation—Delivery of atmospheric air to the alveoli (breathing).
2. Pulmonary diffusion—Transfer of oxygen from the alveoli to the capillary blood.
3. Transport by the blood—Collection and delivery of oxygen in combination with the blood from the lungs to the muscles.
4. Tissue diffusion—Transfer of oxygen from the muscle capillary blood to the muscle cells.

There is no active transport of oxygen at any point in its journey, which occurs via a process of passive diffusion. During diffusion, oxygen moves from an area of high concentration (the atmosphere) to one of low concentration (the muscle). The rate and efficiency of diffusion are directly related to the size of the gradient. Think of a river flowing downhill; the steeper the hill, the faster the water flows.

In theory, any one of the four listed stages could limit the transport of oxygen. In practice, for people with healthy lungs who are at sea level (not at an altitude where the oxygen gradient is reduced), steps 1 and 2 operate with almost 100 percent efficiency in terms of their purpose, which is to oxygenate the blood fully before it leaves the lungs. Steps 1 and 2 are the only steps in the transport of oxygen that can be influenced by breathing, and because the blood is almost 100 percent saturated with oxygen when it leaves the lungs, increasing breathing cannot improve oxygen transport (the oxygenation of the blood is already almost 100 percent).

of respiratory physiology, it comes down to the laws of physics. The exchange of oxygen and carbon dioxide between the 300 million alveoli and the capillaries surrounding them occurs via passive diffusion. For this process to keep pace with the metabolic needs of the average person, especially during exercise, the surface area for diffusion (number of alveoli and capillaries) must be vast. Think of the lungs as being like a huge office building, and think of the oxygen and carbon dioxide as the people who work inside. If all the people are entering and leaving at the same time, and there is only one door (one alveolus and capillary), then the rate at which the people can enter or leave the building (exchange of gases) is very slow. However, by increasing the number of doors (the number of alveoli and capillaries), the rate at which people can enter and leave is increased in direct proportion to the number of doors. Evolution has therefore provided an extremely efficient organ for exchanging oxygen and carbon dioxide—so efficient, in fact, that diffusion in the lung is not a limiting step in the transport of oxygen to the cells (see the sidebar on page 6). This is a little known fact, and most people believe that by breathing more, a person can increase the amount of oxygen in the blood. This widely held belief is also prevalent among coaches and exercise professionals. And it's easy to see how this myth came into being. Breathing must place some limits on exercise tolerance; otherwise, phrases such as "I need to stop to catch my breath" or "I'm taking a breather" would never have come into being. The error in the logic is the assumption that the limit imposed by breathing is due to lack of oxygen, and that breathing harder can fix it. Chapter 2 will explain the real reasons why breathing limits performance and often forces people to "take a breather."

The health of the lungs is assessed by measuring the maximal volumes and airflows that can be generated. In the presence of a disease such as asthma, these can be compromised. Measurements are made using an instrument known as a spirometer, and figure 1.2 illustrates the tracing obtained from such a device. To generate this graph, the participant started by breathing normally at rest; the participant then filled and

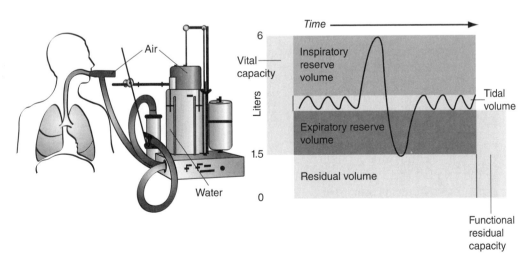

Figure 1.2 Lung volume subdivisions traced by a spirometer.

emptied his lungs as fast as possible. As shown in the figure, when the participant is at rest, only a small proportion of the available lung capacity is used. The participant has both an inspiratory and an expiratory reserve volume to call on when the need arises to increase breathing. Breathing is increased by raising depth (volume) and rate. The changes that occur to the depth and rate of breathing during exercise will be discussed in upcoming sections. The graph from the spirometer also illustrates an important feature of mammalian lungs—they are never completely empty. At the end of a maximal exhalation, there is always about 150 to 200 milliliters of air remaining. This is referred to as the residual volume. Once again, the laws of physics come into play when evaluating why it's impossible to empty the lungs completely. In a nutshell, the forces keeping the airways open reach zero before the lungs are completely empty, resulting in a small amount of air being trapped.

How Breathing Happens

The mechanical actions of breathing are extremely familiar to everyone. These actions involve a rhythmic pumping of the chest "bellows" that sucks air in and blows air out of the lungs. Conceptually, the breathing apparatus can be thought of as a pump consisting of an elastic balloon (lungs) inside an expandable and compressible cavity (thorax). The expansion and compression of the thoracic cavity are brought about by the actions of the complex group of muscles that surround the lungs (i.e., the breathing, or respiratory, muscles). These muscles bring about movements of the cavity that surrounds the lungs; changes in the volume of this cavity produce changes in the pressure within it, and this creates the gradient for movement of air in and out of the cavity.

In high school biology classes, a simple model is often used to explain how changes in volume and pressure bring about the movement of air (physics again!). The model consists of a glass bell jar (rib cage) containing two balloons (lungs); the jar is sealed at its open base by an elastic membrane (diaphragm). The model is imperfect because the walls of the bell jar, which represent the rib cage, do not expand; however, the elastic membrane provides a perfect illustration of what happens in response to movements of the major inspiratory muscle, the diaphragm. It is not difficult to see how moving the walls of the bell jar (expanding the rib cage) would bring about precisely the same changes as moving the diaphragm—that is, an increase in volume and a fall in pressure, which create movement of air.

The balloons in the bell jar model also illustrate another important feature of the lungs—the lungs are elastic. In fact, both the lungs and the rib cage are elastic structures that naturally spring back to their resting positions once the forces acting on them are removed. You can experience this yourself by taking a deep breath and then relaxing; the air "falls" out of your lungs under the pressure generated by the recoil of the lungs and rib cage. During inhalation, the inspiratory muscles expand the thoracic compartment and stretch the lungs and rib cage. This stores some elastic energy within these tissues in the same way that inflating a party balloon stores elastic energy within the wall of the balloon. At the start of an inhalation, the inspiratory muscles are relaxed, and any elastic energy stored within the lungs and chest wall has been dissipated during the preceding exhalation. Each intake of breath is therefore initiated from a point where all of the forces acting on the lungs are in a state of balance. When a person is breathing while at rest, only the inspiratory muscles are active, because exhalation can rely on elastic recoil to provide the energy.

The balloon analogy has one final point to convey about the lungs and rib cage: Because they are elastic, the more they are inflated, the greater the force required to change their volume. In other words, in the case of the balloon, the balloon is relatively easy to inflate at first, but as it becomes larger, you need to use more effort to inflate it. This property has important implications for how a person chooses to breathe during exercise, which will be considered a little later.

Obviously, the breathing pump has a finite volume (lung volume) and pumping capacity, and these define the maximal ventilation that can be achieved during activities such as exercise. If we conceptualize the breathing pump as a bellows, the pumping capacity is equivalent to the rate at which the bellows can be emptied and refilled. The pumping capacity of the lungs is therefore determined by the balance between the factors that limit air movement (such as the resistance of the lung airways) and the ability of the respiratory muscles to overcome these limiting factors (how much power the breathing muscles can generate to drive air into and out of the lungs). All other things being equal, the greater the power-generating capacity of the pump, the greater the pumping capacity of the pump. This latter property lies at the heart of *Breathe Strong, Perform Better* because this property—and this property alone—can be modified by training.

Earlier in this section, the idea that breathing more does not increase the transport of oxygen to the muscles was explained. If breathing more doesn't improve oxygen transport, why would it be beneficial to improve the pumping capacity of the lungs? The answer is underpinned by some very interesting physiology that has emerged in the past decade, which will be discussed in more detail in chapter 2.

However, in the meantime, let's accept the idea that improving pumping capacity *is* good for performance. To rationalize the apparent contradictions just described, we need to recognize the fact that breathing is brought about by the actions of muscles. Muscles require a share of resources (blood flow, oxygen, energy substrates), and they generate sensations that are proportional to the intensity of the work that they are undertaking. Both of these factors can contribute to exercise limitation, but both are modifiable by training (and detraining).

What Happens to Breathing During Exercise?

At rest, the average adult takes 10 to 15 breaths per minute, with a volume of about 0.5 liters, producing a "minute ventilation" of 7.5 liters per minute (15×0.5). The volume of each breath (tidal volume) depends on body size and metabolic rate. Bigger people have larger lungs and take larger breaths; they also require more energy and oxygen to support their metabolism, so they naturally have a larger minute ventilation.

During heavy exercise, breathing frequency rises to around 40 to 50 breaths per minute. In a physically active young male, tidal volume rises to around 3 to 4 liters (minute ventilation is 120 to 160 liters per minute). However, in Olympic-class male endurance athletes, tidal volume can be over 5 liters, resulting in a minute ventilation of 250 to 300 liters per minute.

Pound for pound, Olympic oarsmen can achieve a minute ventilation that is equivalent to that seen in thoroughbred racehorses! Take the rower Sir Matthew Pinsent as an example. In his 20s, this four-time Olympic gold medalist (1992, 1996, 2000, 2004) and 13-time senior world champion possessed the largest lungs of any British athlete. The maximum volume that he was able to exhale after filling his lungs (vital capacity) was 8.25 liters. Sir Matthew stood just under 6 feet 5 inches (2 m) tall and weighed around 240 pounds (108 kg); a man of his size would normally have a vital capacity of about 6 liters, while the average man has a vital capacity of closer to 5 liters. During a 2,000-meter rowing race, Sir Matthew would generate a massive 460 watts for around 6 minutes, requiring a peak oxygen uptake of around 8 liters per minute and a minute ventilation of close to 300 liters per minute. The total volume of air that was moved into and out of his lungs during a race would have been close to 1,700 liters, requiring a power output by his breathing muscles of around 85 watts. These are truly staggering statistics. Next time you go to the gym, set a cycle ergometer to 85 watts, then reflect on whether you could generate the power required to turn the pedals with your breathing muscles instead of your quads!

Clearly, Sir Matthew is an extreme example and a truly exceptional athlete, but sports such as rowing—that is, sports that are undertaken at near maximal intensities for relatively prolonged periods—stretch the ability of the breathing pump to its limits (we will learn more about breathing and rowing in chapter 2). Given these extreme demands, it's logical to ask this question: Do the lungs respond to training? To most people's surprise, the answer is no. Unlikely though it seems, training does not increase lung volumes, improve lung function, or enhance the ability of the lungs to transfer oxygen to the blood, even in athletes who have trained for many years (Wagner, 2005).

Notwithstanding this inability to adapt to training, observations that athletes such as swimmers and rowers appear to possess superior lung function (superior to that of their nonathletic contemporaries) have led to speculation that physical training, especially during childhood and adolescence, may enhance the development of the lungs (Armour, Donnelly, & Bye, 1993). However, one cannot exclude the possibility that, for some sports, having large lungs may provide an advantage that leads to success. Hence, only competitors with larger than normal lungs (like Sir Matthew) succeed and remain to compete in their chosen sport as adults. Until a longitudinal study follows the development of a group of athletes through adolescence and into adulthood, the "nature versus nurture" question will remain unresolved.

So if the lungs themselves don't respond to training, is that the end of the story? Of course not, or the following pages of this book would be blank. The lungs themselves are only part of the system that delivers oxygen and removes carbon dioxide from the body; as mentioned earlier, breathing involves muscles, and these muscles are part of a system that does adapt to training. We will consider how whole-body training influences breathing muscle function a little later, but for now, let's continue our discussion of what happens to breathing during exercise.

During exercise, the rate and depth of breathing are increased, which requires the breathing muscles to contract more forcefully and quickly. When a person is at rest, the expiratory muscles are relaxed, but during exercise these muscles begin to make a contribution to breathing in order to raise tidal volume and expiratory airflow rate. However, at all intensities of exercise, the majority of the work of breathing is undertaken by the inspiratory muscles; expiration is always assisted to some extent by elastic energy that is stored in the expanded lungs and rib cage from the preceding inhalation. This elastic energy has been donated by the contraction of the inspiratory muscles as they stretched and expanded the chest during inhalation. Recent studies have estimated that during maximal exercise, the work of the inspiratory breathing muscles demands approximately 16 percent of the available oxygen, which puts into perspective how strenuous breathing can be.

It's obvious to everyone that exercise requires a person to breathe "more heavily," but what does this mean in terms of changes in tidal volume and airflow rates? Does a person increase tidal volume by breathing in more deeply or breathing out more deeply, and at what point does a person start breathing more quickly? Does it even matter? Well, the answers lie in the interaction of physiology and physics.

Breathing is controlled by a center in the brain (called the respiratory center) that receives a complex array of information from a myriad of sources (e.g., inputs from the brain's motor center, receptors in the exercising muscles, receptors in the cardiovascular system, and so on). A description of the control of breathing is beyond the scope of this book, but suffice it to say, one of the most important control factors influencing breathing strategy is comfort, or rather, the minimization of discomfort.

Figure 1.3 illustrates how tidal volume changes as exercise intensity increases, placing it within the subdivisions of the lung volumes that are illustrated in figure 1.2 (page 7). Initially, during light exercise, tidal volume increases because the person exhales a little more deeply (using the expiratory reserve volume), but this increase is quickly supplemented as a result of the person inhaling more deeply (using the inspiratory reserve volume).

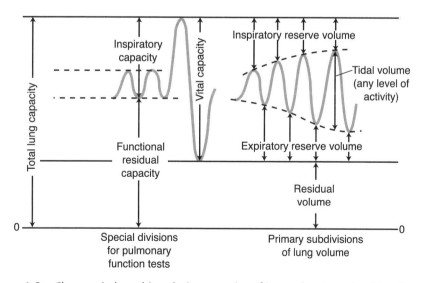

Figure 1.3 Changes in breathing during exercise of increasing intensity. Note how tidal volume increases as exercise intensity increases. This increase in tidal volume results from the person exhaling and inhaling more deeply.

Reprinted, by permission, from P-O Åstrand, K. Rodahl, H. Dahl, and S. Strømme, 2003, *Textbook of work physiology: Physiological bases of exercise,* 4th ed. (Champaign, IL: Human Kinetics), 185.

Eventually, tidal volume reaches a point where it does not increase any further, despite a continuing need to increase minute ventilation. This can be seen more clearly in figure 1.4, which shows how minute ventilation, tidal volume, and breathing frequency change during incremental cycling to the limit of tolerance in a well-trained triathlete. Each point on the plot represents an individual breath, and there are two key features to note: First, the increase in minute ventilation is not a straight line; it rises sharply about two thirds of the way into the exercise. As a result, the amount of breathing required at 80 percent of maximum capacity is not twice the amount required at 40 percent—rather, it is more like four or five times greater. Second, as tidal volume levels off, breathing frequency rises steeply to meet the need for an escalating minute ventilation. Why does breathing change like this? The nonlinear increase in minute ventilation is a result of the role that breathing plays in minimizing changes that occur as the locomotor muscles rely more heavily on anaerobic metabolism during heavy exercise (i.e., when exceeding the lactate threshold). The steep increase in minute ventilation at the lactate threshold is central to the system that minimizes the negative influence of lactic acid on muscle function and fatigue (see the sidebar titled How Breathing Helps Delay Fatigue on page 4).

The increasing reliance on breathing frequency to raise minute ventilation at high intensities of exercise arises because it becomes too uncomfortable to continue to increase tidal volume. As tidal volume increases, it requires progressively greater inspiratory muscle force to expand the lungs; using the analogy of the lungs as balloons, the lungs become stiffer and more difficult to expand when they contain more air. Higher inspiratory muscle force equals more effort and greater breathing discomfort. Eventually, the sensory feedback from the inspiratory muscles signals

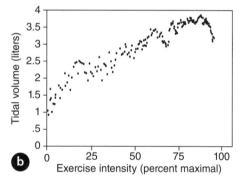

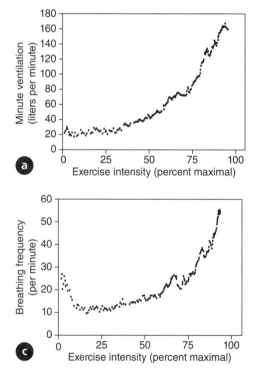

Figure 1.4 Changes in breathing during incremental cycling in a well-trained triathlete. Each dot corresponds to one breath. Note that tidal volume drops away steeply at the end of the test, and that this is accompanied by an increase in breathing frequency that maintains minute ventilation for a short while but quickly drops away. These changes are manifestations of breathing muscle fatigue.

the respiratory center to change tack and to increase breathing frequency more steeply instead of tidal volume. The respiratory center has an exquisite system for minimizing breathing discomfort, which also optimizes efficiency.

If having a high tidal volume spells more inspiratory muscle work and more discomfort, why does the tidal volume increase at all? The answer is that increasing tidal volume offers the most efficient strategy for gas exchange, but this must be balanced against the mechanical cost of expanding the lungs (the elastic work of breathing).

As previously explained, the tubes that channel the air to the alveoli are unable to take part in gas exchange, but they are nonetheless part of the lung volume. This non-gas-exchanging conducting region is called the anatomical "dead space," and the air that it contains reduces the volume of each breath that reaches the alveoli. For example, figure 1.5 illustrates that if you inhale 0.5 liters and your dead-space volume is 0.15 liters, then about 0.35 liters (70 percent) of the breath reaches the alveolar parts of the lung to take part in gas exchange.

Now let's consider the effect of dead space and, more important, tidal volume during exercise. Let's say that in order to meet the gas exchange requirements of running on level ground, the alveolar ventilation must be 54 liters per minute (the volume of each breath that must reach the alveoli). Figure 1.5 and table 1.1 (page 14) illustrate the repercussions of two different breathing strategies that will both deliver this level of alveolar ventilation.

The shallow breathing strategy leads to a doubling of breathing frequency and an increase in the minute ventilation requirement of 5.2 liters (9 percent). Therefore, this strategy is far less mechanically efficient, despite the fact that the elastic work of breathing is reduced. The influence of more than doubling the breathing frequency far outweighs the benefits to the elastic work (and breathing effort) of halving the tidal volume, which is why the control system tends to use a bit of both tidal volume and breathing frequency in order to increase minute ventilation. It's a bit like striking the right balance between stride length and frequency during running; there's a window that is both efficient and comfortable, and this is where one intuitively positions oneself.

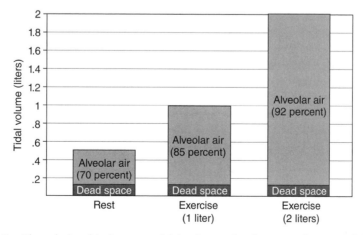

Figure 1.5 The relationship between tidal volume, dead-space volume, and the proportion of each breath that reaches the alveoli.

Table 1.1 Influence of Breath Volume on Breathing Requirement During Exercise

Deep breathing	Shallow breathing
Alveolar ventilation = 54 liters per min	Alveolar ventilation = 54 liters per min
Minute ventilation = 58.3 liters per min	Minute ventilation = 63.5 liters per min
Dead space = 0.15 liters	Dead space = 0.15 liters
Tidal volume = 2.0 liters	Tidal volume = 1.0 liters
Breathing frequency = 29.2 breaths per min	Breathing frequency = 63.5 breaths per min
Dead-space ventilation = 4.3 liters per min	Dead-space ventilation = 9.5 liters per min

Why Breathing Muscles Are Not at the Peak of Fitness

Given that everyone is breathing 24/7 and the fact that breathing can be so strenuous during exercise, a logical question to ask is this: Why aren't the breathing muscles the best trained muscles in the body? The answer requires a look at the relationship between exercise intensity and the corresponding breathing requirement. Figure 1.6 illustrates this schematically and subdivides it into breathing effort domains. These domains are based on the magnitude of the requirement for breathing muscle work associated with the intensity of exercise. The figure also depicts the difference between the actual breathing requirement and the breathing requirement for oxygen supply. The former is much higher because of the role of breathing in delaying fatigue (see the sidebar on page 4).

Moderate-intensity exercise (activities that can be sustained for more than 30 minutes) is within the "comfort" zone of the breathing muscles. Heavy-intensity exercise (activities that can be sustained for only 10 to 30 minutes) is within the

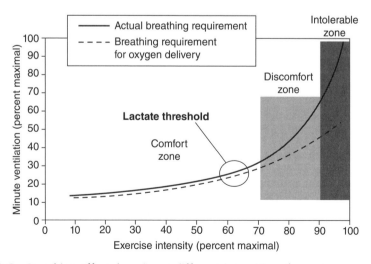

Figure 1.6 Breathing effort domains at different intensities of exercise.

"discomfort" zone of the breathing muscles. Very heavy-intensity exercise (activities that can be sustained for less than 10 minutes) is within the "intolerable" zone of the breathing muscles.

What does all this have to do with the fitness of the breathing muscles? To stimulate any muscle to undergo adaptation (to become fitter), the muscle must be overloaded; this means forcing it to do something that it is not accustomed to doing (this concept will be considered in more detail in chapter 5). The vast majority of aerobic training occurs within the comfort zone of the inspiratory muscles, where the training stimulus to the breathing muscles is very modest and little training adaptation occurs. Unfortunately, the zone that provides the most potent training stimulus to the inspiratory muscles (intolerable zone) is so challenging that it cannot be sustained long enough to provide an effective overload. In other words, the intensity of breathing work that's needed to hone a person's breathing muscles into optimum fitness is the same intensity that makes a person so out of breath that the only option is to stop or slow down—it's a catch 22. This is why normal training doesn't optimize the condition of the breathing muscles and why they need to be trained specifically in order to ensure that the limits they impose are minimized.

The following section provides a more detailed description of the structure and function of the muscles involved in breathing. These properties are described in more detail because they determine the response of these muscles to both exercise and training.

STRUCTURE AND FUNCTION OF THE MUSCLES INVOLVED IN BREATHING

This section describes the anatomy and physiology of the muscles involved in breathing. This includes not only the breathing pump muscles whose functions were outlined earlier, but also the muscles in the upper airway (throat) that keep the airway open, as well as the trunk musculature that is involved in core stabilization and maintenance of posture. The inclusion of the breathing muscles within the group of trunk muscles that have these nonrespiratory roles is an important concept to grasp. This section will help you understand how the breathing muscles function and interact during exercise, how their function can be limited by factors such as lung volume and airflow rate, and why functional training of the breathing muscles can help them to undertake their many functions more effectively.

Breathing Pump Muscles

The breathing pump muscles are a complex arrangement that form a semirigid bellows around the lungs. Essentially, all muscles that attach to the rib cage have the potential to generate a breathing action, but the principal muscles are shown in figure 1.7 (page 16). Muscles that expand the thoracic cavity are inspiratory muscles and induce inhalation, while those that compress the thoracic cavity are expiratory and induce exhalation. These muscles possess exactly the same basic structure as all other skeletal muscles, and they work in concert to expand or compress the thoracic cavity.

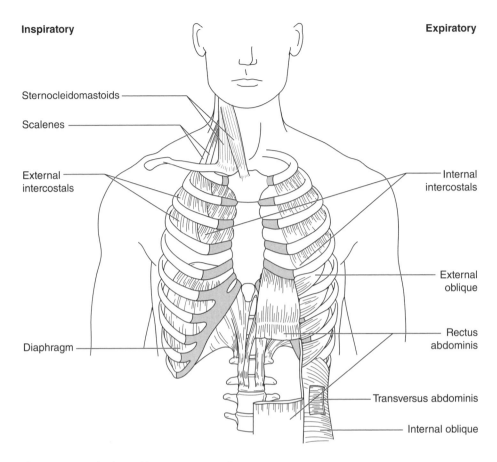

Figure 1.7 The breathing pump muscles.

Inspiratory Muscles

The principal muscle of inspiration is the diaphragm, a domed sheet of muscle that separates the thoracic and abdominal cavities. The diaphragm attaches to the lower ribs, as well as to the lumbar vertebrae of the spine. When the diaphragm contracts, the dome flattens, moving downward into the abdominal cavity like a piston (think of a syringe barrel). This movement increases the volume of the thoracic cavity, creating a negative pressure that is proportional to the extent of its movement, and thus, to the force of contraction. Diaphragm contraction also induces the lower ribs to move upward and forward, which also increases thoracic volume. The ribs move outward because the central tendon of the diaphragm (at the crown of the dome) pushes down onto the liver and stomach, which act like a fulcrum. This has the effect of raising the edges of the diaphragm, which are connected to the rib margins, forcing them upward and outward. When the diaphragm moves downward into the abdominal compartment, it also raises intraabdominal pressure and assists the abdominal muscles in stabilizing the spine.

The muscles of the rib cage are known as the intercostal muscles because they are located in the space between adjacent ribs. Each space contains a layer of inspiratory and a layer of expiratory muscle fibers. The inspiratory intercostal muscles form the outer layer, and they slope downward and forward; contraction causes the ribs to move upward and outward, similar to the raising of a bucket handle. Contraction of these muscles also serves to stabilize the rib cage, making it more rigid, as well as bringing about twisting movements. The stiffening of the rib cage enables it to oppose the tendency to collapse slightly under the influence of the negative pressure generated by the movement of the diaphragm. Without this action, the rib cage would distort, and the action of the diaphragm would be less mechanically efficient, thus wasting energy. Intercostal muscle contraction also brings about stiffening of the rib cage during lifting, pushing, and pulling movements, which makes the intercostal muscles an important contributor to these movements.

Some muscles in the neck region also have an inspiratory action. The scalene and sternocleidomastoid muscles (also known as sternomastoid) are attached to the top of the sternum, upper two ribs, and clavicle at one end; at the other end, they are attached to the cervical vertebrae and mastoid process. When these muscles contract, they lift the top of the chest, but the scalene muscles are also involved in flexion of the neck.

Expiratory Muscles

The principal muscles of expiration are those that form the muscular corset of the abdominal wall. The most well known and visible of these (at least in male models!) is the rectus abdominis (or "six pack"); the other three muscles are less visible but arguably more functionally important to sports—the transversus abdominis and the internal and external oblique muscles. When these muscles contract, they pull the lower rib margins downward, and they compress the abdominal compartment, raising its internal pressure. The pressure increase tends to push the diaphragm upward into the thoracic cavity, inducing an increase in pressure and expiration. However, these muscles only come into play as breathing muscles during exercise or during forced breathing maneuvers; resting exhalation is a passive process brought about by the recoil of the lungs and rib cage at the end of inspiration (due to stored elastic energy).

The four abdominal muscles involved in breathing also have important functions as postural muscles, in rotating and flexing the trunk, and when coughing, speaking (or singing), and playing wind instruments. The compression and stiffening of the abdominal wall generated by contraction of the abdominal muscles also optimize the position of the diaphragm at the onset of inspiration. This also enhances spinal stability and postural control.

The rib cage also contains muscles with an expiratory action. These are the internal intercostal muscles, which slope backward; contraction causes the ribs to move downward and inward, similar to the lowering of a bucket handle. Both internal and external intercostal muscles are also involved in flexing and twisting the trunk.

Functional Properties of Breathing Pump Muscles

The functional properties of any given muscle are determined by the type of muscle fibers it contains. Human muscles have three main types of fibers, and most muscles contain a mixture of these, in differing proportions. The relative proportions of these three fiber types determine the properties of each muscle:

- Type I—Slow contracting and relatively weak, but very resistant to fatigue.

- Type IIA—Moderately fast and strongly contracting, with high resistance to fatigue.
- Type IIX (also known as Type IIB)—Fast and very strong, but with only moderate resistance to fatigue.

Type I and IIA fibers have a high oxidative capacity (ability to use oxygen to liberate energy) and a high to moderate density of blood capillaries (delivering oxygen). These fibers are also known as oxidative fibers, and they are capable of sustaining activity for prolonged periods without becoming fatigued.

Not surprisingly, the proportion of oxidative fibers (Type I and Type IIA) within the diaphragm and inspiratory rib cage muscles is approximately 80 percent, while that of the expiratory rib cage muscles is almost 100 percent. This compares to around 35 to 45 percent for limb muscles. The fibers of the abdominal muscles tend to be much more variable in their composition, reflecting their varied roles. Another important factor determining muscle fatigue is the blood supply to the muscle. Inadequate blood flow (ischemia) not only limits oxygen delivery, but it also limits the delivery of substrates (fuel such as carbohydrates) and the removal of metabolic by-products (such as lactate), all of which can hasten fatigue. The diaphragm and rib cage muscles are supplied by numerous arteries that help to protect them from fatigue.

In the past, the highly fatigue-resistant characteristics of the breathing pump muscles contributed to a key assumption regarding the likelihood that the breathing muscles contributed to exercise limitation. Physiologists assumed that the breathing pump muscles, especially the diaphragm, were so well evolved from their continuous work that they were immune to fatigue. It wasn't until the 1990s that this myth was finally shattered (as will be discussed in chapter 2).

Mechanical Properties of Breathing Pump Muscles

To generate a breath, the breathing pump muscles must produce a pressure differential between the atmosphere outside the body and the inside of the lungs. Broadly speaking, the inspiratory muscles pull outward to expand the thorax, and the expiratory muscles pull inward to compress the thorax. The size and speed of the pressure differential that the muscle contractions generate determine how large the breath is and how fast the air moves into (or out of) the lungs, respectively. During exercise, air must flow in and out of the lungs more quickly than at rest, and the breathing pump muscles must contract more forcefully to generate the required increase in volume and airflow rate. Like other muscles, the breathing pump muscles have a finite ability to generate force (which results in the generation of pressures within the thorax), and this limited ability is one of the limiting factors to breathing during exercise.

The ability of the breathing muscles to generate the pressure differentials that make breathing happen (negative pressure for inhalation and positive pressure for exhalation) is influenced by the act of breathing itself. Breathing results in changes in the length (lung volume) and the speed (airflow rate) of muscle shortening, both of which change the ability of the breathing muscle to generate pressure. The implications of this are important.

The length–tension (volume–pressure) relationship of the breathing pump muscles is illustrated in figure 1.8. As shown in this schematic, which is based on data from a number of studies, the capacity to generate inspiratory pressure is greatest when the lungs are empty and smallest when they are full. Conversely, the capacity to generate expiratory pressure is greatest when the lungs are full and smallest when they are empty (this is not shown in the figure). This makes perfect sense, because it means that inhalation and exhalation commence at the lung volumes where the respective muscles are strongest. So why is this relationship important functionally? Tidal volume increases with increasing exercise

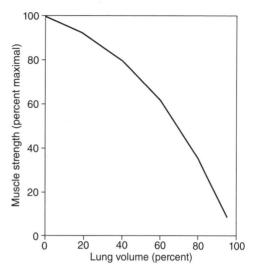

Figure 1.8 The effects of lung volume on the static strength of the inspiratory muscles.

intensity (see figures 1.3 and 1.4, pages 11 and 12), and as a result, the end of inhalation occurs closer to the point where the lungs are full; this is also the point where the inspiratory muscles are weakest (see figure 1.8). This functional weakening of the inspiratory muscles increases their susceptibility to fatigue, because they need to work relatively harder at high lung volumes. For example, inflating the lungs at a low lung volume (where the muscles are strong) may require only 10 percent of the muscles' maximal strength, but at high lung volumes (where the muscles are weaker), this might require 60 percent. Functional weakening also has implications for the perception of breathing effort, as well as how the breathing muscles can be overloaded during resistance training, which will be considered in chapter 6.

The force–velocity (pressure–flow) relationship of the breathing pump muscles also has important repercussions. This is a complex physiological phenomenon that is common to all skeletal muscles. Although complex, this phenomenon is not as difficult to understand as one might imagine. Essentially, the faster a muscle contracts (shortens), the lower the force it is able to generate (figure 3.1, page 53). In real life, muscles shorten when they contract, and this brings about movements, which have a given velocity. To better understand this property of muscle, consider how much more force can be exerted against a door that is closed (static contraction) versus a door that opens when a person pushes on it (dynamic contraction). Or consider how much less force a person can exert on the pedals when cycling in a low gear compared to a high gear.

Thus, as breath volume and airflow rate increase with exercise, a given level of respiratory pressure represents a relatively greater percentage of the system's maximum pressure-generating capacity—and requires correspondingly greater effort from the breathing muscles. In moderately fit, healthy individuals, the peak dynamic pressure generated by the inspiratory muscles (expressed relative to the ability to generate pressure, at the volumes and flows adopted during maximal exercise) is around 40 to 60 percent. However, in circumstances where muscle operating length is reduced (high tidal volumes) or where the velocity of shortening must increase to meet elevated flow requirements, this percentage may increase considerably. Such conditions arise in sports such as swimming, and they render the inspiratory muscles, in particular, vulnerable to fatigue.

Assessment of Breathing Muscle Function

A comprehensive description of assessment is beyond the scope of this book; however, this section will help you develop a working knowledge of the most widely used testing methods.

Assessing the strength of limb muscles is relatively straightforward and involves measuring the force that can be exerted using a device that measures force. However, it's impossible to measure the force output of the breathing muscles directly. Instead, we must measure a surrogate of this—the pressure that the breathing muscles can generate. The most commonly used index of breathing muscle function is the maximal static pressure (measured at the mouth) during maximal inspiratory or expiratory efforts when the mouth is occluded.

As previously mentioned, the respiratory muscles have a potent length–tension (pressure–volume) relationship (see figure 1.8). In other words, muscle strength (pressure) is determined by muscle length (volume). To standardize measurements, maximal mouth pressures are assessed at specified lung volumes where strength is maximal. Maximal inspiratory pressure (MIP or P_{Imax}) is most commonly measured at residual volume (the end of a maximal exhalation), although it may also be measured at functional residual capacity (the end of a relaxed exhalation). Maximal expiratory pressure (MEP or P_{Emax}) is measured with the lungs full, which is known as total lung capacity (the end of a maximal inhalation). Failure to standardize lung volume contributes to lack of reliability in the assessment of inspiratory muscle strength, making this one of the most important factors to control. Proprietary equipment is available for the measurement of mouth pressures (see the equipment recommendations at www.breathestrong.com).

In addition, peak inspiratory airflow rate is proportional to inspiratory muscle strength, showing an increase after training and a reduction in response to fatigue (Romer & McConnell, 2003). Accordingly, this is another index of inspiratory muscle function that can be used when suitable equipment is available (e.g., an electronic spirometer or a mechanical peak inspiratory flow meter). Unfortunately, peak expiratory flow rate is not proportional to expiratory muscle strength, being determined to a large extent by the characteristics of the lung airways. Therefore, it cannot be used as an alternative means of assessing expiratory muscle function.

By their very nature, measures of maximal voluntary muscle function are highly effort dependent, and participant motivation is therefore another extremely influential factor in determining the outcome of the test. Task learning also has an effect, which results in progressive improvement in pressures with repeated measurement. Thus, to obtain representative measures of function, we must familiarize the participants with the measurement, and we must provide coaching and encouragement to obtain maximal effort. A technique for warming up the inspiratory muscles is described in more detail in chapter 6. This technique reduces the effect of repeated measurement and improves reliability.

Upper Airway Muscles

In the context of exercise, the relevant upper airway (throat) muscles are those that control the vocal folds (also known as the vocal cords). Why are these muscles relevant? During normal breathing, the vocal folds are parted (abduct) during inhalation in order to widen the laryngeal glottic opening, permitting unobstructed airflow through the larynx. This occurs via reflex activation of the posterior cricoarytenoid (PCA) muscle—that is, it's not something that occurs consciously; it happens automatically as part of a normal inhalation. Without this activity, the vocal folds would collapse across that laryngeal opening, causing an increase in resistance to upper airway flow and leading to increased breathing effort and breathlessness. The force of contraction of the PCA muscles is proportional to the level of effort of the breathing muscles. During vigorous breathing, the action of the PCA is supplemented by contraction of the cricothyroid muscle (CT), which acts to tense the vocal folds, increasing the anteroposterior (front to back) dimension of the larynx. Active narrowing of the vocal folds (adduction) is performed by the lateral cricoarytenoid muscle (LCA), the thyroarytenoid (TA), and the interarytenoid (IA). During resting breathing, most of the narrowing of the vocal folds is brought about by relaxation of the PCA. Narrowing of the airway provides an important passive braking effect during exhalation, which gives it an important role in controlling breathing frequency, the duration of exhalation relative to inhalation, and end expiratory lung volume. Active narrowing is also associated with activities such as vocalization, coughing, and straining.

The fiber types of human laryngeal muscles have not been studied nearly so extensively as those of limb muscles, but the PCA and CT muscles (airway opening) contain around 66 percent and 45 percent Type I fibers, respectively. The Type II fibers of these muscles are limited to IIA and IIX, but the latter are very few in number. The proportion of fast IIX fibers appears to be larger in the airway-narrowing muscles (TA and LCA), which probably gives them a better ability to contract to protect the lungs from inhalation of foreign materials.

Because of its role in vocalization, the LCA (an airway narrower) has been studied in relation to its fatigability. Prolonged, loud vocalization exercises result in fatigue, and under similarly challenging conditions of vigorous breathing during exercise, the airway opening can become impaired during inhalation, resulting in an increase in breathing resistance. This phenomenon is observed in athletes who present with inspiratory stridor, which is a loud, inspiratory wheeze (see chapter 2).

Core Muscles

A book on functional breathing training would be incomplete without consideration of the breathing muscles as part of the postural control (balance) and core-stabilizing systems. Let's begin by defining the difference between the concepts of stability and control, because these will be revisited many times in *Breathe Strong, Perform Better*.

> **Core stability**—Actions that maintain stability of the trunk and lumbo-pelvic region, protecting the spine from damage and creating a stable platform from which to generate limb movements.

> **Postural control**—Actions that maintain balance in response to destabilizing forces acting on the body.

These nonrespiratory roles of the trunk muscles are often brought into conflict with these muscles' role in breathing. As a result, none of these roles are undertaken optimally. When functional conflicts occur within the muscular system, the risk of system failure can be mitigated by providing the muscles involved with reserve capacity and by establishing (as routine) specific neural activation patterns through training. In this section, the role of the breathing muscles as postural controllers and core stabilizers is considered in order to develop the rationale for such functional breathing training.

Before beginning our discussion, we first need to define core stability. In simple terms, core stability provides a stable platform from which the limbs can perform movements. Without the stable platform provided by the core muscles, people are just "shooting a cannon from a canoe" (Tsatsouline, 2000)—with very similar results! However, an emerging concept in core training is based on the notion that a key function of the core is to oppose rotational movements of the trunk that could be injurious (Boyle, 2010). These seem like sensible and helpful ways to conceptualize the core.

As previously mentioned, anatomically, the core acts as a stable base from which the limbs perform movements; the core is made up of the spine, the pelvis, and a myriad of muscles that stabilize these bony structures. The majority of the prime movers and stabilizing muscles of the limbs attach to the pelvis and spine.

The abdominal muscles (transversus abdominis, internal and external obliques, and rectus abdominis) are a group of large and relatively superficial muscles that act to stiffen the abdominal compartment and increase intraabdominal pressure, thereby stiffening and stabilizing the spine and pelvis. When contracted, these muscles form a rigid cylinder (or corset). Their ability to increase intraabdominal pressure is influenced by the state of contraction of the pelvic floor and the diaphragm, which can be considered as the base and lid of the rigid cylinder formed by the abdominal muscles. The increase in intraabdominal pressure resulting from contraction of the walls of the cylinder (the corset muscles) is dissipated if the lid (diaphragm) is not held in place. Conversely, if the lid moves downward into the cylinder, the increase in pressure can be magnified. Hence, the diaphragm makes a substantial and important contribution to the development of intraabdominal pressure, and thus, to core stability and postural control.

Both the transversus abdominis and the diaphragm have important roles in stiffening the trunk as part of a strategy to protect the spine and to preserve postural control (prevent falling). Both muscles contract automatically in anticipation of actions that destabilize or load the trunk. These contractions occur irrespective of the phase of breathing, but when push comes to shove, the diaphragm's role in breathing always takes precedence over its role in posture (Hodges, Heijnen, & Gandevia, 2001). So in situations of high breathing demand, such as exercise, the postural role of the diaphragm is compromised, which may lead to an increased risk of injury and an increased risk of falling or loss of balance. This has important implications for any sport where breathing demands are high.

Interestingly, when the inspiratory muscles are fatigued, people adopt less efficient postural control strategies than in the unfatigued state (Janssens et al., 2010). This supports the notion that the breathing muscles play a vital role in balance. Another recent study has also shown that if the inspiratory muscles are fatigued before an isometric trunk extension test, fatigue of the back muscles occurs more quickly. This suggests that inhibiting the contribution of the inspiratory muscles to trunk extension places greater demands on the back musculature. These data highlight the vital role played by the inspiratory muscles in postural control and core stability.

Clearly, both inspiratory and expiratory muscles are fundamental to providing postural control and core stabilization. However, although the abdominal muscles are an integral part of most core stabilization training, the same is not true of the diaphragm or other inspiratory muscles. Given the high risk of inspiratory muscle fatigue during exercise, and given the fact that respiratory functions predominate when the diaphragm is overloaded, this appears to be an oversight with respect to effective core conditioning and injury prevention. In chapters 7 to 11, we will consider how to implement functional inspiratory muscle training (IMT) that incorporates challenges to both respiratory and postural control, as well as how to incorporate IMT into core stability training.

EXERCISE-INDUCED ASTHMA

Exercise-induced asthma (EIA) is the most common chronic condition affecting the sporting population. Accordingly, no book on breathing during exercise would be complete without consideration of EIA, especially since there is good evidence that breathing muscle training relieves some symptoms. In some sports, as many as 50 percent of athletes are affected; this is a staggering four times the prevalence observed in the general population. In this section, we consider what asthma is, explore why its prevalence differs between sports, and discuss how breathing muscle training may be used to help manage this condition.

Asthma is defined as a chronic inflammatory disorder of the airways; the main symptoms of this disorder are wheezing, breathlessness, chest tightness, and coughing. An example of an inflammatory response that everyone has experienced at some time in their lives is the tissue swelling and redness after a nettle sting. Asthma symptoms are the result of airway narrowing in response to the swelling and inflammation caused by a trigger (e.g., pollen, animal dander). A complex cascade of biochemical events takes place, starting with the release of inflammatory bio-chemicals and culminating in tissue swelling and the contraction of small muscles around the airways. The resulting airway narrowing is called bronchoconstriction. In addition to this acute narrowing in response to specific triggers, narrowing can become a chronic event due to persistent swelling of the airway lining, which bulges into the lumen of the airway, making it narrower. Additional narrowing may occur because of a buildup of mucus in the airway lining. These events reduce the internal diameter of the airways, inducing the classic symptoms of asthma.

The prevalence of asthma in the general population varies among nations, being highest in the developed Western countries such as the United Kingdom and the United States, where 8.6 percent and 11 percent of the population are diagnosed with asthma. Current estimates of the prevalence of asthma in elite athletes are between 10 and 50 percent, depending on the sport. This higher prevalence in athletes compared to "couch potatoes" comes as a surprise to most people, who see athletes as the epitome of health. So why are athletes more prone to asthma? The difference in prevalence across sports holds some clues.

Winter sport athletes are reported to have the highest prevalence rates, especially those engaged in endurance events. For example, the prevalence of asthma in cross-country skiers is around 50 percent, and it is 21 percent in figure skaters. Other endurance-based events with high prevalence rates include cycling and triathlon. In addition, certain indoor environments are associated with high prevalence rates for asthma (e.g., swimming). Thus, there is a greater prevalence of EIA in endurance and winter sports, as well as those sports where training and competing take place in environments where the air contains irritants, such as chlorinated swimming pools. In these sports, prevalence can be as high as 40 or even 50 percent.

So the question remains, why should athletes be more susceptible to asthma? To understand this, a person needs to know a little about what triggers asthma during exercise. Exercise is believed to trigger bronchoconstriction (narrowing of the airways) because it leads to dehydration of the lung's airways. Inhaled air contains relatively little moisture, so when this air enters the lungs, it's not only warmed (to body temperature) but it's also humidified. This moisture is "sucked out" of the airway-lining cells, causing them to dehydrate. Dehydration induces inflammation and sets off the same cascade of biochemical changes that other asthma triggers initiate in a susceptible individual, ending in bronchoconstriction. The response normally peaks 10 to 15 minutes after exercise has stopped. The degree to which a given bout of exercise provokes bronchoconstriction is dependent on exercise intensity (how much air washes in and out of the lungs) and the temperature and humidity of the inhaled air. Cold air is very dry and therefore causes faster and more severe dehydration. In contrast, warm and humid environments (such as swimming pools) are less provocative from a dehydration perspective (but see the upcoming caveat).

No one knows for certain why asthma prevalence is higher in athletes, but it seems that they may develop the condition over a number of years of heavy training. One plausible hypothesis relates to the phenomenon of "airway trauma." In other words, airway damage due to repeated dehydration or damage caused by inhaled irritants leads to the development of a chronic inflammatory state within the airways. Eventually, airway sensitivity to triggers increases to a level where it becomes clinically significant, and asthma is the result.

Prevalence of Exercise-Induced Asthma in British Olympic Athletes

As part of routine screening of Team GB (Great Britain Olympic team) before the 2004 Athens Olympics, we confirmed the relatively high prevalence of asthma in high-performance athletes (Dickinson et al., 2005). The recorded prevalence for Team GB across all sports was 21 percent, which is more than double the prevalence rate in the United Kingdom's general population. The two sports with the highest prevalence rates were swimming and cycling (both over 40 percent).

Does asthma actually limit exercise performance? Given the world-class athletes who are known to have asthma, you'd think not—some examples include Paula Radcliffe, Haile Gebrselassie, Jerome Bettis, Dennis Rodman, Misty Hyman, and Grant Hackett. However, poorly controlled asthma does impair performance, as well as jeopardizing health and well-being.

Any performance impairment probably derives from the effect that asthma has on a person's ability to fill and empty the lungs during exercise. Narrowed airways impair expiratory flow-generating capacity, making it more difficult to breathe out and causing the end expiratory lung volume to increase (the person cannot breathe out as far). Inhalation therefore begins at a higher lung volume, so to achieve the required breath volume, inhalation must be deeper. This takes end inspiratory lung volume closer to total lung capacity, a phenomenon known as dynamic hyperinflation. Breathing at higher lung volumes requires greater inspiratory muscle work, because hyperinflated lungs are more stretched and resist expansion to a greater extent than deflated lungs (remember the balloon analogy from earlier in the chapter). To conceptualize this, think about how much more difficult it becomes to inflate a party balloon as it approaches full inflation.

Not surprisingly, the main symptom of hyperinflation is a heightened sensation of breathing effort, or breathlessness, due to the increased inspiratory muscle work. Breathlessness contributes to the sensation of total-body effort; consequently, dynamic hyperinflation due to airway narrowing increases the overall sense of effort during exercise. Because most athletes use their perception of effort as a means of pacing, the consequences of dynamic hyperinflation and increased airway resistance for an athlete's ability to achieve and maintain a given pace are obvious. The increased inspiratory muscle work may also exacerbate inspiratory muscle fatigue, which would further intensify the sensation of respiratory effort (as well as have other deleterious effects that are discussed in chapter 2). It is currently unknown whether respiratory effort sensation and inspiratory muscle fatigue are greater in athletes with EIA, but the potential for overloading of the inspiratory muscles in these athletes provides a rationale for specific training. The evidence of a beneficial effect of training on asthma symptoms is described in chapter 4.

PROTECTIVE EQUIPMENT AND BREATHING

Many sports involve the use of protective equipment; for some sports, the use of this equipment (e.g., mouth guards) is a mandatory prerequisite to participation. Unfortunately, some protective equipment interferes with breathing. In this section, we'll consider the implications of this.

Mouth Guards

The use of mouth guards in sport has increased enormously in the past decade and is now a mandatory feature of many contact sports, especially for minors. The American Dental Association has recommended the use of mouth guards for a wide variety of sports, including boxing, field and ice hockey, lacrosse, martial arts, rugby, and wrestling. Used initially as a means of preventing or minimizing orofacial trauma, mouth guards have also been shown to reduce the risk of brain injury by absorbing impact forces that are usually transmitted through the skull to the brain. Because of their presence within the oral cavity, mouth guards increase the resistance to airflow via the mouth. Although this can be minimized by the use of smaller, custom-fit products, even these products can double the resistance to airflow and, consequently, the sense of breathing discomfort associated with their use. The sight of players in team sports removing their mouth guards between plays is commonplace, and this illustrates perfectly the impediments that these devices impose during recovery. Any additional increase in the work of breathing also increases the risk of inspiratory muscle fatigue. These repercussions provide a potent rationale for training the breathing muscles in order to counteract the negative impact of mouth guard use related to breathing difficulty and the risks of breathing muscle fatigue.

Impact Protection

Impact protection equipment takes many forms and is highly sport specific, but there are some common features of such equipment that are relevant to breathing. Much of this equipment is worn on the trunk, and as explained earlier in this chapter, inhalation requires the expansion of the rib cage and outward movement of the abdominal wall; thus, anything that is worn on the trunk has the potential to impede inspiratory movements—and therefore has the potential to impede breathing. The two factors that determine the severity of this impedance are the weight of the equipment and how tightly it fits the body. More often than not, heavy protective equipment is also tight fitting (so that it does not interfere with body movement), which amounts to a double whammy from the perspective of breathing effort and discomfort. A study of the influence of American football shoulder pads on lung function found significant impairments when padding was "game tight." The authors concluded that these impairments may be sufficient to impair performance. This is supported by other evidence that mechanical restriction of rib cage movement exacerbates diaphragm fatigue during moderate exercise and reduces maximal exercise performance. Therefore, we have an excellent rationale for addressing the negative impact of tight-fitting protective equipment using specific training, and this will be covered in the relevant functional training chapters.

Wet Suits

For a wet suit to perform its function efficiently, it needs to be very tight fitting. Unlike other swimwear, which is relatively elastic, even those wet suits that are designed specifically for open-water swimming are relatively noncompliant. Wet suits therefore impose a restriction on breathing movements that is perceptible even at rest. Once the person is immersed, the problem is exacerbated by the additional influence of hydrostatic pressure (see chapter 2). In addition, the high breath volume associated with swimming necessitates larger thoracic movements than those of terrestrial exercise, and the stretching of the suit during the stroke also serves to add further tension around the trunk. As mentioned in the previous section, mechanical restriction of rib cage movement exacerbates diaphragm fatigue, reduces maximal exercise performance, and increases breathing effort. All in all, the wet suit poses a huge challenge to the inspiratory muscles by increasing the work, effort, and discomfort of the breathing muscles, as well as the risk of inspiratory muscle fatigue. Again, we have a particularly strong rationale for using specific training to overcome the detrimental effects of wet suits on breathing, and this will be addressed in chapter 8.

BREATHING CADENCE DURING EXERCISE

A glance at the table of contents of most coaching manuals speaks volumes about how overlooked the importance of breathing is. There is simply no mention of breathing, let alone any advice on how to do it well. This shouldn't be surprising, given the fact that everyone thinks of breathing as an automatic process that takes care of itself. However, a simple awareness of breathing and its interaction with exercise can prompt behavioral changes that improve the comfort of exercise and might also improve performance.

So what is the best way to breathe during exercise? The answer, of course, depends on what you are doing, but the application of some simple common sense is a great place to start. However, the commonsense approach requires an understanding of the factors that interfere with efficient, comfortable breathing during exercise. These are discussed in detail in the context of specific sports in chapter 2, but on a generic level, the main challenges to breathing arise because of the following:

- The effects of gravity
- The influence of momentum
- The dual role of the breathing muscles as postural control and stabilizing muscles
- Involvement of the breathing muscles in locomotion (e.g., rowing)
- Involvement of the breathing muscles in rotation of the trunk

To illustrate how breathing and the natural rhythm of the activity can and should be coordinated (entrained) in order to maximize comfort and efficiency, let's look at three sports—running, cycling, and rowing. The principles involved can be extended to other sports by the application of the aforementioned common sense.

Gravity and momentum pose particular problems during running. These problems arise from the fact that the main inspiratory muscle, the diaphragm, moves between the thoracic and abdominal compartments during contraction (inhalation) and relaxation (exhalation). As the diaphragm contracts, its dome flattens and it moves into the abdominal compartment. This compartment is full of organs (the abdominal viscera) that move up and down during running; these organs can impede or assist diaphragm movement, depending on how breathing and movement of the abdominal viscera interact. Based on this knowledge, it should be obvious that there is a need to synchronize breathing and stride cadence (tempo) in order to optimize these interactions. Some evidence, albeit limited, suggests that entrainment of running and breathing cadences reduces the oxygen cost of running. During a moderate-intensity run, the breath cycle should be completed on every other footfall of the same leg. In other words, inhalation starts as the right foot strikes, and it continues as the left foot strikes (so that inhalation occurs in two "sips"); exhalation starts as the right foot strikes for the second time, and it continues as the left foot strikes (in two sips).

However, bear in mind that faster running cadence or higher-intensity exercise may necessitate modification of this pattern, but that synchrony with movement should be maintained through modulation of breathing frequency and volume.

During cycling, the factors that determine pedal cadence are complex, and cadence varies enormously. However, during flat stages and time trials, professional and highly competitive cyclists typically adopt pedal rates of around 90 rpm, and they use breathing frequencies entrained to either 1:3 (1 breath to 3 pedal revolutions) or 1:2. A shift from a breathing–pedaling ratio of 1:3 to 1:2 occurs as exercise intensity or duration increases. In other words, breathing frequency tends to increase to meet increased demand for breathing. Although cyclists don't have to contend with the influence of gravity and momentum on their abdominal viscera, there is evidence that entraining pedal and breathing patterns reduces the oxygen cost of cycling. This phenomenon may be related to the role of the breathing muscles as core stabilizers—power output may be generated more efficiently from a more stable pelvis, which may be achieved more effectively if breathing and pedal cadence are entrained.

Experienced rowers entrain their breathing to their rowing stroke rate, confining their breathing to two main patterns: 1:1 (one expiration per drive and one inspiration during recovery) or 2:1 (one complete breath during the drive and one complete breath during recovery). During a 2,000-meter race, athletes commonly try to maintain the 2:1 breathing pattern; they breathe out during the initial part of the drive (when the blade is in the water), take a breath as they reach the end of the drive, breathe out again as they begin to come forward, and take a small breath just before the "catch." Unlike most other sports, the drive phase of the rowing stroke involves the breathing muscles in locomotor force transmission (from foot stretcher to blade handle), because they must contract forcefully in order to stiffen the trunk. Stiffening the trunk is achieved more effectively if the lungs are partially inflated and if there is a brief breath hold, which is what a person instinctively does when lifting something heavy. Thus, for actions that involve production or transmission of force using the upper body, the synchrony of breathing with the movement is essential. This is also seen in sports that involve striking or throwing (see chapter 10).

Chapter

2

Performance Limitations of Breathing Muscles

In chapter 1, we discussed the structure and function of the respiratory system, as well as the muscles involved in breathing. This included the muscles that people don't conventionally think of as being linked to breathing, such as those of the upper airway and abdomen. We also considered some common breathing problems encountered in sports, and we discussed the importance of synchronizing breathing with locomotor and other movements. As mentioned in chapter 1, breathing harder does not increase the amount of oxygen delivered to the muscles during exercise. On the face of it, this fact might seem to be a show stopper for a book with the premise that breathing training improves performance. However, in this chapter, we explore the reasons why breathing limits performance, and we lay the foundation for the benefits of functional breathing training. We do this by identifying the sport-specific demands that create conflicts between the breathing and nonbreathing roles of the trunk musculature. This chapter presents a strong, rational argument for investing time, money, and effort in breathing training. The information in this chapter also serves as a prelude to chapter 3, which summarizes the direct research evidence that breathing muscle training improves performance.

For people to understand how breathing training can be a time-efficient, versatile, and effective addition to their training, they need to understand the ways that breathing limits exercise performance. After all, if the condition of a muscle group doesn't limit performance, what's the point of improving its condition through training? If you've taken classes on exercise physiology and you've been told that breathing doesn't limit exercise performance, please don't stop reading. The research in this area is very new (in scientific time scales), having emerged only in the past decade. It's going to take another decade before this information becomes a part of exercise physiology texts and education programs. You're getting it here first.

WHY BREATHING LIMITS TRAINING AND COMPETITION

To explore the ways that breathing can limit training and competition, we'll look at two main areas: how the breathing pump muscles can limit exercise performance and how the upper airway muscles can limit exercise performance.

Limitations of the Breathing Pump Muscles

The physical work undertaken by the breathing muscles during the task of pumping air in and out of the lungs can be immense, and it influences both the perceived effort and the demands placed on the circulatory system for blood flow. Let's consider how these factors contribute to exercise limitation, focusing on the role and repercussions of breathing muscle fatigue.

An important premise in the argument that breathing muscles limit exercise performance is that they function at, or close to, the limits of their capacity. When muscles work in this way, they display fatigue. Accordingly, without some evidence of exercise-induced breathing muscle fatigue, the argument in favor of training these muscles is flimsy at best.

Breathing muscles are separated functionally according to whether they have inspiratory or expiratory actions. Because breathing requires equal amounts of each action, you might expect that fatigue would be present in both groups of muscles under the same conditions. This is not the case. One reason for this is that inspiratory muscle work is always greater than expiratory work (recall the party balloon analogy from chapter 1—the stretching of tissues on inhalation assists exhalation). A second reason is the differing training state of the muscles themselves (expiratory muscles are engaged in many postural activities that improve their training status). A third reason is that different exercise conditions overload the inspiratory and expiratory muscles to differing extents.

The earliest reports of inspiratory muscle fatigue after competitive events appeared in the early 1980s, where significant reductions in inspiratory muscle strength were measured after marathon running. Subsequent studies have confirmed these findings and have also shown that inspiratory muscle fatigue is present after ultramarathon and triathlon competitions. The sidebar on the next page summarizes published data on inspiratory muscle fatigue, which confirms that inspiratory muscle fatigue occurs under a wide range of real-world sporting conditions. Excellent evidence from the highly controlled environment of the research laboratory also indicates that strenuous exercise induces inspiratory muscle fatigue, including fatigue of the diaphragm. The inclusion of the diaphragm in exercise-induced fatigue came as a revelation, because people assumed that the diaphragm was so well evolved and adapted to continuous activity that it would be immune to fatigue. The evidence of diaphragm fatigue led to a complete rethink about the role of breathing muscles in exercise limitation.

So it's now well established that the inspiratory muscles fatigue, but what about the expiratory muscles? The expiratory muscles have been studied much less extensively, and the data are a little confusing because they are contradictory. For example, one study showed that after marathon running that induced inspiratory

Breathing Muscle Fatigue Occurs in a Wide Range of Sports

Under laboratory and field-based research conditions, my own research group has demonstrated inspiratory muscle fatigue after rowing, cycling, and swimming, as well as a sprint triathlon and treadmill marathon running. Figure 2.1 illustrates the relative magnitude of inspiratory muscle fatigue that we have measured for four aerobic sports.

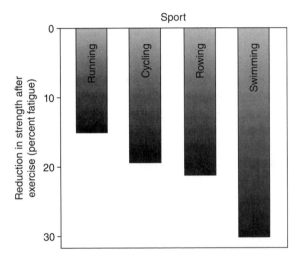

Figure 2.1 Inspiratory muscle fatigue in four sports.

muscle fatigue (IMF), there was no evidence of expiratory muscle fatigue (EMF). Similarly, another study showed that after a triathlon that induced significant IMF, there was no EMF. In contrast, after a rowing time trial that simulated a 2,000-meter rowing race in the laboratory, significant IMF and EMF have been observed. Research on EMF after cycling has only been undertaken in laboratory situations, but the data are no less confusing. Although EMF has been observed after cycling, it doesn't always occur. EMF appears to be specific to certain exercise modalities or intensities of exercise. On balance, EMF seems to arise under conditions where exercise intensity is maximal and where the expiratory muscles have a key role in propulsive force transmission (via trunk or core stabilization), such as in rowing and cycling. Currently, the research evidence points to IMF occurring in response to a wider range of activities than EMF, suggesting that the inspiratory muscles are overloaded to a greater extent than the expiratory muscles.

The next question is, "Does it matter that [some] breathing muscles show fatigue?" One way to answer this question is to prefatigue the breathing muscles by breathing against an external load—and then see what happens during subsequent exercise. In a nutshell, prefatiguing the breathing muscles increases the intensity of breathing and whole-body effort, and it leads to a reduction in the ability to sustain exercise. For example, one study found that when IMF was present, there was a 23 percent reduction in the time that cyclists could sustain high-intensity cycling, and the exercise felt harder.

Prior EMF has also been found to reduce the time that cyclists could sustain high-intensity cycling (33 percent) and increased breathing and leg effort. However, a cautionary note needs to be applied to any studies of EMF. It's been shown that breathing against an expiratory load doesn't just affect the expiratory muscles; it also induces IMF. In other words, the effect of EMF on subsequent exercise performance is "contaminated" by the accompanying IMF. This is because the inspiratory muscles are involved in the transmission of expiratory pressure (think about how much you need to brace your rib cage and diaphragm when you try to inflate a stiff party balloon).

Another way to look at how breathing muscles influence performance is to manipulate the work of breathing during exercise. In theory, if breathing muscles limit exercise performance, then reducing the amount of work they undertake during exercise should improve performance. Similarly, increasing the work of breathing during exercise should impair performance. In a series of studies undertaken at the University of Wisconsin, a special lung ventilator has been used to do just this, with some surprising results.

In the first study, the Wisconsin researchers examined the influence of changes in the work of inhalation on blood flow to the legs during maximal cycle ergometer exercise (Harms et al., 1997). Somewhat surprisingly, they found that if they decreased the work of inhalation using the ventilator, leg blood flow increased (4.3 percent). In contrast, when the work of inhalation was increased by having the person breathe against a resistance, leg blood flow decreased (7 percent). The changes in leg blood flow were mediated by changes in the neural input to the blood vessels in the limbs—the blood vessels narrowed (vasoconstricted) when inspiratory work was increased, and they dilated when inspiratory work was reduced. In a series of subsequent studies, the researchers showed that the trigger for limb vasoconstriction was a reflex originating within the inspiratory muscles, which they called the "inspiratory muscle metaboreflex" (Sheel et al., 2002).

What's a metaboreflex? When muscles work very hard, metabolic by-products, such as lactic acid, accumulate within them. These metabolites stimulate receptors inside the muscles that send signals to the brain to trigger a reflex shutdown of the circulation, including the blood supply to the locomotor muscles. What are the implications of changing the blood flow to muscles in this way? Restricting blood flow restricts the supply of oxygen and impairs the removal of exercise metabolites from exercising muscles. As a result, muscles fatigue more quickly, and exercise performance is impaired. Indeed, this is precisely what has been found; changing the work of breathing to hasten or delay the onset of the inspiratory muscle metaboreflex changes leg fatigue and exercise performance in a highly predictable way—that is, increasing inspiratory muscle work hastens metaboreflex activation, accelerates limb fatigue, and impairs performance (reducing inspiratory muscle work does the opposite). It is thought that this metaboreflex may be a protective mechanism that forces people to slow down or stop in order to prevent catastrophic levels of breathing fatigue.

Earlier, we touched briefly on the effect of IMF and EMF on breathing and limb effort—breathing muscle fatigue intensifies the sense of effort during exercise. The influence on limb effort should now be clear; IMF reduces limb blood flow, thereby reducing oxygen delivery and accelerating limb fatigue. Although it might seem obvious that weak or fatigued muscles generate greater perception of effort than fresh or stronger muscles, the neurophysiological mechanism underpinning this reality merits a few words. The human brain is able to judge the size of the neural drive that it sends to muscles to make them contract. As muscles contract, they return information to the brain about the amount of force that is being generated, as well as about the speed and range of motion of the movement. Heavy objects generate high forces, are moved slowly, and are moved with a more limited range of motion (vice versa for light objects). The sensory area of the brain compares the size of the drive sent to the muscles with the sensory information coming from the muscles. In doing so, it formulates a perception of effort. For example, if the neural drive to the biceps during an arm curl is high (because the muscle is weak or fatigued), and if the sensory feedback suggests that there is a high tension within the muscles and that the bar is moving slowing and through a limited range, the perception of effort is high (i.e., the weight feels heavy).

The size of the neural drive required to generate a given external force is influenced by a number of factors, but principally by the strength of the muscle. A strong muscle requires a lower neural drive to generate a given force, which is why weights feel lighter after a person has become stronger. Similarly, a fatigued muscle requires a higher neural drive to generate a given force, which is why weights feel heavier when a person is fatigued.

These neurophysiological principles apply equally to the breathing muscles as they do to other skeletal muscles, so it is easy to see why and how weakness, fatigue, or strengthening of the breathing muscles can modulate the perception of breathing effort. How might this affect performance? Athletes use their perceived effort as a pacing cue; intolerable effort for a given speed will lead to a reduction in pace. The evidence that strengthening the breathing muscles reduces breathing effort and improves performance is reviewed in chapter 3.

Thus, the past decade or so has seen the emergence of evidence that breathing muscle work has influences far beyond anything that was thought possible. Fifteen years ago, nobody would have suggested that when a person's breathing muscles work hard, it causes that person's legs to fatigue more quickly!

Limitations of the Upper Airway Muscles

The upper airway muscles must operate in a coordinated fashion with the respiratory muscles in order to minimize upper airway resistance. Although there is currently no research (on human beings at least) examining the influence of exercise on fatigue of the upper airway muscles, evidence does exist that points to the fact that exercise can disrupt the normal coordinated function of the upper airway muscles. When this happens, the resulting increase in breathing effort means that exercise intolerance follows swiftly.

Disruption of the normal function of the upper airway occurs most notably in a condition known as inspiratory stridor. This condition is characterized by a high-pitched wheeze that occurs during inhalation, and it is the result of the failure of the vocal folds to move apart during inhalation. The resulting obstruction induces a huge increase in inspiratory muscle work, an increase in the intensity of breathing effort, and abrupt exercise intolerance. The association of inspiratory stridor with exercise leads to a frequent misdiagnosis of exercise-induced asthma.

How do the upper airway muscles contribute to exercise limitation? In people who experience inspiratory stridor, the implications are obvious—abrupt exercise intolerance. But this is not the end of the story for these athletes; they often experience severe disruption to training and an associated decline in performance. Furthermore, the role of fatigue of the upper airway dilating muscles in minimizing the resistance to airflow is, as yet, untested. However, it is reasonable to suggest that if there is even slight upper airway collapse during exercise, this will increase resistance to airflow and increase the work of breathing. As discussed in the previous section, the implications of increasing the work of breathing are wide reaching and could precipitate a decline in performance via increased effort perception, as well as the inspiratory muscle metaboreflex.

Some Myths About Our "Superhuman" Breathing System

The biggest myth in sport science is that breathing doesn't limit exercise tolerance or performance. The myth has arisen because the scientists have been blinded by their incomplete knowledge. It's normally the nonscientists who get it wrong when it comes to sport science (e.g., how many people in the street think that sit-ups will "burn" fat on the abdomen?), but in the case of breathing, the nonscientists actually have it right; breathing does limit exercise. They know this from their own experience. The problem for the sport scientists is that they have been bogged down by some dogma about breathing that needs to be rethought.

Essentially, three "submyths" about breathing have misled the scientists who were taught them:

1. The first myth is that because breathing harder doesn't increase oxygen delivery to the muscles, breathing cannot be a limiting factor in performance. The problem is that this assumes that oxygen delivery is the sole limiting factor in exercise performance. When athletes complete a time trial as fast as they can, they do so at an intensity that is below the maximal ability of their body to deliver oxygen to their muscles (the maximal oxygen uptake, or $\dot{V}O_2$max). The athletes' performance is not limited by their $\dot{V}O_2$max, but by their ability to sustain a critical intensity of exercise for a specified period of time without becoming fatigued. For example, athletes running a 10K will be exercising at a high proportion of their $\dot{V}O_2$max; however, what separates athletes is not their individual $\dot{V}O_2$max, but the proportion of their $\dot{V}O_2$max that they are able to sustain for the duration of the event. The factors that limit their pace are many and varied, but these factors boil down to two things: the athletes' ability to sustain a given intensity of exercise without becoming so fatigued that they must slow down or stop, and the athletes' ability to tolerate the discomfort associated with the exercise. These two factors are not independent of one another, but they do have separate influences. Either way, an athlete's $\dot{V}O_2$max is not a direct determinant of her performance, and the fact that breathing does not limit $\dot{V}O_2$max should not be interpreted to mean that breathing does not limit performance.

2. The second myth is based on the observation that if you ask someone to breathe as hard as he can for 15 seconds, the ventilation that he can achieve exceeds the ventilation that he reaches at peak exercise. In other words, there is a "breathing reserve." However, this is a bit like saying that because you can sprint 100 meters faster than you can run a 10K, you have a "speed reserve"—and therefore your running ability doesn't limit your 10K performance, because you could run faster! A more meaningful index of the limits imposed by your breathing is to see how well you can *sustain* high levels of breathing. Back to the 10K analogy, the index of how your running speed affects your performance is the speed that you can sustain for the duration of a 10K race. When we use a test of the ability to sustain high levels of breathing, we find that the level is roughly the same as the minute ventilation at peak exercise. This suggests that during heavy exercise, the breathing pump is operating at a level that is very close to its maximal capacity for sustained breathing. Furthermore, when we also take into account the effect of fatigue on the breathing muscles during sustained exercise, it is clear that they are likely operating close to their capacity during many real-world sporting situations.

3. The third myth is that breathing muscles are highly evolved and developed for their function and do not show fatigue during exercise. Research has now shown that even the "superhuman" diaphragm exhibits fatigue after exercise (see the main text).

With these three myths about breathing and exercise dispelled, the path is now clear to explore the ways in which the breathing muscles limit exercise tolerance and performance.

BREATHING MUSCLE LIMITATIONS IN SPECIFIC SPORTS

Different sports impose differing demands on the breathing, postural control, and core stabilizing roles of the trunk muscles. In some sports (e.g., soccer), these roles must be met simultaneously; failure to do so can lead to a loss of postural control and an increased risk of injury. In other sports (e.g., golf), the breathing muscles play a key role in generating the stability and anchoring that are required to generate striking movements. In others, such as swimming, the entire trunk musculature contributes to propulsive movements, creating a different sort of competing demand for the breathing muscles. Fundamentally, the role of the breathing muscles in a given sport needs to be considered in all its contexts, because each aspect contributes to performance. In addition, a muscle that is performing multiple roles simultaneously is more susceptible to fatigue. Finally, in some sports, the work of breathing is rendered greater because of the restriction of normal inspiratory movements by the environment (e.g., swimming) or by body position (e.g., rowing), which also heightens the risk of fatigue. Breathing muscle fatigue makes a major contribution to exercise limitation, and it increases the risk of injury; avoiding this kind of fatigue is therefore a "no-brainer" in terms of optimizing performance. The following sections consider the role of the breathing muscles in a range of popular sports. By considering the factors described, people can develop an insight that enables them to examine their sport in order to undertake their own analysis.

Running

On the face of it, you might think that breathing while running is a piece of cake compared to sports such as swimming, in which breathing is so completely dominated by the locomotor activity. However, running is a state of almost continuous instability, and the core muscles have to work hard—not only to ensure that you remain upright, but also to ensure that the sacroiliac joints (SIJs) and spine function properly and that the spine is protected from damage. The SIJs connect the fused section of your lower spine (the sacrum) to the pelvis (hip girdle); they are nature's shock absorbers, protecting your spine from the shock wave that hits your pelvis each time your foot strikes the ground. These joints also provide positional information that allows the trunk and legs to work in harmony. Therefore, the SIJs must be allowed some movement and compression, but not too much, and this is where the core stabilizers of the pelvic girdle come in. The core stabilizers add stability to the SIJs, promoting compression and allowing them to move within safe limits. The core stabilizers therefore protect the spine and SIJs from damage (Hodges et al., 2005).

What does this have to do with breathing? As described in chapter 1, the breathing muscles are a particularly important part of the core-stabilizing system. If you've ever had sore ribs and sore abdominal muscles after a cross-country run, then you have experienced the role of the core muscles in postural control firsthand; the soreness is a sign that your core stabilizers have been put through their paces by the postural challenges produced by running on uneven terrain. What most people don't appreciate is that the diaphragm is a vital component of the core, and that the rib cage muscles are also involved in making compensatory adjustments for postural instability. In effect, these muscles "catch" and restrain the trunk when it is thrown outside the center of gravity by an unstable foot placement. Research has shown that people with SIJ pain show impaired diaphragm contribution to SIJ stabilization, and that people with breathing-related disorders also have higher rates of low back pain. These observations highlight the vital role played by the diaphragm in postural control and injury prevention. During an activity such as running, the diaphragm and other breathing muscles are subjected to competing demands for postural control, core stabilization, and breathing. This has obvious implications for their risk of fatigue, as well as for the risk of injury—overloaded muscles fatigue more rapidly, and muscle fatigue increases the risk of injury. In chapter 8, we will consider how to mitigate these risks with functional training of the diaphragm and other breathing muscles for running.

The key to efficient, comfortable breathing during running is synchronizing breathing with the running cadence; this minimizes the competition between the stabilizing and breathing functions of the breathing muscles. In addition, if breathing and running cadences are not synchronized, respiratory movements of the diaphragm in particular are impeded by movements of the abdominal viscera (liver, stomach, gut), which bounce up and down in synchrony with running cadence. If the viscera are moving up as the diaphragm is moving down, diaphragm movement is impeded, increasing the work of the diaphragm and possibly impeding its blood flow. But, this "visceral pump" can also be used to your advantage. By breathing in time with stride frequency, a runner can ensure that the diaphragm is assisted by the downward movement of the abdominal viscera.

A sign that the respiratory muscles are working at the limits of their capacity to meet the demands of breathing and postural control during running is the high prevalence of stitch pains during running (i.e., localized and focused discomfort in the thoracic region). In a survey of almost 1,000 people engaged in a number of sports, 69 percent of runners had experienced stitch pain within the previous 12 months. The most common stitch pain for runners is a side stitch. Although there is currently no clear consensus regarding the cause of a side stitch, one theory is that it represents diaphragm ischemia (insufficient blood flow for the metabolic demand) or a diaphragm spasm (cramp). One of the most surprising untimely exits from a sporting event in recent times was Haile Gebrselassie's DNF in the 2007 London Marathon. The double Olympic 10,000-meter champion dropped out of the lead group shortly after the 30-kilometer mark, clutching his ribs. "I had a stitch here in my chest and could not continue. I'm not injured, I just couldn't breathe," he told BBC Sport, with more than a tinge of exasperated disbelief in his voice. This shows that a stitch can strike anyone at anytime and is no respecter of past sporting achievement or training.

In addition to pain around the rib cage, runners can also develop discomfort around the collarbone and lower neck region, which sometimes radiates from the collarbone down the biceps. These are signs that the inspiratory accessory muscles of the rib cage and neck (inspiratory intercostals, sternomastoids, scalenes) are overloaded and undertaking too much of the work of breathing.

Running efficiently also requires the maintenance of a stable core and the minimization of counter-rotational movements of the shoulders. Many inexperienced runners illustrate this need perfectly, especially when they are tired. One of the most noticeable deficits in their style is that their trunk and hips buckle and flex as they run. Also, their shoulders roll from side to side with each stride during the enforced counter-rotation of the upper and lower halves of their body. When this happens, propulsive forces are dissipated (think of them as leaking away like water through loose-fitting joints), and the efficiency of movement is reduced, making the runner slower. Maintaining control over trunk movements places extraordinary demands on the trunk musculature, which must accommodate this need as well as the need to control posture and to meet the demand for breathing.

Running presents a huge challenge to the breathing muscles. It requires them to function not only as breathing muscles, but also as a central part of the systems that control posture, protect the spine from injury, and optimize force transmission during the leg drive. In addition, running is an integral part of most terrestrial sports, which superimpose yet more demands. Chapter 8 includes specific guidance on functional breathing training to meet the demands of running, and chapter 9 deals with a range of sprint- and power-based team sports.

Cycling

As discussed in chapter 1, the breathing muscles form an important part of the system that stabilizes the trunk, forming a central anchoring point from which the limb muscles are able to generate forces that bring about locomotor and other movements.

An analysis of the biomechanics of cycling is beyond the scope of this book, but the relationship between core stability and cycling is pertinent to our discussion, because the breathing muscles form an important part of the core-stabilizing system. As has already been discussed, when there is competition between the breathing and core-stabilizing roles of the trunk muscles, there is potential for both impairment to performance and injury.

Currently, there is very little scientific information about the influence of core function on performance measures in cycling, but one study has noted that prior fatigue of the core musculature induced changes in cycling mechanics that placed greater stresses on the knee joints. The authors of the study concluded that this might predispose cyclists to an increased risk of overuse injuries. In addition, another study found that cyclists with chronic low back pain had impaired function of the muscles that control flexion and rotation in the lumbar region (the experience of low back pain, especially toward the latter stages of a long ride, is an all-too-familiar experience among cyclists at any level). In other words, these data suggest that, aside from any performance-related issues, normal function of the core-stabilizing system is essential for the maintenance of normal cycling mechanics and the reduction of injury risk.

In most sports, including cycling, the core provides the foundation from which force is generated. The stabilizing action of the core is very important for the production of cycling power. This is illustrated by the fact that external stabilization of the trunk (i.e., relieving the core muscles of the need to stabilize the trunk) significantly reduces the metabolic cost of cycling. The effect is greatest at pedaling speeds that induce the highest pedal forces. In other words, cyclists expend a lot of energy stabilizing their trunk in order to optimize power production.

The entrainment of breathing to pedaling cadence occurs more often and for longer periods in experienced cyclists, suggesting that it may provide some advantage. Professional and highly competitive cyclists typically adopt pedal rates of around 90 rpm, and they use breathing frequencies of either 1:3 (1 breath to 3 pedal revolutions) or 1:2. A shift from a breathing–pedaling ratio of 1:3 to 1:2 occurs as exercise intensity or duration increases. In other words, breathing frequency tends to increase to meet increased demands for breathing. This probably reflects two phenomena: that continuing to increase breath volume is unsustainable because of the increased inspiratory muscle work and breathing effort that is required (see chapter 1), and the onset of inspiratory muscle fatigue, which also increases unpleasant breathing sensations.

A characteristic of professional cyclists is that the shift toward higher breathing frequencies does not occur, and they are able to meet increased demand for breathing by increasing their breath volume. The maintenance of breath volume may reflect a higher training status of the cyclists' inspiratory muscles, and this may be a key factor in minimizing the energetic cost associated with breathing, thereby enhancing performance.

If the core provides the foundation from which force is generated during the pedal stroke, and if the stability of the core is influenced by breathing, a question then arises regarding the best time to breathe during the pedal cycle. Because a complete respiratory cycle (breathing in and out) occurs only once every two or three pedal revolutions, it is inevitable that force will not always be exerted on the pedals during, for example, an exhalation. To date, no studies have examined the potential benefits of breathing during particular phases of the pedal stroke, and this is probably because it's unlikely to have a large impact on performance. However, more than just performance should be considered. Exerting force on the pedals during the pedal downstroke requires the coordination of more than just the leg muscles. The stability of the upper body also needs to be maintained in order to ensure that it provides a stable foundation and that spinal movements are controlled. If a vital part of this stabilizing system is otherwise engaged (in breathing), the potential exists for impaired function of the core. As previously discussed, this has implications for injury risk.

At high pedal rates (greater than 70 rpm), the forces transmitted to the pedals are relatively small compared to the maximum force-generating capacity of the muscles involved; therefore, the competition between the postural role of the trunk muscles and their role in breathing is not as problematic as it is in sports such as rowing. However, during steep hill climbing, pedal rates drop, and pedal forces increase. During climbing, cyclists may find it advantageous to synchronize breathing and pedal cadence; indeed, this tends to occur intuitively, especially on very steep climbs. Notwithstanding this, evidence from elite cyclists suggests that the most important aspect of breathing and pedal synchrony is keeping a steady rhythm for each and maintaining a 1:3 ratio (1 breath for every 3 pedal revolutions). This ratio will optimize the efficiency and comfort of breathing, but a cyclist needs to work at maintaining the ratio; the reason that cyclists slip into a 1:2 ratio is because their inspiratory muscles are not sufficiently strong and fatigue resistant to maintain tidal volume. This is where specific breathing muscle training can help. Chapter 8 includes specific guidance on how to enhance breath control and optimize inspiratory muscle training (IMT) for cycling by using functional training techniques.

Finally, let's touch on the topic of upper body posture during cycling. Three main postures can be adopted during cycling: completely upright, leaning forward onto the brake hoods or drops of drop handlebars, or crouched forward over aerobars. Studies suggest that there are differences in the metabolic cost (energy cost) of cycling in these different postures—and that adopting a streamlined body position is advantageous. This is because minimizing the frontal area of the cyclist reduces aerodynamic drag, which reduces the metabolic cost of cycling for any given speed. However, the crouched body position associated with the use of aerobars is not without its disadvantages. Cyclists who are inexperienced in the use of aerobars exhibit detrimental effects on their breathing and mechanical efficiency compared to cycling in the upright position. For example, one study compared upright cycling to the use of aerobars, finding a lower maximal oxygen uptake and lower maximal ventilation with the use of aerobars. In addition, breathing appeared to be constrained, such that tidal volume was lower and breathing frequency was higher. This is a very inefficient breathing pattern (see the section called What Happens to Breathing During Exercise? in chapter 1); indeed, the mechanical efficiency of the cyclists was lower when using aerobars—that is, the same amount of cycling work required more energy.

The explanation for these findings resides in the influence of a crouched body position on inspiratory muscle mechanics during cycling. First, there is an effect on diaphragm movement caused by the large organs of the abdominal compartment (stomach, liver, and gut). These organs lie immediately below the diaphragm, and they are effectively a noncompressible mass (visceral mass) that must be pushed out of the way by the descending diaphragm (see figure 2.2). When a cyclist is crouching forward, the abdominal organs press against the diaphragm, impeding its movement; the volume of the abdomen is also reduced, which means there is less space to accommodate movement of the visceral mass during breathing. The abdominal wall, which normally bulges forward during inhalation, is also stiffer because it contributes to core stabilization, increasing diaphragm work still further. In addition, the extreme hip flexion brings the thighs closer to the abdominal wall, where they can also impede its outward movement during inhalation. These effects conspire to impede the free movement of the diaphragm and rib cage muscles, increasing inspiratory muscle work (see figure 2.2). Second, if cyclists are forced to adopt a higher breathing frequency (because breathing deeply is too uncomfortable in the crouched position), the resulting increase in breathing frequency means that inspiratory flow rate must be higher. This forces the inspiratory muscles to work in a region of their force–velocity relationship where fatigue and effort perception are greater (see Mechanical Properties of Breathing Pump Muscles on page 18 of chapter 1). Because studies appear to show that the aerobar position has fewer detrimental effects in cyclists who have used aerobars for a prolonged period, it appears likely that the inspiratory muscles adapt to the increased demands imposed by aerobars. A shortcut to this adaptation is to train the inspiratory muscles so that they are able to cope with the mechanical changes induced by the aerobar posture.

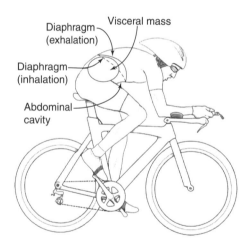

Figure 2.2 The effect of the aero position on the interaction of the incompressible abdominal organs and the diaphragm. Because the organs cannot be compressed, they must be moved within the abdominal cavity. In the crouched position, the space within the abdominal cavity is smaller, resulting in a greater impedance of movement and an increased reliance on forward movement of the abdominal wall.

Thus, some specific additional demands are placed on the breathing muscles during cycling. These include the muscles' contribution to the maintenance of core stabilization (for optimization of cycling mechanics and injury prevention) and the increase in inspiratory muscle work that is created by crouched body positions. Chapter 8 includes specific guidance on how to optimize breathing training for cycling with aerobars, as well as how to undertake breathing muscle training using functional training principles.

Rowing

Experienced rowers entrain their breathing to their rowing stroke rate. They tend to confine their breathing to two main patterns: 1:1 (one expiration per drive and one inspiration during recovery) or 2:1 (one complete breath during the drive and one complete breath during recovery). Research has shown that tidal volume (the volume of each breath) is constrained above a certain power output, and further increases in ventilation are brought about by increasing breathing frequency. Some researchers have gone as far as to suggest that at high work rates, stroke rate may be dictated by the urge to breathe, which reinforces the potent interrelationship of these two factors.

The linkage between stroke rate and breathing pushes the breathing muscles to their limits. During a 2,000-meter race, athletes commonly try to maintain the 2:1 breathing pattern; they breathe out during the initial part of the drive (when the blade is in the water), inhale as they reach the end of the drive, breathe out again as they begin to come forward, and take a small breath just before the "catch." This small breath at the catch is very important in terms of allowing the effective transmission of force from the stretcher to the blade handle.

In rowing, the same muscles that are used to breathe are also used for maintaining posture, maintaining core stability, and transmitting force during the drive phase of the stroke. Differing demands are placed on the breathing muscles at a number of critical points in the stroke. At the finish, the hips are partially extended, and the shoulders are behind the hips. This means that the muscles of the trunk must work against gravity to prevent the rower from falling backward. At the same time, the rower needs to take a large, fast breath, which means that the inspiratory muscles are subjected to competing demands for postural control and breathing. Once the rower reaches the catch, he must take another breath, but in this position, the movement of the diaphragm is impeded by the crouched body position (see the previous description of this effect during cycling). At the catch, the abdomen is compressed by the thighs pushing the abdominal viscera upward against the diaphragm. This compression makes it more difficult for the diaphragm to contract, flatten, and move downward, as it must do in order to inflate the lungs. During the drive, the inspiratory muscles are subjected to competing demands for breathing and force transmission, because they must contract in order to stiffen the trunk. All in all, rowing places some varied and extreme demands on the breathing muscles.

The combination of these demands renders the breathing muscles of rowers at heightened risk of becoming fatigued. Indeed, research has shown that the strength of the inspiratory muscles is 12 to 20 percent lower after a simulated 2,000-meter race (Volianitis, McConnell, Koutedakis, McNaughton, Backx, & Jones, 2001; Griffiths

& McConnell, 2007). Falls in inspiratory muscle strength after national or international indoor rowing competitions can be over 20 percent in world-class rowers.

The mechanics of rowing are such that breathing must be entrained to stroke rate (as previously described). Failure to do so is not only uncomfortable, but also jeopardizes the efficiency of the mechanical linkage between the blade handle and the major force producers of the lower body. In open-class oarsmen, the forces driven from the stretcher, through the body, and to the blade handle can be in the order of 900 newtons (the weight of two bags of cement). Because the main force generators for the rowing stroke are located below the waist, if force is to be transmitted effectively to the blade handle, it must be transferred effectively through the trunk. By increasing intraabdominal pressure, the diaphragm plays an important role in stiffening the trunk to transmit forces efficiently and to protect the rower's spine from injury.

So what's this got to do with breathing? The muscles that provide trunk stiffness are all breathing muscles. On the one hand, this creates a huge potential for conflict between the respiratory and nonrespiratory roles of these muscles, but on the other, it creates a requirement for a high level of synergy between these roles. For example, the precatch breath is important for maintaining the safe transmission of force, because the structural stability of the rib cage and lower back is affected by the pressures inside the chest and abdominal cavities, respectively. During the drive, the muscles of the trunk brace against the partially inflated lungs, allowing the internal pressures within the chest and abdomen to increase; this stiffens the trunk. Failure to maintain adequate internal pressures (because of an inadequate lung volume) may lead to an increased risk of rib stress fractures and low back injury (common problems in rowers).

So the muscles of the trunk have several important roles during rowing, including contributing to the transmission of propulsive force, maintaining structural stability of the spine and other bony structures, and breathing. These roles must be accommodated as well as coordinated. However, these roles may become contradictory from time to time, which can have a negative effect on both performance and injury risk. As previously mentioned, when push comes to shove, the diaphragm's role in

---

Inspiratory Muscle Fatigue Reduces Force Transmission During Rowing

In an unpublished pilot study, my research group demonstrated that when the inspiratory muscles (including the diaphragm) were fatigued, the maximal static force generated in the catch position was reduced by over 9 percent. This suggests that the inspiratory muscles play a role in determining either the magnitude of the force generated by the lower body or the efficiency of the transmission of force through the trunk, or both. Either way, it underscores the vital role played by the inspiratory muscles in supporting force production during rowing.

breathing takes precedence over its role in postural stability. This means that when breathing discipline breaks down during rowing, the risk of injury increases, and performance is impaired. Thus, the breathing muscles must be trained specifically to accommodate all of their roles in order to ensure that breathing discipline is maintained at all times. Chapter 8 includes specific guidance on how to optimize breathing muscle training to meet the specific functional demands of rowing.

Swimming

The aquatic environment is one of the most challenging for the breathing muscles, so it is worth considering this challenge in more detail in order to appreciate the potential benefits offered by breathing training. Competitive swimming presents one of the ultimate challenges for breathing. This is exemplified by the fact that swimming induces the most severe inspiratory muscle fatigue of any sport studied to date (Lomax & McConnell, 2003)—a 29 percent fall in inspiratory muscle strength postexercise, compared with around 10 to 20 percent for terrestrial sports (see the sidebar on page 31). Furthermore, that 29 percent fatigue was induced by a 200-meter swim at an intensity of 90 to 95 percent race pace. The swim lasted just over 2.5 minutes and required only 70 breaths.

Why is swimming so innately challenging? Essentially, swimming is challenging for three reasons. First, breathing with the chest immersed in water requires more inspiratory muscle force and effort, because in order to expand, the chest must overcome the extra hydrostatic pressure exerted by the water. This pressure can be thought of as an extremely tight-fitting jacket that is squeezing the chest. The inspiratory muscles are also around 16 percent weaker when a person is lying horizontal in the water compared to standing upright on dry land. Second, the breathing pattern requires a high degree of "respiratory gymnastics" in order to minimize the detrimental influence of breathing on stroke mechanics. As a rule, swimmers strive to reduce the number and duration of the occasions when their face is out of the water. Swimmers must therefore inhale quickly and must maximize the volume of each breath. Maximizing the breath volume helps the swimmer to maintain minute ventilation and also to maintain a higher body position by increasing buoyancy (see the sidebar on page 132 of chapter 8). This breathing pattern increases the relative work of breathing and the intensity of breathing effort because of the functional weakening of the inspiratory muscles induced by high lung volumes and rapid inhalation rates (remember the balloon analogy from chapter 1 and the fact that higher speeds of muscle contraction induce functional weakening of muscles). Finally, minimizing the number of breaths can compromise delivery of oxygen and removal of carbon dioxide. For example, during a 200-meter maximal swim using the front crawl, when the time between breaths is increased (i.e., the number of strokes per breath is increased), the resulting changes in oxygen delivery and carbon dioxide removal lead to an increase in inspiratory muscle fatigue (Jakovljevic & McConnell, 2009). This is somewhat counterintuitive, because less breathing (four strokes per breath versus two strokes per breath) results in greater inspiratory muscle fatigue. In addition, with less breathing, blood lactate concentration is paradoxically lower, heart rate and stroke rate are significantly higher, and swim time is significantly slower. All of this suggests that oxygen delivery and carbon dioxide removal are compromised by breathing too little, and that there is a threshold beyond which it is disadvantageous to reduce breathing frequency during swimming.

In summary, swimming forces the inspiratory muscles to work at the extremes of their capabilities, creating a "quadruple whammy" for swimmers:

1. A greater demand for work is placed on the inspiratory muscles because of the hydrostatic pressure and the higher elastic work of breathing.
2. The inspiratory muscles are weaker because of the horizontal position in the water.
3. High inhalation rates and volumes are needed (functional weakening).
4. Very low breathing frequency can accelerate fatigue of the inspiratory muscles.

As if this weren't enough, swimmers also need to deal with the breathing muscles being engaged in the swimming stroke, meaning that these muscles are subjected to the competing demands of breathing and locomotion. This functional overload almost certainly contributes to the incredible fatigue of the inspiratory muscles that has been observed; it also creates a compelling rationale for the functional training that will be discussed in chapter 8.

Team Sports

Team sports encompass a huge range of activities involving a variety of physical and physiological requirements. However, most team sports have three things in common—they require intermittent bursts of high-intensity activity, involvement of the upper body in contact and noncontact activities, and continuous tactical decision making. Each of these requirements involves the breathing muscles, either because they place added demands on the breathing muscles or because the added demands affect the performance in these three areas (e.g., it's difficult to think clearly about your next pass when you feel as though you're suffocating after the effort of winning possession in the first place).

The telltale signs that players are out of breath during a game include bending forward and unloading their trunk muscles by placing their hands on their thighs. Another sign is when the players stand upright with their hands on their head. Both of these postural adjustments provide some unloading on the postural role of the trunk muscles, allowing them to focus on breathing movements. However, this behavior also indicates that the player is struggling to keep up with the pace of the game, and that the likelihood of performance impairment and injury may be heightened. This is a sign opponents will exploit and teammates will worry about!

Although many team sports are noncontact (e.g., soccer), modern high-level competition requires a good deal of tussling and fending off. These activities require the involvement of the trunk muscles; in addition, because these activities normally arise while running or changing direction, this involvement brings the breathing, core-stabilizing, and postural control roles of the trunk muscles into direct conflict. In team sports where contact with opponents is an integral part of the game (e.g., rugby football), there are even greater demands placed on the breathing muscles, because the forces that must be applied and overcome are even larger. In addition, sports such as rugby, soccer, and American football often result in players being knocked from their feet repeatedly during the course of a match or game. This not only carries a risk of injury, but also necessitates repeated additional energy expenditure in order for the player to stand up again.

Sports such as rugby football also require players to perform unique activities such as scrums, rucks, and mauls. These necessitate huge amounts of stabilizing activity for the upper body and core. Other sports, such as basketball and hockey, require the upper body to be maintained in a forward-flexed position, which also places huge demands on the core-stabilizing role of the breathing muscles. Because these games are played at a very high intensity, there is direct conflict between the respiratory and nonrespiratory roles of the trunk muscles.

In addition, contact team sports involve the compulsory use of mouth guards, which can obstruct airflow, as well as the use of padding, which increases the work of breathing and the risk of respiratory muscle fatigue. This all spells an increase in the work of breathing and breathing effort.

Finally, the importance of a stable core in performing efficient ball kicking should not be overlooked; accuracy and distance are the first casualties of an overloaded core. Furthermore, conflicts between the breathing and core-stabilizing roles of the trunk muscles during simultaneous running and kicking will exacerbate the loss of performance. Chapter 9 focuses on helping players to be conscious of the multiple roles of the breathing muscles and on developing specific functional exercises that enable players to cope with these demands.

High Altitude

Human beings go to high altitude for many reasons—to climb, to hike, to ski, or even to train. Whatever the motivation, everyone experiences an unprecedented increase in their perception of breathing effort when they are at high altitude. This arises because the breathing requirement of all activities, including rest, increases. This increased demand is stimulated by a reduction in the amount of oxygen in the atmosphere, and in order to boost the amount of oxygen in the lungs, the respiratory controller senses the reduction in blood oxygen and increases minute ventilation. For a given level of oxygen demand, the ventilatory requirement may be 3, 4, or even 10 (at very high altitude) times as great as at sea level. At 9,800 feet (3,000 m), the amount of oxygen in the air decreases by 30 percent; at 16,400 feet (5,000 m), the amount of oxygen is half that at sea level. This means that at around 3,300 feet (1,000 m), breathlessness occurs during moderate exercise, and at 13,100 feet (4,000 m), most people will be breathless at rest.

To put the challenge of high altitude into perspective, consider this: While resting at sea level, minute ventilation is around 12 liters per minute. At the summit of Mount Everest (at 29,000 feet [8,848 m]), almost maximal levels of breathing are required (in excess of 150 liters per minute) just to put one foot before the other. This level of breathing can be sustained for only a couple of minutes at a time, because the respiratory muscles fatigue rapidly as a result of the combined challenge of the increased work and the low oxygen environment. At sea level, the ability to exercise is limited by the capacity of the heart to pump blood to the exercising muscles. At high altitude, the limitation is the ability to pump air in and out of the lungs, and this is determined by how "fit" the breathing muscles are.

The ability of the breathing muscles to meet their role as postural stabilizers is compromised severely by the increased demand for respiratory work, as well as by the fatigue associated with high altitude. Accordingly, conditions where postural stability and control are challenged, such as carrying heavy backpacks or hiking on uneven terrain, increase the risk of injury due to failure of the postural role of the breathing muscles. Chapter 8 describes a functional approach to breathing training for hiking and mountaineering that incorporates postural challenges.

Finally, athletes who want to train at high altitude typically do so at 6,600 to 9,800 feet (2,000 to 3,000 m). At these altitudes, the athlete's ability to train at the same intensities that are achievable at sea level is severely compromised by the increase in respiratory work. Breathing muscle fatigue and its repercussions therefore arise (and impede performance) earlier and at lower exercise intensities when at high altitude. The effect of altitude on performance should be viewed as an exacerbating demand that altitude adds to the existing demands of the sport itself. Altitude training is accepted as an essential prerequisite to competing at high altitude; an integral part of the benefits of this training is the additional stimulus delivered to the breathing muscles, as well as the familiarity with the increased breathing requirement. The former can be achieved through functional breathing training at sea level, which is far less demanding of time and money.

Sliding Sports

Sports that involve sliding—either on snow, ice, or rollers—place multiple demands on the respiratory, core-stabilizing, postural control, and propulsive roles of the trunk muscles. An obvious additional demand posed by skiing and snowboarding, for example, is that these sports are normally undertaken at high altitude (see the previous section). Who hasn't been taken aback at some time by the disproportionate breathlessness elicited by a short stretch of poling or by trudging up a ski slope?

Cross-country (Nordic) skiing has much in common with rowing in that it places multiple simultaneous demands on the trunk muscles for breathing, core stabilizing, and propulsion. The risks of respiratory muscle fatigue and the associated repercussions are therefore especially high for this sport.

Ice skating and roller skating or in-line skating require continuous high levels of postural adjustment, and the breathing muscles play a key role in this. In addition, if speed is the goal, skaters will adopt forward-flexed postures that heighten postural demands and may also restrict inspiratory movements, as they do in cycling (see figure 2.2, page 40). Thus, the risks of inspiratory muscle fatigue and its associated repercussions are correspondingly increased in sports such as speedskating. Indeed, a sign that a skater is breathless is when the skater abandons an aerodynamic posture periodically in order to relieve her breathlessness—the skater stands up and takes a large breath coming out of a bend. This illustrates how breathing and the sense that it is inadequate can indirectly (as well as directly) affect performance.

Striking and Throwing Sports

Striking and throwing sports are considered together because they have one vital thing in common: The trunk muscles are involved in providing a stable platform from which to generate arm movements. These muscles are also involved in generating twisting movements to propel an object in the hand, whether it's a javelin, tennis racket, baseball, or golf club.

There is no obvious conflict between the breathing and core-stabilizing roles in activities such as pitching a baseball; however, this does not mean that there is not merit in optimizing the contribution of breathing muscles to core stability and rotational movements, because training may bring benefits to both injury prevention and performance (see the sidebar below). Rib muscle tears and rib injuries are very common in sports that involve vigorous twisting movements of the trunk, including golf, racket sports, baseball, and so on. These injuries take a long time to recover from, which can have a devastating impact on training and can result in an athlete refraining from competition. From a performance perspective, maximizing the velocity of the arms and hands requires a stable core that forms the vital first stage in the transfer of energy to projectiles and implements. Basic physics dictates that the greater the stability of the base from which movement takes place, the more efficient the transfer of energy will be to a distal body segment such as a hand. A useful analogy is to consider the cracking of a whip, where the velocity of the tip of the whip (distal end) is greatest when its base (proximal end) is stationary. Giving speed to a projectile also requires excellent coordination and contractile performance of the muscles that rotate the trunk. These muscles all have a breathing role, which means that training to optimize their function should involve functional movements that incorporate breathing. This approach is taken to breathing muscle training in chapter 10.

In the case of racket sports, the conflict between the breathing, postural control, and core-stabilizing roles of the trunk muscles is ever present. For example, sports such as badminton, tennis, and table tennis are played at a high intensity, and it is not uncommon for players (even at the highest level) to take their time during their own service games in order to "get their breath back." However, the biggest impact of the breathing muscles in these sports is their role in both breathing and contributing to propelling a bat or racket (via their role as core stabilizers and as generators of rotational movements of the trunk). The potential for conflict between these roles is obvious. For example, if a player is so out of breath that he is unable to coordinate his breathing with the movement of his racket, the resulting contact between racket and ball will be suboptimal (also see the sidebar titled The Tennis Grunt in chapter 10). Chapter 10 includes specific guidance on how to optimize breathing muscle training to meet the specific functional demands of complex sports that require striking and throwing.

Strengthening Rib Cage Muscles Reduces Incidence of Injury

A number of years ago, I discovered an unexpected by-product of adding inspiratory muscle training (IMT) to the training schedule of a cricket team (an English first-class county team)—the incidence of side strain injuries (a rib cage muscle tear) was reduced. This is an injury that can ruin the season of bowlers and is essentially an intercostal muscle tear. It appears that strengthening these muscles increases their resistance to damage. This benefit will also be gained in other sports where injuries to the rib cage muscles are common (i.e., any sport that involves striking or throwing).

THE RATIONALE FOR FUNCTIONAL BREATHING TRAINING

In the preceding sections, some sport-specific challenges faced by the breathing muscles were explored. These challenges are common to many sports. The resulting overload and functional compromise to the trunk muscles are due to the multiple roles of the trunk muscles in breathing, postural control, core stabilization, trunk rotation and propulsion; as well as the impedance of inspiratory movements because of posture (e.g., the catch of the rowing stroke). This overloading may predispose the breathing muscles to fatigue (the consequences of this were also considered earlier in this chapter). Because of the multiple roles of the trunk muscles, these muscles must be trained functionally, and the training must not be delivered using an exclusively "isolationist" model of training—that is, if optimal function is to be achieved, the core-stabilizing role of the diaphragm must be trained in the context of an activity that challenges core stability. Notwithstanding this, there remains a role for foundation training (see chapter 6), which involves isolated training that provides the foundation onto which functional training is built. *Breathe Strong, Perform Better* takes the "isolate, then integrate" approach to breathing muscle training.

The rationale for functional breathing training is the same as the rationale for any kind of functional training—sport movements are complex, imposing differing demands on muscles, both within and between movements. Muscles respond to training in highly specific ways that limit the transferability of training benefits when the training stimulus is nonfunctional (e.g., an isolated leg extension will not improve running performance). In functional training, muscles are subjected to forces during functional movements in order to develop the neuromuscular system in ways that are transferable to real-world performance. To date, a missing element from the functional training repertoire has been any consideration of the role of breathing muscles (major trunk stabilizers and controllers) in functional movements.

In addition to satisfying the demands of breathing, the muscles of the trunk are responsible for a wide range of movements during sports and other physical activities (flexion, extension, rotation, stabilization, and so on). Imagine for a moment a parallel evolutionary present in which your legs were not only responsible for locomotion, but also had sole responsibility for pumping blood around your body—you'd think this was a pretty tall order and certainly something that warranted specific training. But something akin to this is precisely what the breathing muscles are expected to contend with—all sports involve movements that perturb posture or require stabilization or compression of the trunk, while simultaneously increasing the demand for breathing. The breathing muscles therefore have to accommodate all of these functions simultaneously. For example, basketball imposes conflicting demands on the trunk muscles because the high breathing requirement must be balanced against the need to use the trunk musculature to maintain postural balance while running, changing direction at high speed, passing the ball (or faking), and managing physical interactions with other players.

Failure to address breathing as part of the conflicting roles of the trunk musculature during functional training also fails to create a truly functional training stimulus. After all, when is any physically demanding sport ever undertaken without a considerable increase in breathing demand? Functional training never re-creates this demand because the exercises are brief, isolated rehearsals of functional movements. The only contexts in which breathing is trained as part of a functional training activity are yoga and Pilates. Indeed, breathing is at the very heart of both yoga and Pilates training. In his excellent new book on yoga training, Kaminoff observes that ". . . life on this planet requires an integrated relationship between breath (prana/apana) and posture (sthira/sukha). When things go wrong with one, by definition they go wrong with the other" (Kaminoff, 2009). However, even in the context of yoga, the approach taken to the conflicting roles of the trunk muscles is to minimize the imposition that breathing makes on the physical movement and control by minimizing breathing movements (Kaminoff, 2009). The role of breathing in Pilates has been described very eloquently by Isacowitz (2006), who observes that it is advantageous to synchronize breathing movements so that the actions of the inspiratory and expiratory muscles coincide with extension and flexion movements of the trunk. However, the focus remains on minimizing conflicts between breathing movements and, for example, maintaining abdominal compression. These strategies are possible during the largely static poses of yoga and Pilates, but minimizing breathing movements is not practical for sports with high metabolic and breathing requirements. For this reason, in sport training, the trunk muscles need to be trained (overloaded) functionally to meet the breathing and other demands placed on them.

In his book on low back disorders, Professor Stuart McGill rightly highlights the specific challenge that elevated ventilation represents to spine stability, as well as the increased risk that it poses for back injury in athletes (McGill, 2007). The therapeutic approach suggested by McGill is to undertake a range of stabilizing exercises (e.g., side bridge) immediately after an activity that raises ventilation—the idea being that the resultant heavy breathing is superimposed on exercises that challenge the stabilizing musculature. The aim is to produce what McGill calls a "grooved" pattern of muscle activation, similar to a rope running in a well-worn slot, so that breathing and stabilization take place simultaneously but without any compromise to either. Often, athletes will cope with their inability to meet the conflicting demands on their breathing muscles by holding their breath during exercises such as a side bridge. This is clearly a bad "groove" to get stuck in.

The breathing challenge that is recommended in *Breathe Strong* is not limited to raising ventilatory flow rate (as recommended by McGill); rather, the functional exercises that are recommended will also increase the requirement for inspiratory pressure (force) generation by the inspiratory muscles. These exercises involve breathing against an inspiratory load during functional movements. This is actually no different from using any external resistance during functional training (e.g., a cable machine or dumbbell); its purpose is to challenge the neuromuscular system's ability to bring about controlled movements.

In addition to providing a stable platform, the breathing muscles play an important role in postural control during brief perturbations to balance. A good example of this is the automatic, anticipatory activation of specific trunk muscles immediately before swinging a tennis racket overhead for a serve. The role of the diaphragm in this type of postural control is preprogrammed ("grooved"); this is known because diaphragm activation *precedes* movements that destabilize the body. However, this automatic activation does not mean that the program is not dynamic or adaptable; rather, the program varies according to the movement parameters of the task and according to factors such as the prevailing postural conditions (stable or unstable), muscle fatigue, injury, pain, and so on. For muscles that are involved in automatic anticipatory postural adjustments, such as the transversus abdominis, isolated specific training can normalize previously abnormal patterns of motor activation—that is, restore a program to normal (flip the rope back into the groove). In other words, isolated voluntary training of muscles involved in automatic anticipatory postural adjustments leads to improvement in complex automatic control strategies. The similarity of the diaphragm's role to that of the transversus abdominis makes it extremely likely that this effect is also present for the diaphragm. Therefore, isolated voluntary training of the diaphragm (the kind of training undertaken during foundation inspiratory muscle training, or IMT) can reestablish its automatic functioning during complex movements. The implications of this preprogrammed role of the diaphragm also need to be considered, and they are incorporated within the information on functional training provided in part II of this book.

Finally, in some sports, the body position or equipment restricts breathing by impeding inspiratory (outward) thoracic movements. A good example of this is the aero position in cycling, which is adopted in order to minimize aerodynamic drag. This position has unintended consequences for breathing. These situations also provide a rationale for context- and posture-specific breathing training. In other words, by overloading the inspiratory muscles in situations where thoracic or diaphragm movement is already impeded, we are effectively training for 20 rounds in a fight that we know will only last 15.

Chapter

3

Training Response of Breathing Muscles

In chapter 2, we considered how breathing muscles contribute to sport performance, thereby establishing the rationale for breathing muscle training. In chapter 3, we consider how the breathing muscles respond to specific training. This will set the scene for chapter 4, which describes the benefits of these changes for sport performance.

This chapter explores what adaptations are possible within the breathing muscles if the right training stimulus is provided (chapter 5 describes how the training stimulus can be manipulated and implemented). Essentially, muscles adapt to training by changing their structure, and this causes a change in muscle function. For example, when we lift weights, muscle fibers become larger, and the strength of the muscle increases. On the other hand, if a muscle is subjected to prolonged continuous bouts of exercise, muscle fibers undergo structural and biochemical changes that increase their endurance. Broadly speaking, training can be subdivided into two main types: One type increases strength, and the other increases endurance. The equipment needed to implement these two different types of breathing training also differs; it's a little like comparing a leg press machine with a treadmill—both machines train the leg muscles, but the end results are very different. In the case of specific strength training for inspiratory and expiratory muscles, devices are used to impose a resistance to the breathing muscles at the mouth (similar to lifting a dumbbell). In contrast, endurance training for the breathing muscles consists of hyperventilating for prolonged periods (similar to running on a treadmill). For endurance training of breathing muscles, it's not possible to separate inspiratory and expiratory muscle contributions, so this method trains both sets of muscles simultaneously. We will explore training methods and equipment in much more detail in chapter 5.

MUSCLE STRUCTURE AFTER BREATHING MUSCLE TRAINING

Structural adaptations in response to specific breathing muscle training have been studied by using microscopic examination of muscle fiber samples (biopsies), as well as by measuring changes in the thickness of muscles using ultrasound. To date, the only type of breathing muscle training studied in this way has been resistance (weight) training of the inspiratory muscles.

As one might expect, taking small pieces of breathing muscle (biopsies) is not something that is undertaken routinely, and it has never been undertaken on a live healthy person. At the time of this writing, the only study in which biopsy samples of inspiratory muscle have been obtained both before and after inspiratory muscle training (IMT) was undertaken on patients with chronic lung disease. The study found that training induced an increase in size (hypertrophy) of the intercostal (rib cage) muscle fibers, which was accompanied by an improvement in inspiratory muscle strength and endurance.

Studies using ultrasound imaging of the inspiratory muscles have done so in healthy people, because this is a routine technique that is perfectly harmless. Using ultrasound, it is very easy to get an image of the diaphragm, and the thickness of the diaphragm can be conveniently and reliably measured. Measurements are made where the base of the dome is in close proximity to the lower ribs.

In healthy young people, the thickness of the diaphragm increases about 12 percent after 4 to 8 weeks of inspiratory muscle resistance training (Downey et al., 2007). As would be expected, the increase in thickness is accompanied by improvements in inspiratory muscle strength (24 percent and 41 percent after 4 and 8 weeks of training, respectively). Interestingly, the changes in diaphragm thickness were the same after 4 and 8 weeks of training, yet the changes in strength differed. This clearly indicates that diaphragm hypertrophy is not the only source of improvement in inspiratory muscle strength. Inspiratory muscle strength can also increase through improvements in accessory muscle function and through neural adaptations. These neural adaptations include an enhanced ability to coordinate the contraction of synergistic muscles, as well as an enhanced ability to maximize the activation of individual muscles.

In keeping with the diaphragm's key role as a postural control and core-stabilizing muscle, diaphragm thickness and inspiratory muscle strength have also been shown to increase after 16 weeks of training consisting of sit-ups and biceps curls (DePalo et al., 2004). Expiratory muscle strength increased 37 percent, which is to be expected because the rectus abdominis is an important expiratory muscle. These data highlight the close interrelationship of the breathing and postural stabilizing functions of the trunk muscles, thereby reinforcing the potential benefits of functional breathing training.

MUSCLE FUNCTION AFTER BREATHING MUSCLE TRAINING

Collectively, the data just presented on structural adaptations indicate that the breathing muscles are highly adaptable and show structural changes that are consistent with the well-established evidence relating to limb muscle training. In the following section, we'll consider the functional adaptations that occur after breathing muscle training.

Resistance Training

Principally, muscles respond to training by improving their strength, speed of contraction, power output, endurance, or any combination thereof. Because muscles respond to training stimuli in highly specific ways, different training regimens tend to elicit slightly different changes in each property. For example, training that consists of maximal static efforts with high forces improves strength but does not improve contraction speed. However, there is also a good deal of crossover, and training regimens that are ostensibly strength orientated can also give rise to improvements in endurance, but generally not vice versa. The following section describes what is known about improvements in each functional property after resistance training.

A useful method of characterizing a muscle's functional properties is to plot a graph of the relationship between its strength and its contraction speed; this is the force–velocity relationship. A third dimension can also be added to this in the form of the muscle's power output, which is the product of force and velocity. Figure 3.1 illustrates these interrelationships for the inspiratory muscles, and it encapsulates the three key and interrelated functional properties of muscles—strength, speed, and power. All three of these can be improved by appropriate training.

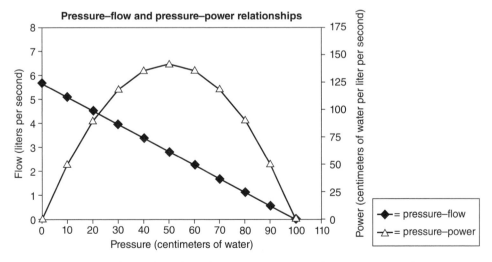

Figure 3.1 Interrelationship of the three key properties of inspiratory muscles—pressure (strength), flow (velocity), and power (strength × velocity).

Inspiratory Muscle Adaptations to Resistance Training

The inspiratory muscles have been by far the most widely studied, which clearly illustrates their supreme functional importance. As previously described, inspiratory muscle training (IMT) elicits hypertrophy and improvements in strength; summaries of the extensive evidence base for this are provided in other sources (McConnell & Romer, 2004). When IMT is undertaken using moderate loads (about 60 percent of inspiratory muscle strength) that allow rapid muscle contraction, improvements in strength are accompanied by increases in maximal shortening velocity (peak inspiratory flow rate) and maximal power (see figure 3.2) (Romer & McConnell, 2003). These loads can typically be sustained for around 30 breaths,

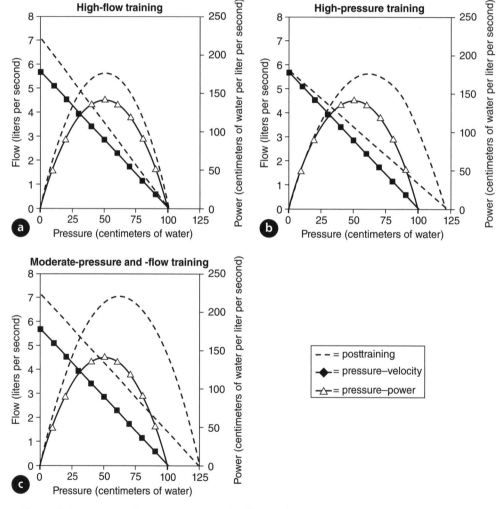

Figure 3.2 Changes in pressure (strength), flow (velocity), and power (strength × velocity) in response to different training stimuli (data derived from Romer & McConnell, 2003).

Adapted, by permission, from L.M. Romer and A.K. McConnell, 2003, "Specificity and reversibility of inspiratory muscle training," *Medicine & Science in Sports & Exercise* 35(2): 237-244.

and they have also been shown to improve endurance. Figure 3.2 shows the changes in strength, peak flow, and power induced by different IMT regimens in healthy young people. Clearly, different types of training induce changes in different functional properties, and this is explored in more detail in chapter 5, which describes the specificity principle of training (i.e., muscles adapt according to the nature of the training stimulus). For example, it is clear from figure 3.2 that high-pressure training (maximum static muscle contractions) led to improved strength but did not improve the velocity of shortening. The opposite was true for high-flow training (unloaded maximal inhalations).

As mentioned earlier, strength training can also improve endurance. There is no single accepted method of assessing breathing muscle endurance; however, borrowing the methods used to assess endurance during whole-body exercise, IMT improves inspiratory muscle endurance measured using incremental and fixed-intensity loaded breathing tests, as well as tests requiring the maintenance of maximal hyperventilation. In addition, an improvement in endurance after IMT can be implied from the absence or reduction of fatigue after a task that had previously induced fatigue, which also occurs after IMT (see chapter 4).

Expiratory Muscle Adaptations to Resistance Training

Specific expiratory muscle training (EMT) has been much less widely studied in healthy young people, primarily because the rationale for specific EMT is much weaker than for IMT. For example, in chapter 2, the evidence for functional overload of the breathing muscles was examined, and although fatigue of inspiratory muscles appears commonplace, the same is not true for expiratory muscles. However, the key question is whether specific EMT provides any performance benefits, and research suggests that it does not (see chapter 4). In addition, the main expiratory muscles are those of the abdominal wall, and these muscles can be overloaded functionally using nonspecific training methods. Notwithstanding the dearth of data and the absence of a rationale for EMT, there is every reason to believe that the expiratory muscles would show the same broad responses to specific EMT as the inspiratory muscles do to IMT.

Simultaneous Resistance Training of Both Inspiratory and Expiratory Muscles

You might predict that combining IMT and EMT would result in improvements in the function of both muscle groups. However, the results of two studies that have implemented specific EMT and IMT within the same breath cycle suggest that this approach actually impairs the training response. For example, a study on young swimmers found no change in inspiratory or expiratory muscle strength despite a strenuous training regimen, while a study on rowers found only modest changes in inspiratory and expiratory strength (Griffiths & McConnell, 2007). People generally find the simultaneous loading of both breath cycles to be uncomfortable, and they report that they are unable to train with maximal effort when both phases of breathing are loaded. No studies exist of concurrent IMT and EMT when the loads are applied separately, but it's reasonable to suppose that functional changes would be similar to those seen after isolated IMT and EMT.

Endurance Training

Pure endurance training of the breathing muscles is undertaken using a sustained high-intensity hyperventilation task. This type of training uses both inspiratory and expiratory muscles simultaneously. This endurance training improves the person's ability to sustain high levels of hyperventilation (an index of endurance). The training also improves the volume of air that can be respired during a brief maximal burst of hyperventilation, typically 15 seconds (an index of power output) (Verges, Boutellier, & Spengler, 2008). The latter finding is also consistent with improvements in peak velocity of muscle contraction, although there is no direct evidence of this to date. This type of training does not improve the strength of the respiratory muscles (Verges, Boutellier, & Spengler, 2008), which is not surprising because the training stimulus required to improve strength must include an increase in the force of muscle contraction. Thus, functional adaptations are confined to flow, power, and endurance.

In summary, functional adaptations to specific resistance training of the inspiratory muscles include improvement in all four key functional properties—strength, speed of contraction, power output, and endurance. It's unclear how expiratory muscles adapt, or more importantly, whether there is a rationale for specific expiratory muscle training. Attempts to resistance train inspiratory and expiratory muscles simultaneously have so far ended in failure. Endurance training that is specific to respiratory muscles improves speed, power, and endurance, but not strength.

That's all well and good, but the important question is, "What are the functional benefits of these changes for sport performance?" We'll explore this in chapter 4.

Chapter

4

Performance Benefits of Breathing Muscle Training

In chapter 3, we considered how the breathing muscles respond to specific training at the level of the muscles themselves. In chapter 4, we consider the benefits of these changes in relation to exercise performance.

To get the most from this chapter, you need to understand how breathing limits exercise performance (as described in chapter 2). In short, two major factors arise from the breathing pump muscles that cause athletes to slow down or stop: the perception of breathing effort and the consequences of activation of the inspiratory muscle metaboreflex. The former makes exercise feel harder, and this intensifies as the inspiratory muscles become fatigued; the latter reduces limb blood flow, hastens limb fatigue, and exacerbates the perception of limb and whole-body effort.

Logically, making the breathing muscles stronger and more fatigue resistant should delay or abolish the negative influences of breathing on exercise tolerance. But what's the scientific evidence supporting this, how big are any improvements, and what types of activities are improved? The first part of this chapter describes the ways in which we can measure improvements after breathing muscle training in the laboratory; it also identifies what types of training work and what don't. The chapter then looks at how these improvements translate into performance in a number of sports in order to illustrate the sport-specific benefits. Finally, we'll consider how two common breathing disorders in athletes can be managed using breathing muscle training—asthma and inspiratory stridor.

PERFORMANCE IMPROVEMENTS IN ENDURANCE SPORTS

Most of the studies of breathing muscle training have examined endurance sports, and two types of exercise tests have been used: fixed-intensity exercise undertaken to the limit of tolerance (Tlim) and time trials. There are no competitive events that require athletes to keep going at the same intensity for as long as they can (a Tlim), but this type of test does provide an excellent laboratory model for studying the effects of "ergogenic aids" such as breathing training (i.e., interventions that purport to improve performance). This is because Tlim tests are extremely sensitive to small physiological improvements; they yield large changes (greater than 30 percent) and allow physiological and perceptual responses to be studied under identical conditions before and after the intervention. In contrast, the obvious advantage of using a time trial to assess performance is that it simulates a race. However, for this very reason, the magnitude of the changes that are typically observed after ergogenic interventions is extremely small (less than 5 percent). In addition, it is impossible to compare physiological responses in a meaningful way before and after the intervention because the exercise conditions are not identical. For example, if performance is enhanced, then the athletes will be working at a greater intensity, which cannot then be compared to the preintervention test. Both types of tests have provided useful insights into the effects of breathing muscle training.

Typically, Tlim tests are conducted at intensities that are just above the lactate threshold. The ability to sustain exercise above the lactate threshold is limited, and the more the intensity of exercise exceeds the lactate threshold, the faster the onset of exercise intolerance (fatigue). Studies of breathing muscle training have used exercise intensities that can be tolerated for 20 to 40 minutes. In contrast, time trials have varied considerably, depending on the sport being studied—for example, studies have used as little as 6 minutes for rowing or as much as 1 hour for cycling.

Let's begin by exploring studies that have used resistance training of the breathing muscles. These have assessed performance during cycling, rowing, and running. In the case of cycling and running, this has been undertaken using both Tlim tests and time trials. For rowing only time trials have been used. Table 4.1 summarizes the findings of placebo-controlled studies (i.e., those where sham training was undertaken to control for psychological factors). Many more studies have been conducted, but their quality is variable, so the table is limited to the best.

The information in table 4.1 clearly shows that inspiratory muscle training (IMT) produces improvements in performance, but that expiratory muscle training (EMT) does not. Improvements occur whether you test using time trials (1.9 to 4.6 percent for tests lasting 6 to 60 minutes) or Tlim tests (greater than 30 percent for a 30-minute test). For higher-intensity, shorter-duration Tlim tests, the improvements are smaller (4 percent for a test lasting less than 4 minutes). This difference in the size of the improvements occurs because of differences in the factors that lead to people stopping exercise and the rate at which these factors accumulate and lead to intolerance.

Let's turn our attention to endurance training of the breathing muscles, which involves hyperventilation at high levels for prolonged periods. Table 4.2 (page 60) summarizes the controlled trials. Despite the profound difference in the training

Table 4.1 Placebo-Controlled Studies of the Influence of Resistance Breathing Muscle Training on Endurance Performance

Type of training	Exercise modality	Type of exercise test	Duration or intensity of test	Training duration	Performance change	Physiological changes in training group	Comments	Author
Resistance IMT	Cycling	Tlim	21 min	4 weeks	33%	Attenuation of [La]b & RPE		(Caine & McConnell, 1998)
Resistance IMT	Cycling	TT	20 km & 40 km (~30 & ~60 min)	6 weeks	3.8% & 4.6%	Attenuation of breathing & leg effort	Inspiratory muscle fatigue also attenuated	(Romer, McConnell, & Jones, 2002a)
Resistance IMT	Cycling	Tlim	75% $\dot{V}O_2$max	10 weeks	36%	Attenuated fc, V_E, & perception of effort		(Gething, Williams, & Davies, 2004)
Resistance IMT	Cycling	TT	25 km (36 min)	6 weeks	2.6%		Inspiratory muscle fatigue also attenuated	(Johnson, Sharpe, & Brown, 2007)
Resistance IMT	Running	Tlim	3.8 min	4 weeks	4%			(Edwards & Cooke, 2004)
Resistance IMT	Running	TT	5,000 m (~20 min)	4 weeks	2%	Attenuation of RPE		(Edwards, Wells, & Butterly, 2008)
Resistance IMT	Rowing	TT	6 min & ~20 min (~2 km & 5 km)	4 weeks & 11 weeks	1.9% & 2.2%	Attenuation of [La]b & breathing effort; increased V_T	Performance improved at 4 & 11 weeks; inspiratory muscle fatigue also attenuated	(Volianitis et al., 2001)
Resistance IMT and EMT	Rowing	TT	6 min (~2 km)	4 weeks & 10 weeks	2.7%	Attenuated fc, [La]b, & perception of breathing effort	Performance & other outcomes only improved in response to IMT; inspiratory muscle fatigue also attenuated	(Griffiths & McConnell, 2007)

IMT = inspiratory muscle training; EMT = expiratory muscle training; RMT = respiratory muscle training; Tlim = fixed intensity to the limit of tolerance; TT = time trial; $\dot{V}O_2$ = oxygen uptake; $\dot{V}O_2$max = maximal oxygen uptake; fc = heart rate; V_E = minute ventilation; V_T = tidal volume; [La]b = blood lactate concentration; RPE = rating of perceived exertion.

Table 4.2 Controlled Studies of the Influence of Endurance Breathing Muscle Training on Endurance Performance

Type of training	Exercise modality	Type of exercise test	Duration or intensity of test	Training duration	Per-formance change	Physiological changes in training group	Comments	Author
Endurance RMT	Cycling	Tlim	70% peak power	15 weeks	24%		No placebo group, just non-RMT control group	(Markov et al., 2001)
Endurance RMT	Cycling	Tlim	70% peak power	15 weeks	24%		No placebo group, just non-RMT control group	(Stuessi et al., 2001)
Endurance RMT	Cycling	Tlim	85% peak power	4-6 weeks	~20%		No placebo group, just non-RMT control group	(McMahon et al., 2002)
Endurance RMT	Cycling	Tlim	40 min	6 weeks	4.70%			(Holm, Sattler, & Fregosi, 2004)
Endurance RMT	Running	TT & Tlim	TT = 4 miles; Tlim = 80% $\dot{V}O_2$max	4 weeks	TT = 4% Tlim = 50%	Attenuated V_E, $\dot{V}O_2$, [La]b		(Leddy et al., 2007)

IMT = inspiratory muscle training; Tlim = fixed intensity to the limit of tolerance; TT = time trial; $\dot{V}O_2$max = maximal oxygen uptake; fc = heart rate; V_E = minute ventilation; [La]b = blood lactate concentration.

method, the results are strikingly similar to those for resistance training—Tlim typically increases by 20 to 50 percent, while a time trial shows around a 4 percent improvement. This similarity is quite unlike the response to whole-body endurance and resistance training, which suggests that breathing muscle training taps into a unique and profoundly important mechanism—that is, the metaboreflex that is explained in chapter 2.

It's impossible to separate the inspiratory and expiratory effects of hyperventilation training, but when this has been done for resistance training, the independent roles of the two groups of muscles in performance changes become clear (Griffiths & McConnell, 2007); only IMT improves performance. Indeed, adding EMT to IMT during the same breath cycle seems to impair inspiratory muscle responses to IMT, which provides a strong argument against using this approach or undertaking EMT at all. Simultaneous IMT and EMT is also discussed in relation to swimming later in this chapter.

Tables 4.1 and 4.2 also summarize some of the physiological changes that accompany breathing muscle training, and these help to shed some light on the mechanisms that lead to the improvement in performance. Why should we be interested in the mechanisms? Because if we know these, we can optimize training to maximize benefits, and we can also predict the type of sports and activities most likely to benefit from training. Specifically, after IMT there are reductions in blood lactate concentration, heart rate, and perception of breathing and limb effort. In addition, breathing becomes deeper and slower. IMT delays or abolishes inspiratory muscle fatigue, and in doing so, it delays activation of the reflex from the inspiratory muscles that shuts down circulation to the limb muscles (metaboreflex). This preservation of blood flow reduces limb fatigue, lactate production, and limb effort. In addition, if the inspiratory muscles don't fatigue, the perception of breathing effort is reduced, and it is possible to maintain a more efficient deep, slow breathing pattern. In short, the physiological changes point directly to the ergogenic effect of IMT being underpinned by preservation of limb blood flow and reduction in breathing effort.

Finally, the cost and benefit of any training adjunct needs to be considered, given that athletes have any number of additions that they could make to their training that would improve their performance. Table 4.3 compares the training requirements of

Table 4.3 High-Intensity Interval Training Versus IMT for Time Trial and Repeated Sprint Performance

	High-intensity cycle interval training (Laursen et al., 2002)	IMT (Romer, McConnell, & Jones, 2002a)
Performance enhancement in 40 km time trial	5% 3 min	4.6% 2.76 min
Duration of training	4 weeks	6 weeks
Type and intensity of training	$\dot{V}O_2$max on a cycle	50% of MIP
Session regimen	8 intervals of 2.4 min	30 breaths, twice daily
Session duration	53 min	<3 min
Session frequency (per week)	2	14
Total training time (per week)	106 min	<42 min
	High-intensity running interval training (Impellizzeri et al., 2008)	IMT (Tong et al., 2008; Nicks et al., 2009)
Performance enhancement in yo-yo intermittent sprint test	12%	16%
Duration of training	4 weeks	5-6 weeks
Type and intensity of training	Sprinting at 90-95% fc_{max}	50% of MIP
Session regimen	4 intervals of 4 min	30 breaths, twice daily
Session duration	28 min	<3 min
Session frequency (per week)	2-3	11
Total training time (per week)	56 min	<33 min

MIP = inspiratory muscle strength

$\dot{V}O_2$max = maximal oxygen uptake

fc_{max} = heart rate

two studies that assessed performance in a 40-kilometer cycle time trial. One study added IMT twice daily (Romer, McConnell, & Jones, 2002a), while the other added cycle interval training twice weekly at a very high intensity (Laursen et al., 2002). Both training adjuncts enhanced time trial performance by around 5 percent. The total duration of interval training required to elicit a 5 percent increase in time trial performance in 4 weeks was 7 hours. Compare this to the total time required to attain a 4.6 percent improvement in performance after 6 weeks of IMT, which is around 1.8 hours. Another very salient point is the intensity and duration of each training session (53 minutes at $\dot{V}O_2$max versus less than 3 minutes of moderate inspiratory muscle loading), not to mention the fact that IMT can be undertaken anywhere; there's no need for a bike, or even to break into a sweat . . . so the choice is yours.

The research on endurance sports indicates that for sports involving a sustained effort against the clock of 6 to 60 minutes, IMT will improve performance by 1.9 to 4.6 percent. Although there is no direct research evidence that similar improvements will be derived during longer events (e.g., marathons or triathlons), the fact that inspiratory muscle fatigue has been demonstrated after these events means that performance in these events is limited by breathing-related factors. Accordingly, there is every reason to believe that IMT also will improve performance in these longer events.

PERFORMANCE IMPROVEMENTS IN TEAM AND SPRINT SPORTS

Sprinting is such a brief activity that the benefits of breathing training are not immediately obvious. However, the changes that IMT induces in underlying physiology are so fundamental that it's now clear that performance in sprint sports can also benefit from IMT.

Repeated sprinting is an integral part of team and racket sports, as well as interval training. A sense of increased breathing effort between sprints has a profound influence on an athlete's ability to sprint again, and in competition, this has implications for the quality of the athlete's contribution to the match or game. The first study to examine the effect of IMT on sprinting was a placebo-controlled trial that used perceived rate of recovery during continuous bouts of repeated sprinting (Romer, McConnell, & Jones, 2002b). The expectation was that IMT would reduce breathing effort between sprints and delay the onset of inspiratory muscle fatigue, thereby making the participants feel as if they had recovered more quickly. However, because the sprint was very brief (3.2 seconds) and punctuated with periods of recovery, there was no expectation that actual sprint performance would improve. These expectations were confirmed; the athletes showed a faster rate of recovery, but no change in sprint performance. The implications of these findings for sport performance are considered later in this chapter, where sport-specific benefits of IMT are reviewed.

Using a slightly different approach, two controlled studies have explored the benefits of IMT to actual repeated sprint performance. The sprint test used was developed originally as a sport-specific performance assessment for soccer. The so-called yo-yo intermittent recovery test consists of repeated 20-meter sprints with progressively increasing speed, and it simulates the physiological demands of intermittent sprint sports such as soccer, football, rugby, and basketball. The test is also applicable to racket sports such as tennis and badminton. Performance in the yo-yo test is influenced by both effort perception and factors related to blood flow such as oxygen delivery and metabolite removal. As we've already discussed, both of these factors are influenced by IMT via the effect on breathing effort and the inspiratory muscle metaboreflex. This being the case, we'd predict that IMT should improve yo-yo test performance. But does it? Of course it does! Both studies found that performance improved by around 17 percent (Tong et al., 2008; Nicks et al., 2009). Accompanying the improvement in performance were reductions in perception of breathing and whole-body effort, as well as markers of metabolic stress. The similarity with the changes seen in endurance sports is to be expected, given that IMT is operating via the same underlying mechanisms.

How does a 17 percent improvement in yo-yo test performance compare to improvements from other interventions? A study of junior soccer players showed that a 4-week program of aerobic interval training produced a 12 percent improvement (Impellizzeri et al., 2008). Thus, the benefits of IMT are at least as good as those produced by interval training. But do the cost–benefit equations stack up? The details are in table 4.3, but the total additional training time for IMT averaged 3 hours. By contrast, the interval training adjunct required an extra 5 hours of training. As was the case for the previous comparison of the 40-kilometer time trial (also in table 4.3), the time and physical commitment required by IMT are a fraction of those required by interval training. Furthermore, the same IMT protocol shows unique versatility, improving both endurance performance and repeated sprint performance; contrast this with the highly specific nature of interval training, which needs variations in intensity, duration, and repetitions in order to vary the training outcomes.

In summary, IMT was once thought to be of benefit only for performance in activities in which aerobic metabolism dominates. However, studies suggest that IMT is more versatile than this, and that its influence on breathing effort and blood flow to the limb muscles make it an effective adjunct for athletes whose sports require repeated high-intensity efforts. This benefit has been confirmed experimentally using a test that correlates well with match performance in sports such as soccer; however, IMT is also likely to be of benefit to any athletes whose training involves repeated high-intensity efforts, because IMT enhances the ability to sustain the intensity of such activities. The latter should improve the quality of activities such as interval training, thereby enhancing the traditional training benefits from these activities.

PERFORMANCE IMPROVEMENTS IN SWIMMING

The aquatic environment is one of the most challenging for the breathing muscles, and competitive swimming presents one of the ultimate challenges for breathing. High-intensity swimming using the front crawl is associated with the most severe (29 percent fall in MIP) and fastest developing (2.5 minutes) states of inspiratory muscle fatigue of any sport thus far studied.

Bearing this in mind—along with the obvious "respiratory gymnastics" that are such an integral part of swimming—it is surprising that there have been so few studies of IMT in the context of swimming performance. At the time of this writing, only two studies have examined the influence of breathing muscle training on surface swimming performance. The first study employed simultaneous IMT and EMT, and the training failed to elicit significant improvements (above the similarly modest changes of the placebo group) in either respiratory muscle strength or swim performance. Because breathing muscle function did not improve, it would be surprising if anything else did. Most recently, the influence of IMT on performance in the 100-meter, 200-meter, and 400-meter front crawl was studied in 16 club-level swimmers (Kilding, Brown, & McConnell, 2009). After 6 weeks of IMT, perceived exertion during incremental swimming was reduced, and there were improvements in 100-meter (1.7 percent) and 200-meter (1.5 percent) swim performance, but no change in 400-meter performance. The absence of an effect on 400-meter performance is puzzling and is most likely a statistical anomaly, because there is no physiological reason why the response over 400 meters would differ from 100 or 200 meters.

A series of studies have also been conducted on the underwater swimming performance of experienced divers after breathing muscle endurance training and IMT. These studies have demonstrated improvements in underwater swim performance. In two of these studies, improvements were found in endurance (Tlim) for both underwater (33 to 50 percent) and surface (38 to 88 percent) fin swimming. In common with terrestrial exercise, tidal volume also increased (12 percent), and breathing frequency was lower (19 percent) after RMT. This more efficient breathing pattern may have been responsible for the small reduction in energy cost of the underwater swim (7.8 percent).

These data from fin-swimming divers are not directly comparable to those of surface swimmers using the front crawl, breaststroke, and so on, but they provide strong evidence to support the limited data on IMT in surface swimming. When IMT is undertaken with the correct training equipment and regimen, surface swimmers are also extremely likely to experience improvements in their performance. This may be especially relevant to novice swimmers, as well as swimmers coming back from injury or an off-season period, because inspiratory muscle deconditioning may affect performance under these conditions.

Given the many hours that swimmers spend trying to improve their performance using traditional training interventions, IMT must rank as one of the quickest fixes around. Most coaches would agree that breathing discipline is central to an efficient swim technique—unfortunately this discipline is very difficult for most swimmers to achieve and maintain (it tends to break down at the end of a race, and the stroke shortens accordingly). From an anecdotal perspective, experience has shown that swimmers who have previously struggled to master their breathing, sometimes for months or even years, find that IMT provides the kick start that enables them to make progress. IMT is therefore a win–win, because it improves stroke mechanics (via its effect on breathing discipline) and also improves performance (via its effect on breathing effort and inspiratory muscle fatigue or metaboreflex activation).

PERFORMANCE IMPROVEMENTS FOR ALTITUDE

Like swimming, activities performed at high altitude place additional demands on the breathing muscles. Therefore, people who perform activities in this environment are obvious candidates for breathing muscle training. To date, only one placebo-controlled study has assessed the influence of IMT on exercise tolerance and physiological responses to exercise, although there have been a handful of field trials. The results of the randomized controlled study were both impressive and surprising. During exercise at a simulated altitude of about 12,000 feet (3,500 m), the following changes occurred after 4 weeks of IMT:

- The breathing requirement of exercise was reduced by 25 percent.
- The oxygen requirement of exercise was reduced by 8 to 12 percent.
- The cardiac output requirement of exercise was reduced by 14 percent.
- The arterial oxygen saturation was increased by 4 percent.
- The diffusing capacity of the lungs was increased by 4 percent.
- Perceived exertion and breathlessness were reduced.

The changes included a reduction in the breathing requirement of exercise along with an improvement in arterial oxygen saturation. These two changes appear to be completely at odds with one another; increase in saturation normally requires a higher level of breathing. The clue to explaining this resides in the improvement in the diffusing capacity of the lungs, because this can only increase if the lung diffusion surface area increases (i.e., the amount of blood and air in close proximity with one another within the lung increases). Once again, the answer lies in the metaboreflex. If the inspiratory muscle metaboreflex is delayed or abolished after IMT, then blood flow will be preserved in the pulmonary circulation. The result is an increase in diffusion surface area and an increase in arterial oxygen saturation. The other physiological changes that were seen in this study all follow as logical consequences of this fundamental change in metaboreflex activation.

The findings of this laboratory study of IMT at altitude are consistent with field data collected during a study conducted as part of a medical expedition to one of Nepal's highest peaks (Mount Kanchenchunga). Some members of the expedition, who were all well-trained mountaineers, undertook IMT before departure for Nepal. Those who did *not* undertake IMT experienced a significantly greater increase in their sense of effort at altitude than those who did. They also experienced greater inspiratory muscle fatigue and a reduction in inspiratory muscle endurance. This attenuation of the normal increase in breathing effort experienced at high altitude has been a common experience of people in the handful of such expeditions that have incorporated IMT into their preexpedition preparations. These expeditions have included some of the toughest and most experienced mountaineers in the world, attempting feats that are at the very limits of human endurance (including the British Army Everest West Ridge team); all have reported an improvement in their breathing when incorporating IMT.

High altitude is the one environment where the lungs limit oxygen transport. When you also consider that IMT improves performance at sea level, undertaking IMT before ascent to high altitude becomes a complete "no-brainer." In addition, it's not just mountaineers who can benefit from IMT; athletes who are training at high altitude can also benefit from both the altitude-specific benefits and the generic performance-enhancing improvements that occur.

BENEFITS FOR ATHLETES WITH BREATHING PROBLEMS

The preceding section has presented evidence that breathing muscle training improves athletic performance. The following sections consider how IMT can be used as a method of managing two common respiratory problems in athletes. Exercise-induced asthma is the most common chronic illness in athletes, affecting around 20 percent of Olympians (which is twice the prevalence in the general population). Although asthma is no barrier to competing at the highest level or even becoming a world-record holder (e.g., Paula Radcliffe), it has a potentially negative impact on performance and may prevent athletes from achieving their true potential. Anything that can minimize the potentially negative impact of asthma is therefore worthy of serious consideration. Dysfunction of the upper airway muscles manifests itself in sport as inspiratory stridor. Both asthma and inspiratory stridor have been treated very successfully using IMT. When it comes to asthma, IMT is particularly helpful for those athletes in whom the severity of their condition just falls short of the International Olympic Committee (IOC) criteria for granting a Therapeutic Use Exemption (TUE), which permits the use of asthma medication in competition.

Asthma

The main symptom of asthma is being out of breath, and IMT is an extremely effective method of decreasing the intensity of breathing effort, even in people with perfectly healthy lungs. Studies of the benefits of IMT for people with asthma have thus far been confined to nonathletes; however, there is every reason to believe that the benefits experienced by nonathletes will be just as good, if not better, in athletes. This is confirmed by anecdotal evidence indicating that athletes with asthma show greater perceptual responses to IMT than nonasthmatic athletes, as well as improvement in their specific asthma symptoms. The former may be because the work of breathing is often elevated in people with asthma, which will tend to fatigue the inspiratory muscles more quickly. Athletes with asthma therefore not only benefit from relief of asthma symptoms, but may also experience a larger ergogenic effect; in addition, it's likely that these benefits are additive (see the sidebar on the next page).

So what does the scientific research on IMT for people with asthma tell us? Well-controlled studies (including those with placebo designs) have demonstrated improvements in inspiratory muscle strength, lung function, breathlessness, quality of life, and symptom severity, as well as reductions in hospital visits, acute flare-ups, and use of medication.

Case Study of IMT in a Distance Runner With Asthma

Tom was a national standard distance runner who competed on the track as well as in cross country. He developed asthma as a child and was treated by his GP using inhaled medication. "As a child, my asthma was quite well controlled and didn't used to impede me at all. But as I got older, my symptoms became less easy to control, and I developed a series of chest infections in my late 20s that really knocked my training back," Tom explained.

After this run of setbacks, Tom found that his breathing always troubled him during training—and especially during racing—and his performances suffered accordingly. On the verge of giving up the sport completely, Tom read an article about IMT (an article that I'd written for a popular running magazine), and he decided to give it a try. Tom completed about 2 months of IMT, during which he saw his 10K personal best improve to a time he'd not run for more than 5 years. He also found that his asthma symptoms improved considerably, and that he wasn't using his inhaler other than immediately before exercise.* In short, he felt like a new man.

Around this time, Tom contacted me to let me know of his experiences with IMT. I love it when this happens, because there's nothing quite so gratifying as hearing success stories like Tom's. I also like to use these points of contact as opportunities to encourage athletes to develop their IMT further by introducing some of the functional breathing training exercises that I have developed. As it happened, Tom did report that he found the transition into cross country each season quite challenging for his breathing, and he'd always put it down to the fact that it was colder and that this just irritated his lungs more (which it does); however, I thought there was more to it than this, especially when Tom told me that he did no core or stability training at all—the only thing he did was run. I prescribed some of the functional breathing training exercises that I have developed (see chapter 8) and asked Tom to report back in 4 weeks. Four weeks later, Tom contacted me with yet more good news. He'd finished 4th in his first cross country event of the season. This was a race he had entered every year for the past 10 years (lungs permitting), and he'd failed to finish higher than 18th in any previous year. "It was quite surreal; for the first time during a [cross country] race, I felt like I was running on air," said Tom. "I normally feel like I'm wading through treacle [syrup], especially that early in the season, but I just felt so balanced and strong—it was amazing." Tom went on to have the best winter and summer seasons he'd had since leaving the junior ranks.

Bolstered by this success, Tom has made IMT and the functional breathing training exercises an integral part of his training. He's fitter and healthier than he's been in almost a decade, and he's become an enthusiastic ambassador for all things related to breathing training. As for his asthma, he's not had a chest infection since he took up IMT, and he still only uses his inhaler immediately before exercise.

*People must be sure not to change their medication regimen without consulting their doctor.

However, despite these impressive improvements, IMT is not a miracle cure for asthma, and it should be considered as an adjunct to conventional treatments (i.e., something to use in conjunction with medication in order to optimize treatment). Notwithstanding this comment, IMT seems to be associated with substantial reductions (40 to 80 percent) in the consumption of "reliever" inhaler medication. Why this happens is not known, but it is likely related to the fact that increasing inspiratory muscle strength reduces breathlessness. Because people with asthma use breathlessness as their main cue for the current state of their asthma—and as a prompt to take medication—some of the changes observed in the research studies may be linked directly to the relief of breathlessness.

All in all, the data suggest that athletes with asthma have even more reason to add IMT to their training regimens, because it will not only enhance their performance, but will also improve their asthma.

Before closing this section, it is worth mentioning that because of the rules in place, a small group of international athletes with mild asthma are not allowed to use medication during competition. Not all sports apply these rules, but the International Olympic Committee does, and some athletes' asthma is not sufficiently severe to justify the granting of a Therapeutic Use Exemption. For these athletes, IMT offers the only "legal" means of managing their symptoms and is therefore highly recommended.

Inspiratory Stridor

Dysfunction of the muscles that control the upper airway, especially those controlling the larynx, can lead to extreme breathlessness and sudden exercise intolerance. The latter arises because inspiratory airflow is obstructed if the vocal folds collapse across the airway opening to the lungs. The condition is known as inspiratory stridor (because of the noisy breathing it creates) and is most common in adolescent female athletes, though it is not confined to this group. The precise causes remain unknown, but they may be related to fatigue of the muscles that open the vocal folds and maintain the upper airway opening.

How can IMT help? Breathing against a breathing muscle trainer produces a negative pressure inside the lungs and the airways during inhalation. This negative pressure is transmitted to all of the cavities inside the respiratory system (lungs, thoracic airways, upper airways, nose, and mouth). For the upper airway (located outside the thoracic cavity), the negative pressure inside the lungs and airways creates a pressure gradient that tends to collapse the airways. In its relaxed state, the upper airway is essentially a floppy tube, and if the muscles that stabilize this tube are not activated when using a breathing muscle trainer, the upper airway will collapse. Fortunately, we don't have to activate these muscles consciously, because there is an automatic reflex activation of these stabilizing muscles that prevents the airway from collapsing. Because these muscles are activated during IMT, we can use IMT as a means of training the upper airway muscles and treating inspiratory stridor.

Traditional treatments for inspiratory stridor are based on speech therapy techniques, and in extreme cases, surgery is used to stabilize the upper airway mechanically. However, IMT offers a very effective evidence-based alternative. A number of case studies have shown that exercise-induced symptoms of stridor subside after a short period of IMT (4 to 6 weeks), without recurrence. The case studies have also shown that IMT can be used very successfully in athletes across a wide range of sports and at all levels of competition.

It is not necessary to modify the IMT in any way when using it as a treatment for inspiratory stridor (see chapter 6). However, during IMT, the athletes should concentrate on activating the upper airway muscles during inhalation and emphasizing these muscles' dilatory effect on the airway. This is best conceptualized as "opening up the throat" during inhalation. The same conscious awareness of upper airway activation should also be applied during normal whole-body training sessions, along with a focus on deep, controlled breathing.

ANALYSIS OF SPORT-SPECIFIC BENEFITS

The preceding sections pointed out that there is strong scientific evidence indicating that breathing muscle training improves performance and resolves breathing-related problems in a wide range of sports. However, this research evidence underestimates the wider, more subtle benefits that can be achieved by adding IMT to normal training. What other benefits might be expected? Because of the role of the breathing muscles, especially the diaphragm, in core stability and postural control, IMT improves functional core stability, movement efficiency, and injury prevention. Of course, improvements such as these are almost impossible to measure in a laboratory, but that doesn't make them any less valuable.

The following sections review the specific benefits of breathing muscle training for a range of sports (before reading these sections, you may want to review chapter 2, which describes how the specific demands of different sports increase the demands placed on the breathing muscles). This is not a comprehensive list of sports, but it does provide an overview of the situations in which IMT can bring direct performance benefits of the kind observed in the laboratory, as well as more subtle benefits that cannot be quantified in research studies (e.g., an enhanced ability of the inspiratory muscles to meet their dual role in breathing and delivering trunk stiffness in a sport such as rowing).

The sport-related challenges to breathing muscles are common to many sports, resulting in overload and functional compromise to the trunk muscles because of their simultaneous contribution to breathing, core stabilization, postural control, and propulsion, as well as their overcoming of the impedance of inspiratory movements because of posture (e.g., the catch of the rowing stroke). This overloading may predispose the breathing muscles to fatigue. Thus, the addition of IMT—especially when undertaken using the functional approaches described in part II of this book—serves to mitigate the risk of performance limitation due to inspiratory muscle fatigue, while also reducing the risk of injury. The next sections summarize the functional benefits of IMT for a range of sport contexts. Table 4.4 (page 74) provides a summary of benefits by sport.

For every sport and fitness category described in the following sections, IMT will improve exercise tolerance or performance by delaying the onset of the inspiratory muscle metaboreflex and reducing the perception of breathing and whole-body effort. These sections summarize the additional benefits.

Exercise and Fitness

For those engaged in general fitness training, IMT will make exercise feel easier, which enables people to maintain higher exercise intensities for longer durations. This enhances the fitness gains and caloric expenditure of general fitness conditioning.

The rate of perceived recovery will also improve, which will enhance the ability to maintain the tempo of activity during exercise-to-music classes and the intensity of circuit training. The enhancement of core stability will reduce injury risk and improve weight training.

Weight trainers will benefit from improved core stability, which may produce an improvement in maximal lift performances for lifts where trunk stiffness and stability contribute to the ability to overcome a load (e.g., Olympic lifts).

Endurance Sports

A wide range of endurance sports are reviewed here, but the principles that have been applied can be adapted to suit any sport.

Running

IMT will improve the runner's ability to maintain a deeper, slower breathing pattern. It will also enhance the efficiency of respiratory and locomotor coupling (entrainment), enhance core stability (reducing spinal loading and improving leg drive efficiency), and improve postural control (balance). IMT may also reduce the risk of developing a side stitch.

Cycling

IMT will improve the cyclist's ability to maintain a deeper, slower breathing pattern. It will also enhance the efficiency of respiratory and locomotor coupling (entrainment) and enhance core stability (reducing spinal loading and knee stress and improving pedaling efficiency). IMT will also allow the inspiratory muscles to operate more comfortably in extreme cycling positions (e.g., when using aerobars), especially when the IMT is undertaken using the functional training guidance provided in part II of this book.

Swimming

The addition of IMT to swim and other aquatic training will improve the swimmer's ability to maintain a deeper, slower breathing pattern and will enhance the efficiency of respiratory and locomotor coupling (entrainment). IMT can also enhance the swimmer's ability to inhale rapidly and to achieve and sustain high lung volumes. As a result, the swimmer's body position and stroke mechanics will be improved. A decrease in the number of breaths per stroke will also be possible. In addition, the muscles of the trunk will be better able to meet the dual demands for breathing and providing propulsive force, especially when IMT is undertaken using the functional training guidance provided in part II.

Those using scuba will also benefit from a deeper, slower breathing pattern, which reduces air use and extends cylinder wear time. Furthermore, free divers and surfers may also experience an improvement in breath-holding time. Breathing restrictions imposed by wet suits will also be easier to overcome or tolerate after IMT.

Multisport

The addition of IMT to multisport training will provide the benefits summarized for each component, especially when undertaken using the functional training guidance provided in part II. Most triathlons involve a wet suit swim, and IMT will enhance the swimmer's ability to breathe efficiently and comfortably. Furthermore, the unique breathing-related disruption that occurs during the transition from cycling to running will be alleviated.

Rowing

The addition of IMT to rowing training will improve the rower's ability to maintain a deeper, slower breathing pattern; enhance the efficiency of respiratory and locomotor coupling (entrainment); and enhance core stability and trunk stiffness (reducing spinal loading and improving force transmission to the blade). Furthermore, improvements in intercostal muscle function and the ability to generate and maintain high intrathoracic pressure may reduce the risk of rib stress fractures. IMT will also allow the inspiratory muscles to operate more comfortably at the catch and finish positions, especially when the IMT is undertaken using the functional training guidance provided in part II.

Sliding Sports

People taking part in sliding sports have a number of factors influencing their performance, including the effects of altitude and the challenges associated with maintaining balance. IMT will improve their ability to maintain a deeper, slower breathing pattern. It will also enhance the efficiency of respiratory and locomotor coupling (entrainment), enhance core stability (reducing spinal loading and improving leg drive efficiency), and improve postural control (balance) and trunk stiffness. The ability to maintain aerodynamic postures for longer periods without the associated breathing discomfort is another benefit of IMT.

Hiking and Mountaineering

Hikers and mountaineers have to contend with the effects of altitude, the impact of carrying heavy backpacks, and the challenges associated with maintaining balance on unpredictable terrain. IMT will improve their ability to maintain a deeper, slower breathing pattern; enhance the efficiency of respiratory and locomotor coupling (entrainment); and enhance core stability (reducing spinal loading). The challenges to postural control (balance) imposed by carrying a backpack and by traveling on uneven terrain will be minimized by IMT, and trunk stiffness will be improved. In addition, the ability to overcome the resistance to normal breathing movements of the trunk that are induced by backpacks will be improved, especially when the IMT is undertaken using the functional training guidance provided in part II.

Team and Sprint Sports

Team sports are diverse in their challenges, but they all have three important factors in common: They involve repeated high-intensity efforts that drive breathing to its limits; they require the contribution of the upper body and the core-stabilizing system (e.g., fending off opponents, changing direction quickly, or passing objects to teammates); and they require tactical decision making at a time when the distraction from breathing discomfort is high. IMT will improve the rate of perceived recovery between sprints, which will enhance repeated sprint performance and the quality of interval training. These improvements in perceived recovery should enable players to maintain the intensity of their involvement in the match or game, rather than back off for a period of "cruising" recovery. In addition, the damping down of breathlessness will lessen the distraction that this sensation imposes on tactical decision making.

Improvements to core stability will advance a player's effectiveness during physical interactions with opponents (e.g., tackling, fending off) and in activities such as kicking and throwing.

For contact sports and those that involve activities requiring the application of whole-body isometric forces (such as a rugby scrum), players will benefit from the increased ability of the inspiratory muscles to function as breathing muscles. This is important in situations where the demand for breathing is high but the requirement for maximal core-stabilizing activity is also present.

Finally, in those contact team sports requiring the use of mouth guards and other protective equipment, IMT can improve breathing comfort and reduce the risk of inspiratory muscle fatigue that results from the restrictions imposed by the equipment.

Racket, Striking, and Throwing Sports

Sports falling under this heading most commonly require the participants to use an implement to strike a ball—such as a racket (e.g., tennis, squash, badminton), club (e.g., golf), or bat (e.g., baseball, softball, cricket)—or they may be sports that involve throwing a ball (pitching and bowling). In the case of racket sports, the player is required to direct the ball within the bounds of the court using a range of strokes. Matches are fast paced, requiring speed, agility, and skill. In contrast, in sports such as golf or baseball, the player is able to square up to the ball or pitcher and is stationary as the ball is struck. These two scenarios create very different demands on the breathing muscles, but there are two common denominators: the involvement of the trunk musculature in providing a stable platform and in protecting the spine; the contribution of the entire trunk musculature to the task of accelerating a racket, club, bat, or arm.

After using IMT, players in racket sports will be able to maintain a higher tempo of performance during rallies, and they will experience a reduction in unforced errors. Rate of perceived recovery between rallies will also improve, which will enhance the ability to maintain and dictate the pace and tempo of the game. In addition, the damping down of breathlessness will lessen the distraction that this sensation imposes on tactical decision making. The enhancement of core stability and improved contribution of the trunk musculature to racket head speed and precision will increase the likelihood of aces and shots that are "winners," as well as reduce the risk of injury.

Many of these sports require high levels of core stability and a contribution from the trunk musculature to the swinging of implements (such as clubs and bats) or the launching of projectiles (such as in field sports). Players in these sports will benefit from the enhanced function of the diaphragm and the enhanced contribution of the inspiratory accessory muscles to these movements. This will result in an increase in striking and throwing velocities, especially when IMT is undertaken using the functional training guidance provided in part II. In addition, there will be a reduction in injury risk because of the enhanced spinal stability and the improved resistance of rib cage muscles to tearing.

Table 4.4 Summary of Sport-Specific Benefits of IMT

		Improved performance due to delayed metaboreflex activation	Improved performance due to reduced effort	Enhanced core and spinal stability	Enhanced postural control and balance	Improved breathing pattern and breathing entrainment
Exercise and fitness	Core training adjunct			Y	Y	
	Weight loss	Y	Y	Y	Y	Y
	General fitness	Y	Y	Y	Y	Y
	Weight training adjunct	Y	Y	Y	Y	Y
Endurance sports	Running	Y	Y	Y	Y	Y
	Cycling	Y	Y	Y	Y	Y
	Swimming	Y	Y	Y	Y	Y
	Multisport	Y	Y	Y	Y	Y
	Rowing	Y	Y	Y	Y	Y
	Sliding sports	Y	Y	Y	Y	Y
	Hiking and mountaineering	Y	Y	Y	Y	Y
		Improved performance due to delayed metaboreflex activation	Improved performance due to reduced effort	Enhanced core and spinal stability	Enhanced postural control and balance	Improved breathing pattern and breathing entrainment
Team sports	Football	Y	Y	Y	Y	Y
	Soccer	Y	Y	Y	Y	Y
	Basketball and netball	Y	Y	Y	Y	Y
	Ice hockey and roller hockey	Y	Y	Y	Y	Y
	Field hockey	Y	Y	Y	Y	Y
	Rugby football	Y	Y	Y	Y	Y
		Improved performance due to delayed metaboreflex activation	Improved performance due to reduced effort	Enhanced core and spinal stability	Enhanced postural control and balance	Enhanced breathing and movement synchrony
Racket, striking, and throwing sports	Racket sports	Y	Y	Y	Y	Y
	Striking sports			Y	Y	Y
	Throwing sports			Y	Y	Y

Note: The absence of a benefit for a particular sport does not imply that this benefit is not present, but that this benefit is not relevant to the specific sport (e.g., a reduced risk of rib fracture is not present for running because rib fracture is not a risk associated with running).

Reduced risk of "stitch"	Enhanced breathing comfort during thoracic compression	Enhanced breathing comfort during postural challenges	Enhanced trunk stiffness	Reduced risk of rib fractures or intercostal tears	Improved isometric trunk strength	Reduced impairments due to equipment
	Y	Y	Y		Y	
Y		Y			Y	
Y		Y			Y	
		Y	Y		Y	
Y		Y	Y			
Y	Y (aerobars)	Y	Y			
Y	Y (water)	Y	Y	Y	Y	Y (wet suit)
Y	Y (water)	Y	Y	Y	Y	Y (wet suit)
Y	Y (catch)	Y	Y	Y	Y	
Y		Y	Y		Y	
Y		Y	Y		Y	Y (backpack)

Reduced risk of "stitch"	Less distraction from breathlessness during decision making	Improved ability to fend off opponents and maintain balance	Improved kicking and throwing ability	Reduced risk of rib fractures or intercostal tears	Improved isometric trunk strength	Reduced impairments due to equipment
Y	Y	Y	Y	Y	Y	Y
Y	Y	Y	Y		Y	
Y	Y	Y	Y		Y	
Y	Y	Y			Y	Y
Y	Y	Y			Y	
Y	Y	Y	Y	Y	Y	Y

Improved striking or throwing ability	Enhanced trunk stiffness	Reduced risk of rib fractures or intercostal tears				
Y	Y	Y				
Y	Y	Y				
Y	Y	Y				

Breathing Muscle Training

In part I of *Breathe Strong, Perform Better,* we learned about the physiological principles that underpin breathing. We also learned that breathing muscle training induces laboratory-proven performance enhancements in a wide range of sports. These enhancements arise from reductions in effort perception and the maintenance of limb blood flow during exercise. Part II of *Breathe Strong* will consider some general and specific principles that underpin muscle training (chapter 5), demonstrate how to get started with a program of foundation training (chapter 6), and show how to apply functional training principles to breathing training.

As is the case with conventional functional training, the exercises recommended in this book employ external resistances to challenge the neuromuscular system, including applying resistances to the breathing muscles. Initially, the breathing element of the exercises is simply a focus on deep and purposeful breathing. As the ability to perform the exercises improves, external resistances to breathing can be applied, including a pressure threshold breathing muscle trainer (BMT; see chapters 5 and 6).

The approach taken in chapters 7 to 10 is similar; for each sporting or exercise context, a brief analysis is presented of the main demands imposed on the breathing muscles by the activity. This provides the rationale for specific inspiratory muscle training (IMT), which is followed by identification of specific training objectives that are based on movements and scenarios that typify the competing demands for breathing and movement. Finally, a series of specific exercises are suggested (chapter 11). Illustrating the analytical process will help you learn to undertake the analysis for yourself. In this way, you will not be limited to the exercises that are presented in *Breathe Strong, Perform Better;* you will be able to apply your own knowledge to creating new exercises (you can share these at www.breathestrong.com). In formulating the exercises presented in this book, the guidance of expert practitioners has been sought, and their collaboration is acknowledged in the relevant sections.

Analyzing Your Sport

To devise functional breathing training exercises for your sport, you need to take a long hard look at its demands from both a respiratory and functional movement perspective. For example, a team sport such as soccer is typified by short bursts of high-intensity sprinting lasting about 3 seconds that are followed by about 30 seconds of active recovery. A typical work–rest ratio when the ball is in play is 1:4.3. During the recovery phase, what do you think will be happening to breathing? Obviously, it will be elevated hugely by the repeated anaerobic sprint efforts. In addition, soccer is also typified by rapid changes of speed and direction—which must be performed while winning, passing, or receiving the ball. Players must also cope with challenging semi-contact interactions with opponents. When devising a functional training program for soccer, all of these factors need to be taken into account. Similarly, when devising a functional *breathing* training program, the simultaneous breathing and functional demands placed on the trunk musculature must be considered.

Here is a list of some questions you need to consider in order to devise a functional breathing training program:

1. Does your sport require sprinting and jumping, or does it involve continuous moderate activity?

2. How often do you sprint, for how long, and how much rest do you get? In other words, how high is your breathing demand and how long do you have to recover?

3. Does your sport involve your upper body (e.g., interactions with opponents or the use of a racket)?

4. Does your body position or your equipment constrain your breathing (e.g., the aero position on a cycle, a mouth guard, or padding)?

5. Can you only breathe at specific points in a movement (e.g., swimming), or is breathing optimized at particular points (e.g., rowing)?

6. Do you need to breathe heavily during high-intensity static efforts (e.g., a rugby scrum)?

7. Do you need to resist externally imposed rotational forces (e.g., being turned over in rugby)?

8. Is your postural control challenged (e.g., ice hockey)?

9. Do you need to "fight" opponents who are trying to dislodge you from your position, or do you need to dislodge opponents from their position (e.g., basketball)?

10. Does your sport combine a high breathing demand with sudden or heavy spinal loading (e.g., American football)?

11. Is core stabilization important to your performance or risk of injury, and does breathing or movement challenge your core stability (e.g., racket sports)?

12. Are particular activities in your sport associated with breathing discomfort or increased breathing effort (e.g., running on uneven ground)?

Chapter
5
Training the Breathing Muscles

In common with the heart, the breathing pump muscles function continuously throughout our lives. This makes them unique among skeletal muscles, and for many years it was assumed that their continuous activity resulted in a state of optimal training adaptation. As we saw in chapter 1, the structural and functional properties of the breathing muscles are consistent with these muscles being highly trained and adapted for continuous work. However, as we saw in chapter 2, contrary to expectations, the breathing pump muscles have not achieved a state of optimal training adaptation, because the diaphragm shows fatigue after exercise. The presence of fatigue in any muscle is an indication that it is working at, or beyond, the limits of its capacity.

In chapter 3, an overview of the changes induced by strength and endurance training of the breathing muscles was provided, including evidence that these muscles respond to training in the same way as limb muscles. In chapter 4, evidence was presented that specific breathing muscle training improves performance in a wide range of sporting contexts. This research provides very strong support for the argument that the breathing muscles are a weak link in the performance chain—but one that can be overcome by the application of the right kind of training.

To get the most out of any training program, a person must identify the weak links in the performance chain and must understand how they can be overcome with different kinds of training. For example, if the weak link is not being strong enough to overwhelm your opponent in a rugby tackle, then no amount of endurance training will fix it. Armed with knowledge about how muscles respond to training, as well as an understanding of the principles that need to be applied in order to achieve specific training outcomes (strength, power, endurance, and so on), people can devise interventions to overcome specific weaknesses. For example, in a sport such as basketball, poor jumping ability is a weakness, but it can be overcome by applying very specific training stimuli (e.g., plyometric training).

This chapter opens with a description of the principles that underpin muscle training generally. We'll consider how these principles can be applied to the breathing muscles to generate improvements in their function, which can translate into improvements in performance. The chapter also provides an overview of the various training methods that can be used to train the breathing muscles, along with the changes in muscle function that each method produces. Information is also provided on the relative merits of the equipment that is commercially available for breathing muscle training.

GENERAL TRAINING PRINCIPLES

Three universal training principles have been established for all skeletal muscles: the principles of overload, specificity, and reversibility. These three principles guide the formulation and implementation of muscle training. The following sections provide an overview of these principles as they have been shown to apply to the breathing muscles. If you are already familiar with the three training principles, you will be struck by the similarity of the training responses of the breathing and limb muscles. Armed with this knowledge, it is possible to formulate specific training programs to achieve specific training outcomes (for any muscles); furthermore, these training programs will be based on scientific principles, not guesswork.

The Overload Principle

To obtain a training response, muscle fibers must be overloaded. Implicit within this principle is the concept of training *duration, intensity,* and *frequency.* In other words, muscles can be overloaded by requiring them to work for longer periods, at higher intensities, or more frequently than they are accustomed to. Most training regimens combine two or three of these factors in order to achieve overload.

In research to date, two main forms of overload have been imposed: external breathing loads at the mouth (intensity) and voluntary hyperventilation (increased breathing volume and flow rate) for extended periods (intensity and duration). In both cases, the training takes place daily or at least three times per week (frequency).

Studies employing external loading of inspiratory muscles have typically used loads in excess of 50 percent of breathing muscle strength, once or twice per day, for 5 to 7 days per week. Loading at 50 to 70 percent of maximal strength (moderate loading) typically yields "failure" within 30 breaths, or 2 to 3 minutes (intensity = 50 to 70 percent; duration = 30 breaths; frequency = twice daily). Changes in muscle function can be measured within 3 weeks; a plateau in improvement begins to occur after 6 to 9 weeks of training (see the moderate load in figure 5.1), despite continuous increases of the training load (Romer & McConnell, 2003).

Changes in strength occurring within the first 2 weeks of strength training have traditionally been attributed to a neural adaptation process—that is, improving the coordinated activation of synergistic muscles. Although this adaptation undoubtedly makes a contribution to the immediate short-term improvements seen in respiratory muscles, studies have shown increases in diaphragm thickness after just 4 weeks of inspiratory muscle training (IMT), confirming the presence of rapid fiber growth (hypertrophy) in response to loading. These changes in diaphragm thickness were accompanied by improvements in inspiratory muscle strength.

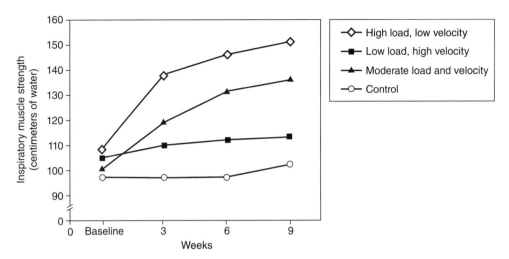

Figure 5.1 Changes in inspiratory muscle strength in response to three different training regimens during a 9-week training program.

Data from L.M. Romer and A.K. McConnell, 2003, "Specificity and reversibility of inspiratory muscle training," *Medicine & Science in Sports & Exercise* 35(2): 237-244.

There is a minimum intensity for overload, below which no changes in strength are observed. For strength training of the inspiratory muscles, this is around 15 percent of inspiratory muscle strength. In fact, a load of 15 percent has been used in many studies as a placebo condition. The loading region between 15 and 50 percent has not been studied in detail, but a 30 percent load (with 300 repetitions) generates improvements in strength of only around half those elicited by a 50 percent load (30 repetitions) over a 4-week period of training (Caine & McConnell, 1998). So to achieve meaningful changes in strength, inspiratory muscle overload in healthy people requires loads of at least 50 to 70 percent of maximal strength. This loading regimen elicits structural and functional adaptations within 3 to 4 weeks.

Studies using hyperventilation training have typically induced overload at intensities corresponding to 70 percent of maximum voluntary ventilation (MVV; maximum flow that can be sustained for 15 seconds) for 15 to 40 minutes per day, once per day, for 4 or 5 days per week (Verges, Boutellier, Spengler, 2008). In the case of hyperventilation training, overload is achieved by increasing the rate of airflow; the inspiratory muscles work against the inherent resistance and elastance (elastic resistance) of the respiratory system (intensity = 70 percent; duration = 15 to 40 minutes; frequency = 4 or 5 days per week). This level of external loading is so low that it does not increase the strength of the breathing muscles, but it does increase their endurance; the changes are evident within 4 weeks. There is currently no data to indicate the point at which functional improvements plateau after commencing training, but this probably also occurs within 6 to 9 weeks.

The intensity and frequency dimensions of overload warrant specific mention, because they need to be balanced carefully in order to avoid tipping the respiratory muscles into a state of overtraining. Most studies have implemented moderate-intensity IMT (50 to 70 percent) daily, but the intensity and frequency balance has yet to be studied systematically or with consideration for other concurrent training. It's possible that there may be "too much of a good thing." Data on healthy young soccer and rugby players suggest that twice daily high-intensity IMT (80 to 90 percent of maximal strength) may induce a state of chronic inspiratory muscle fatigue in athletes who are undergoing intense, concurrent whole-body training. These training conditions may elicit suboptimal improvements in function. Thus, evidence suggests that low- to moderate-intensity loading (30 to 60 percent of maximal strength) can be implemented daily, while high-intensity loading (greater than 70 percent of maximal strength) should be implemented no more than once every other day (see Why Loading Heavy Doesn't Deliver What You Expect on page 100 of chapter 6).

Finally, in the context of overload, it is also worth pointing out that, unlike limb muscle resistance training, breathing muscle training is without an eccentric phase. In other words, there is no parallel for the lowering of the weight once it has been lifted. Thus, the training stimulus received by the breathing muscles is effectively halved, compared with that received by a limb muscle. This may explain why it is possible to achieve quite high numbers of repetitions at relatively heavy loads during breathing muscle training. While the lack of an eccentric phase does not appear to limit the trainability of the breathing muscles in any way, it nevertheless needs to be taken into account.

The Specificity Principle

The specificity principle dictates that the nature of a training response depends on the type of stimulus delivered; in other words, muscles tend to respond to strength training stimuli (high intensity and short duration) by improving strength, and they respond to endurance training stimuli (low intensity and long duration) by improving endurance. This property of specificity also means that muscles tend not to improve properties that are not integral to the training stimulus. For example, training with heavy loads and slow movement velocities does not make muscles contract faster (figure 3.2, page 54).

Training for Strength and Speed

Generally, breathing muscles respond to high-load, low-frequency (strength) loading by getting stronger (Romer & McConnell, 2003). However, when considering the characteristics of a training stimulus, both the load and the speed with which it can be overcome must be taken into account; heavy loads cannot be overcome as quickly as light loads, and the laws of specificity dictate that this limits the range of adaptations that can be achieved using a heavy load. Thus, in addition to considering the load specificity of the training outcomes, one must also consider the airflow specificity, because it's impossible to maximize airflow rates while breathing against high loads. Training stimuli with high loads and low flow rates elicit increases in maximal strength, but they do not elicit increases in maximal flow rate. Conversely, training with low loads and high velocities of shortening (e.g., unloaded hyperventilation) elicits increases in maximal flow rates but not in strength. Interestingly, training stimuli with intermediate loads and flow rates elicit improvements in both maximal strength and flow rate, which has the added benefit of increasing power output; this is arguably the regimen that provides the "best of all worlds" (Romer & McConnell, 2003). (See figure 3.2, page 54.)

Training for Endurance

An endurance conditioning response can be elicited with low-load, high-frequency contractions. For the breathing muscles, this type of stimulus has typically been imposed using prolonged voluntary hyperventilation. However, it is also possible to improve endurance through strength training. This may seem to be at odds with everything in the preceding paragraphs, but it's not contradictory in the least, and here's why: Stronger muscles perform any given task at a lower percentage of their maximum capacity than weaker muscles do; strong muscles are therefore able to sustain a given activity for longer periods. For example, if the threshold for muscle fatigue is 60 percent of maximal strength, and the muscle becomes 30 percent stronger as a result of training, then a load that was 60 percent of maximal strength before training is only 46 percent of maximal strength after training (i.e., below the threshold for fatigue). In other words, making the muscle stronger improves its endurance. Thus, strength training provides a *dual conditioning response* (strength and endurance), and this has been shown experimentally for the inspiratory muscles (Caine & McConnell, 1998). Unfortunately, there is no evidence that a specific endurance training stimulus, such as hyperventilation, improves strength, making it less versatile than strength training.

Collectively, the current research data suggest that breathing training regimens with a moderate strength bias (50 to 70 percent of maximal strength) have the capacity to improve maximal strength, inspiratory airflow rate, and power output, as well as endurance. In addition, strength training has considerable time efficiency advantages over endurance training (less than 5 minutes compared with 15 to 40 minutes). This versatility and convenience support the use of moderate-intensity strength training regimens.

The Effect of Lung Volume

Research on limb muscles has established that the specificity principle applies to the range of motion during training. In other words, if range of motion is limited to the first few degrees of movement, improvements in strength will be limited to the same range of movement. This is why good form for a biceps curl encompasses the full 140 degrees of movement. The biceps is a simple muscle, bringing about an equally simple movement; imagine then the importance of specificity to a complex system such as the breathing muscles. It is no surprise that muscle length plays an important role in determining the adaptations that can be achieved for the breathing muscles.

In the context of the breathing muscles, muscle length is determined by lung volume; training at low lung volumes improves strength at low lung volumes to a larger extent than at high lung volumes and vice versa. However, training at low lung volumes appears to be more versatile than training at high lung volumes. In other words, when training takes place at low lung volumes, improvements are larger, and strength is increased over a greater span of lung volume. Thus, IMT should be conducted over the greatest range of lung volume possible, starting as close as possible to residual volume (maximal exhalation) and finishing as close as possible to total lung capacity (maximal inhalation).

Interactions Between Training Load and Lung Volume

In the context of lung volume specificity, a caveat that must be kept in mind is the volume–pressure relationship of the breathing muscles that was described in chapter 1. The inspiratory muscles become progressively weaker as the lungs inflate; therefore, under conditions of inspiratory loading, the breath may be curtailed ("clipped") before the lungs are completely full. This occurs because a load that is 50 percent of the maximal strength when the lungs are empty rapidly becomes equivalent to 100 percent of maximal strength as the lungs fill—the result is that the load can no longer be overcome, and inhalation stops before the lungs are full. This clipping of inspired volume occurs earlier with heavier loads or if the inspiratory muscles are fatigued. Does this really matter? A recent study suggests that it does; at loads greater than 70 percent of maximal strength, not only was it impossible to complete more than a handful of breaths, but these loads also decreased the amount of work done per breath (McConnell & Griffiths, 2010; see the sidebar titled Why Loading Heavy Doesn't Deliver What You Expect on page 100 of chapter 6). This happens because both load and breath volume contribute to the amount of work done during inspiratory loading (work = force × distance = load × volume). Because heavy loading reduces breath volume, the amount of work completed during a session with heavy loading is much lower than the amount that can be completed during moderate loading. Again, does this matter? Research on limb muscles indicates that the larger the amount of work completed by a given muscle, the greater the training improvements will be. To optimize training overload during IMT, it is important to strike a careful balance between (a) maximizing the load and the number of repetitions and (b) minimizing the reduction in work caused by the smaller breath volume. The practicalities of dealing with this compromise between loading and breath volume are dealt with in chapter 6.

The Reversibility Principle

The phenomenon of "use it or lose it" (detraining) describes the reversibility of training, and sadly, it applies as much to breathing muscles as it does to limb muscles. The reversibility principle also influences strategies for maintenance of training benefits during periods of reduced training.

Detraining

Compared with limb muscle training, the extent and time course of detraining of the inspiratory muscles have been studied comparatively little, but here's what we know. The regression of IMT-induced changes in inspiratory muscle function has been studied over 12-week (Caine & McConnell, 1998) and 18-week periods of detraining (Romer & McConnell, 2003). In the earlier of the two studies, only minor decrements in function were observed after 12 weeks of detraining (Caine & McConnell, 1998). In the later study, a loss of 32 percent of the strength gain from IMT was observed after 9 weeks of detraining, with no further changes in strength after 18 weeks of detraining. In contrast, endurance continued to decline during the period between 9 and 18 weeks of detraining. Over the full 18-week detraining period, there was a loss of around one third of the strength gain from IMT, two thirds of the gain in maximal flow rate, and three quarters of the gain in endurance. This suggests that inspiratory muscles respond in a similar manner to other muscles when a training stimulus is removed. It also suggests three other things: Most of the losses of function occur within 2 to 3 months of the cessation of training; functional gains are reasonably well preserved for the first month, and strength remains well preserved after more than 4 months; and the loss of endurance gains is larger than for other measures of function. The implication of these findings is that short periods of detraining (1 to 2 months) can be accommodated without too much regression of functional gains. However, as described in the following section, loss of function can be avoided completely by implementing a maintenance training program.

Maintenance

There's actually no need to lose any of the gains achieved in training, provided that a program of maintenance training is used. In fact, improvements in inspiratory muscle function can be sustained with training frequency reduced by as much as two thirds, or reduced to just twice a week (Romer & McConnell, 2003). The practicalities of moving to maintenance training are described in chapter 6.

In summary, the scientific literature supports the notion that the general training principles of overload, specificity, and reversibility apply equally to the training of breathing muscles as they do to limb muscles. This means that breathing training interventions should apply these principles in order to obtain specific functional outcomes, such as increasing and maintaining strength.

RESISTANCE AND ENDURANCE TRAINING OF BREATHING MUSCLES

Muscle training interventions can be subdivided broadly into two types: resistance training in which the muscles are subjected to external loading that is similar to lifting a weight, and endurance training in which muscles are required to work at high shortening velocities (rates of contraction) for prolonged periods of time, such as the legs receive during marathon training. In the case of endurance training of breathing muscles, the only loads imposed on the muscles are those of the inherent flow and elastic resistances of the respiratory system. The following sections describe the various methods of applying resistance and endurance training to the breathing muscles, including the specific training benefits that each method produces.

Resistance Training of Breathing Muscles

This method is similar to weightlifting; in this case, the "weight" is applied in the form of a resistance to airflow, via a mouthpiece. The resistance can be generated using two main methods: flow resistive loading or pressure threshold loading. The load can be limited to only one phase of breathing by using a valve that permits unimpeded airflow during either inhalation or exhalation.

Inspiratory Flow Resistive Loading

The simplest method of applying a resistance to breathing is by impeding airflow using a device that increases the force required to move air into the lungs—for example, by breathing through a straw. This type of breathing training is known as inspiratory flow resistive loading (IFRL), and typical training products allow users to select from a range of different sized holes that occlude the inspiratory port of the device. In theory, for a given rate of inhalation, the smaller the orifice, the greater the load to breathing (see the section on equipment later in this chapter for examples of such products). Studies using IFRL have reported increases in inspiratory muscle strength in the range of 20 to 50 percent. However, an inherent limitation of IFRL is that the training load varies with the rate of airflow and not just with the size of the hole; the faster a person breathes through a given hole, the more difficult it is to inhale (and vice versa for slow inhalation). Thus, to obtain a reliable training load using IFRL, a person must either monitor and control inspiratory flow rate or monitor and control the pressure load that is generated at the mouth. Otherwise, IFRL is a bit like pulling a bus that people keep jumping on and off; the load is never constant or predictable.

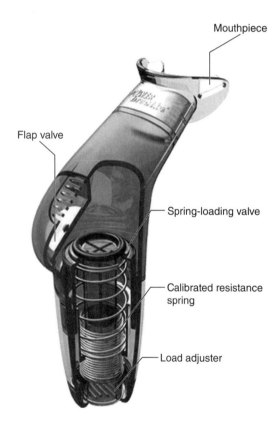

Mouthpiece

Flap valve

Spring-loading valve

Calibrated resistance spring

Load adjuster

Figure 5.2 A pressure threshold inspiratory muscle trainer illustrating the spring-loaded poppet valve that provides the training load to the inspiratory muscles.

Courtesy of POWERbreathe.

Inspiratory Pressure Threshold Loading

Inspiratory pressure threshold loading (IPTL) is the most widely used and studied method of breathing training. It is also more similar to weightlifting than any other form of breathing training. Users breathe via a device that contains a pressure-loaded inspiratory valve and an unloaded expiratory flap valve. To generate airflow, they must first overcome the pressure load and lift open the pressurized inspiratory valve. The pressure load is independent of the rate at which a person breathes through the device, and it can be adjusted to almost any level (weight). A pressure-loaded valve can be achieved in several ways, but the most common is in the form of a spring-loaded poppet valve (Caine & McConnell, 2000) (see figure 5.2). Threshold loading, as it is known, has been shown by several published studies (more than 20 at the time of this writing) to induce improvements in inspiratory muscle strength of up to 45 percent in healthy young adults. Maximum rate of muscle shortening (peak inspiratory flow rate) is also improved, as are maximal power output and inspiratory muscle endurance. Threshold loading therefore offers great versatility from the perspective of training benefits.

Because of its flow independence, training using an IPTL device can be undertaken effectively without the need to regulate breathing pattern. In addition, an IPTL device with a mechanical poppet valve is relatively inexpensive, portable, and easy to use.

Expiratory Pressure Threshold Loading

Expiratory pressure threshold loading (EPTL) is the precise parallel of IPTL, requiring the production of an expiratory pressure sufficient to overcome a positive pressure load and thereby initiate expiration. As is the case with IPTL, loading can be imposed at a quantifiable intensity by providing resistance to expiration that is nearly flow independent. This type of training has been far less extensively studied than IPTL, but EPTL has been shown to generate increases in expiratory muscle strength. However, the performance benefits of doing so remain doubtful.

Simultaneous IPTL and EPTL

Because breathing involves both inspiratory and expiratory muscles, a reasonable presumption might be that training both sets of muscles would be twice as good. This is discussed in more detail in chapters 3 and 4, but it is also worthy of mention here. Far from being twice as good, imposing pressure threshold loads on the inspiratory and expiratory muscles during the same breath cycle seems to be counterproductive. For example, when IPTL was added to EPTL after a period of 4 weeks in well-trained rowers, the increase in inspiratory muscle strength over the subsequent 6 weeks of concurrent training was just 13 percent, which is less than half the value typically attainable when IPTL is implemented without concurrent EPTL. Similar findings were made for young swimmers who undertook simultaneous IPTL and EPTL. After 12 weeks of training with incrementally increasing inspiratory and expiratory loads, inspiratory and expiratory muscle strength improved by only 8 percent. This was identical to the change shown over the same period in the sham training control group. These findings suggest that concurrent IPTL and EPTL generates suboptimal improvements in respiratory muscle strength, and it is therefore not recommended. In some ways, these results are not entirely surprising, because this approach to training would be similar to simultaneous biceps and triceps training—that is, it is fated to generate a suboptimal training stimulus to both muscles. In a world where fitness equipment manufacturers are always looking out for the "next big thing," it is significant that machines allowing simultaneous training of agonist and antagonist muscles simply don't exist.

Endurance Training of Breathing Muscles

If we take training specificity to its logical conclusion for breathing, the type of training that most closely resembles breathing during exercise is hyperventilation. However, there are some problems with this assumption, including the fact that people use their breathing muscles differently when they voluntarily hyperventilate compared to when breathing is driven by exercise. In addition, hyperventilation leads to the loss of carbon dioxide from the body (a state known as hypocapnia), inducing light-headedness and eventually leading to a state of involuntary muscle spasms and convulsions if continued for more than a few minutes. For hyperventilation to be a viable training method, hypocapnia must be prevented, and this requires equipment to maintain the normal level of carbon dioxide in the body (a state known as isocapnia).

Thus, endurance training of the breathing muscles employs a technique known as voluntary isocapnic hyperventilation (VIH) training, which requires participants to maintain high target levels of ventilation for up to 40 minutes. To prevent hypocapnia, a partial rebreathing circuit is used, whereby a proportion of the exhaled breath is breathed again so that its carbon dioxide is returned to the body. In research studies of VIH, training sessions are typically conducted three to five times per week at an intensity equivalent to 60 to 90 percent of maximum voluntary ventilation (MVV). Using VIH, several studies have shown increases in breathing endurance during sustained isocapnic ventilation, as well as increases in maximum sustainable ventilatory capacity (MSVC) and MVV. The latter is consistent with improvements in the peak velocity of muscle contraction (i.e., peak inspiratory flow rate).

Voluntary isocapnic hyperpnea is a relatively time consuming (typically 30 minutes per session) and physically demanding mode of breathing muscle training, requiring a high degree of participant motivation. It also requires special equipment in order to prevent hypocapnia. Although VIH improves indices of respiratory muscle endurance, it does not improve the strength or power of the respiratory muscles (Verges, Boutellier, & Spengler, 2008). Thus, unlike strength training, there is no dual conditioning response after VIH.

In summary, the preceding evidence points to resistance training as being the most versatile, least time consuming, and least arduous method of improving respiratory muscle function. The following section considers commercially available training equipment (including information on portability and relative cost), thus providing the final pieces of information required to select a suitable training method.

TRAINING EQUIPMENT

This section provides information about proprietary respiratory training equipment; this equipment falls into two main categories: resistance and endurance. The pros and cons of each device are summarized in order to help identify the most appropriate devices for a given application.

The products described here are limited to those that have been demonstrated in clinical or laboratory-controlled trials to generate improvements in respiratory muscle function (that is, trials for which the results have been published in peer-reviewed professional or scientific journals). In other words, they are limited to those products with laboratory-proven efficacy.

Resistance Training Equipment

Resistance training equipment is grouped into two main classes based on how the load is generated:

- Passive flow resistance
- Pressure threshold valve

Passive Flow Resistance Trainers

The mechanical products in this class employ simple dials that allow the user to select inspired airway orifices with differing surface areas; the smaller the surface area, the larger the inspired resistance. However, because these loads are passive and are generated by the inspired airflow (no flow equals no load), they are highly sensitive to the influence of inspiratory flow rate, which makes loading unreliable. These products are simple and inexpensive to manufacture; therefore, many devices are available to choose from. However, because of the inherent limitations of this type of device (see the previous section on resistance training), this class contains only one mechanical product that is laboratory proven; this product is the Pflex, which is manufactured by Philips Respironics Inc. (United States). (See table 5.1.) The main advantages of the Pflex are its price (less than $30) and convenience. However, training load and progression are impossible to quantify without providing simultaneous feedback of inspiratory flow rate using another piece of equipment. When the product is used in this way (referred to as targeted-flow resistive training), there is no difference in the quality of the improvement in strength that can be achieved compared with pressure threshold loading products, which are inherently more reliable.

The addition of pressure measurement, other electronics, and software to a simple flow resistor makes load setting reliable and quantifiable, but this also adds considerably to the cost and bulk of the equipment. The only product of this type to be laboratory proven is the TrainAir (Project Electronics Limited [United Kingdom]). The equipment requires an interface to a laptop, and its cost (about $1,000) makes it the preserve of clinics and professional sport. The training is also very strenuous and time consuming (around 30 minutes per session). The advantages of this product are the continuous biofeedback of training intensity and the built-in assessment of inspiratory muscle function.

Pressure Threshold Trainers

In the category of pressure threshold trainers, two laboratory-proven products are available. One has been applied in both the medical and sport settings (POWERbreathe from HaB International Limited); the other has been applied in just the clinical environment (Threshold from Philips Respironics Inc.). Both products are supported by extensive, high-quality published research. The principal differences between the products are their loading ranges, mouthpiece, separation of inspiratory and expiratory flow paths, and price (Threshold costs about $30, while POWERbreathe costs about $60). (See table 5.1.) The loading range of the Threshold renders it unusable by anyone whose baseline inspiratory muscle strength (i.e., maximal inspiratory pressure, or MIP) exceeds around 60 cmH$_2$O (typical MIP values in healthy young males and females are about 130 cmH$_2$O and 100 cmH$_2$O, respectively). This is because the Threshold's load-setting range of 9 to 41 cmH$_2$O is unable to accommodate an adequate training load (greater than 50 percent MIP) for individuals whose inspiratory muscle strength is greater than 80 cmH$_2$O. Thus, someone starting training with a strength value of 60 cmH$_2$O and improving by 30 percent will rapidly reach the limits of the loading mechanisms; for this person, the product will then be unable to provide an adequate training stimulus. The other product, POWERbreathe, is supplied in a range of models with load settings spanning 17 to 98 cmH$_2$O, 23 to 186 cmH$_2$O, and 29 to 274 cmH$_2$O. This product also separates inspiratory and expiratory flow paths so that the inspiratory valve is protected from damp exhaled air. Finally, the Threshold (like the Pflex) provides only a hard plastic mouthpiece that makes it challenging for some users to maintain an airtight seal, while the POWERbreathe has a flexible flanged mouthpiece that is both comfortable and airtight.

Endurance Training Equipment

Only one commercial product—the SpiroTiger from Idiag AG (Switzerland)—provides endurance training of the respiratory muscles. Like the two pressure threshold trainers, the efficacy of the SpiroTiger is supported by a large number of published research papers, primarily covering use of the product in a sport setting. As described in the earlier section on endurance training, the overloading stimulus is provided by vigorous hyperventilation for periods of around 30 minutes. Because the product requires a rebreathing circuit and a method to monitor the training intensity, it is bulky and expensive (about $1,000), which renders it primarily a clinic- or club-based training system. The training is also time consuming and extremely strenuous, requiring a very high level of user commitment in order to achieve and sustain the prescribed training intensity of 60 to 90 percent of maximum voluntary ventilation.

Pros and Cons of Various Training Methods and Equipment

Table 5.1 summarizes the pros and cons of the various training equipment, taking into consideration factors such as reliability, range of functional outcomes, price, ease of use, and training session duration. This table can be used to review the factors that are important for a given application and to select the most appropriate form of apparatus. The table also provides an overall score for each piece of equipment.

Table 5.1 Comparison of Proprietary Laboratory-Proven Breathing Training Products

Training equipment	Strength	Power	Shortening velocity	Endurance	Overload range	Overload reliability	Portability	Ease of use	Mouthpiece comfort
Pflex	2				2	1	5	2	1
TrainAir	5			3	5	5	2	2	5
POWER-breathe	5	5	5	3	5	5	5	5	5
Threshold	5	5	5	3	2	5	5	5	1
SpiroTiger	1			5	5	5	2	3	5

1 = poor

5 = excellent

No score indicates no evidence.

The overall scores for the equipment in table 5.1 suggest that the most versatile, cost-effective, convenient, and time-efficient method of respiratory training currently available is provided by inspiratory pressure threshold loading. This method is also the most widely used and the best supported by research evidence. **Accordingly, all subsequent advice and guidance in this book will be provided for pressure threshold IMT.**

For the latest information on equipment and accessories for breathing muscle training, please visit www.breathestrong.com.

The following chapters of this book focus on the practical implementation of IMT for various user groups using inspiratory pressure threshold IMT.

Suitability for home use	Participant motivation	Session duration	Ease of load setting	Quantification of function	Contraindica-tions	Expense	Overall score	Ranking
5	3	3	1	1	4	5	35	5
1	1	1	5	5	4	1	45	3
5	5	5	4	1	4	5	72	1
5	5	5	4	1	4	5	65	2
1	1	1	5	5	3	1	43	4

The Future of RMT: Dynamically Adjusted Flow Resistance Training

All of the training methods described in this chapter have their limitations, some more serious than others. As someone involved in breathing muscle training research for almost 20 years, I have gained a very clear insight into what I believe provides the optimal characteristics for a breathing muscle training device. As part of a development team that included engineers and designers from Brunel University (United Kingdom) and the manufacturer of a leading IPTL product (POWERbreathe), I have participated in the development of the world's first dynamically adjusted flow resistance trainer.

The design overcomes the inherent limitation of a passive flow resistor by using real-time, dynamic adjustment of the flow resistor. In essence, the surface area of a variable-flow orifice is varied within a breath according to the prevailing respiratory flow rate. The controlled variable can be either the pressure load or the respired flow rate.

The first product of this type is the POWERbreathe K-Series (HaB International Limited), which was launched in 2010. At the time of this writing, the product ranges in price from $400 to $470. The ability to make adjustments within and between breaths makes this type of device extremely versatile from the loading perspective. The many unique features offered by this method include the ability to taper the load according to the prevailing strength of the muscles. In the case of inspiratory loading, for example, the load can be profiled to maintain it at the same percentage of inspiratory muscle strength, irrespective of lung volume. This means that the premature curtailment of inspiration (breath clipping) that occurs with heavy-pressure threshold loading does not arise, so higher loads and higher tidal volumes can be achieved, thus maximizing the work done. The system also performs a pretraining assessment of inspiratory muscle function and sets an appropriate training load automatically. The versatility of this method in terms of functional improvements in muscle strength, power, shortening velocity, and endurance awaits further research, but preliminary data are extremely promising with respect to the superiority of the training outcomes that can be achieved.

Chapter

6

Building Your Foundation

T his chapter focuses on the initial foundation phase of inspiratory muscle training (IMT)—that is, the first six weeks of intensive IMT in which training is undertaken twice per day while standing. This is unashamedly "isolationist" in its approach, which at first sight may appear contradictory for a book that champions the necessity for breathing training to be functional. However, foundation training should be considered as the first part of a phased approach to functional training. The adoption of this approach is a direct response to the recognition that, for some muscle groups, it is necessary to undergo a phase of isolated training in order to optimize the integrated function. In other words, you need to isolate before you integrate.

In addition, for some people, the benefits of foundation IMT may be sufficient for their needs and time constraints. Therefore, even if you never progress beyond foundation IMT, by following these guidelines, you can be assured that the benefits to be accrued are both real and substantial (see chapter 4).

This chapter focuses on the fundamentals of IMT, such as using the optimal breathing technique, setting and optimizing the training load, monitoring progress, and performing maintenance training. It also explains how IMT will affect your whole-body training (and vice versa). In addition, the chapter explains how to warm up the breathing muscles and how to use them to optimize recovery.

Note: The advice provided in this chapter is tailored specifically to the most widely used form of IMT—pressure threshold training (see chapter 5). For the latest information on equipment and accessories for breathing muscle training, please visit www.breathestrong.com.

GENERAL PRINCIPLES OF IMT

This section provides guidance on the best posture to adopt during foundation training, as well as how to optimize breathing technique to achieve the best possible results.

Posture During IMT

The position of the trunk has a profound influence on how the breathing muscles operate as breathing muscles, and this must therefore be considered during IMT. For example, in chapter 1, we learned that the trunk muscles not only operate as breathing muscles, but also have important and demanding roles in trunk flexion and rotation, postural stabilization, and maintenance of balance. These functions directly affect the function of trunk muscles in breathing, even in the foundation phase of training. Posture is relevant to IMT for three main reasons:

1. If the postural requirements imposed on the inspiratory muscles are reduced, more effort can be focused on activating the muscles in their breathing role, thereby maximizing tolerable training loads.

2. Challenging the respiratory and nonrespiratory roles of the inspiratory muscles simultaneously can enhance their ability to meet multiple demands more easily (the basis for part II of *Breathe Strong, Perform Better*).

3. Certain sports include postures that restrict breathing movement (e.g., the aero position in cycling), and training in these postures can minimize the restrictions imposed on breathing during training and competition (another important aspect of part II of *Breathe Strong, Perform Better*).

Points 2 and 3 are considered in detail in chapters 7 to 10, but note that foundation IMT still minimizes the detrimental influence of these two factors on performance. Later chapters focus specifically on optimizing breathing training in order to overcome these factors more comprehensively.

People embarking on IMT commonly ask this question: "Is it best to stand or sit?" Generally, the standing position allows a person to overcome and sustain higher training loads during a training session. So, to optimize the initial development of inspiratory muscle function during the foundation phase, the training should be undertaken in the standing position. The main objective during this phase is to maximize strength gain for the breathing function of the inspiratory muscles. This foundation should be laid before the respiratory and nonrespiratory functions are challenged simultaneously. The best way to maximize strength gains is to maximize muscle activation, and the best way to achieve this is to minimize the competing postural stabilizing role of the inspiratory muscles. Hence, in the foundation phase, the emphasis is on standing IMT with postural unloading (i.e., isolation). Postural unloading can be achieved by leaning forward and taking the weight of the upper body through the arms (e.g., leaning on the thighs, a chair back, or a windowsill). This unloads the postural role of the inspiratory muscles and allows them to be focused on overcoming the inspiratory load on the training device. The logic of this is immediately apparent when you consider what people do at the end of an intense bout of exercise that has made them breathless; they instinctively lean forward and place their hands on their knees so that their breathing muscles can be focused on the job of breathing.

Optimizing Breathing Technique

Maximizing the training stimulus to the inspiratory muscles, as well as the range of adaptations it elicits, is arguably the most important objective in terms of achieving the best possible training results. Choosing the right type of training device is the first step in maximizing results (see chapter 5). For the methods described in this book, the focus is on pressure threshold IMT, for which two evidence-based products are available (see table 5.1). Once you have selected your training device, the second step is to optimize the training stimulus that it generates. Unfortunately, simply breathing through a training device will not achieve this. For this reason, the following sections explain the optimal approach for pressure threshold IMT and the physiology that underlies this approach. First, the fundamentals of good breathing technique will be considered (i.e., how to develop efficient, comfortable, diaphragm-focused breathing). Second, the optimization of breathing pattern (the combination of respiratory flows, breath volumes, and the timing of breaths) for IMT will be explained.

Developing an Efficient Breathing Technique

This first phase of the process of developing an efficient breathing technique can be thought of as "getting in touch with your diaphragm." Most people lose touch with their diaphragm in the first few years after infancy. Human babies breathe almost exclusively with their diaphragms, but most human beings gradually lose touch with their most important breathing muscle and become chest breathers—that is, they breathe using the accessory muscles of the rib cage. To become a belly breather again, you need to rediscover how to use your diaphragm. Without this important reconnection, IMT will neglect the most important inspiratory muscle. The emphasis on diaphragm breathing should not be confused with an objective of focusing the IMT on the diaphragm. This is not what is being advocated (the reasons for this are explained in the section called Breathing Pattern During IMT). Instead, the objective is to ensure that the complex inspiratory musculature is used holistically (as one) and in concert during both training and everyday life activities. This section provides guidance on how to reintroduce the diaphragm into the normal, instinctive process of breathing. If you can accomplish this, your diaphragm will be a subconscious, central part of your response when your breathing is challenged.

At first, you should begin getting in touch with your diaphragm without using an inspiratory muscle trainer; the following staged method of developing efficient, diaphragm-focused breathing is recommended. This involves using a wide elastic exercise band as a means for generating a sense of increased effort within the diaphragm (see figure 8.2, page 133). The band is wrapped around the lower rib cage, and it can be placed over a single layer of light clothing or directly over the skin. The latter is preferable because it allows the breathing movements to be seen more clearly.

Begin with a small amount of tension in the band, and stand in front of a mirror (one that is large enough for you to see your torso). Place the palms lightly on the bottom of the ribs, with the fingers facing forward and the tips of the fingers almost touching (see figure 6.1 on page 96, shown without the band for clarity). Begin at the end of a full exhalation; then relax the abdomen, shoulders, and chest; take a deep, slow inhalation through your nose; and observe the movement of the abdomen and rib cage in the mirror. If the diaphragm is being used effectively, you should be able to see and feel the ribs move sideways and forward, and the abdomen will also bulge forward. In addition, the fingertips will move apart, making it easier to visualize the

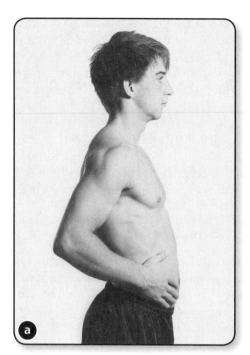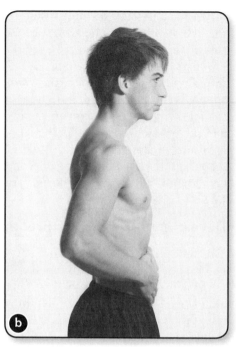

Figure 6.1 Diaphragm breathing: *(a)* inhalation using the diaphragm, and *(b)* exhalation.

movement of the lower rib cage. The movements occur because diaphragm contraction results in a flattening and downward movement of the diaphragm dome (into the abdominal cavity), which causes the lower rib margins to move outward. This also causes the abdominal contents (liver, stomach, intestines) to be pushed outward and forward. If the chest rises, the diaphragm is not being activated properly, and you need to relax the shoulders and chest. Exhalation should be relaxed, with no muscle activity; just allow the air to fall out of the chest as the lungs and rib cage spring back passively. In preparation for IMT, you can begin to squeeze more air from your lungs as your technique improves. Be careful not to hold the breath at the end of the inhalation; relax and let the air fall out.

The resistance of the band intensifies the sensation of working with the diaphragm, but if you cannot complete the previous exercise with the band in place, then try it first without the band (if it is still too challenging, see the alternative method described later in this section). This exercise should be practiced until you feel confident that you know how to activate the diaphragm—and that you know what a diaphragm inhalation feels and looks like. Once you have mastered this technique, try it with eyes closed, focusing on the sensation of the air filling the lungs and the sensation of the diaphragm plunging down into the abdomen.

In this exercise, the breathing rate should be no more than 12 breaths per minute, preferably 8. With practice, you should be able to reduce this to 6 breaths per minute. The inhalation phase will be slightly longer than exhalation, because exhalation is mostly passive; the only phase that is actively controlled is inhalation. Try counting the breath in and out. For example, if the objective is 10 breaths per minute, this means that each breath should take 6 seconds (60/10); count "1-2-3-4" during inhalation and "5-6" during exhalation. The extension of the inhalation phase must not be achieved by breath holding at the end of inhalation; the increase in duration should come about through a slower, deeper, and more controlled inhalation so that exhalation starts immediately when inhalation ends. Remember that exhalation should be passive and that the air should "fall out" of the lungs.

Complete 4 minutes of diaphragm breathing exercise each day until relaxed diaphragm breathing has become second nature (2 minutes with visual feedback and 2 without). In addition, keep checking periodically throughout the day to make sure that these newfound skills are being put into practice. Introduce the technique into everyday activities such as walking up stairs (e.g., breathe in for three steps and out for two), as well as during routine workouts.

When practicing the breathing technique during exercise-related activities, people need to switch from nose to mouth breathing, because nose breathing cannot accommodate the flow rates required during exercise. The aim of this process is to use conscious control of breathing to restore the unconscious control of breathing to a more diaphragm-focused activity.

If the exercises previously described are too challenging, here's an alternative method of getting in touch with your diaphragm: This method involves lying on your back, rather than standing in front of a mirror. When you are lying down, a number of beneficial things happen. First, the breathing muscles are no longer involved in postural activities (holding the trunk upright), which makes it easier to focus on relaxing everything except the diaphragm. The second thing that happens is that the abdominal contents (liver, stomach, and so on) rest against the underside of the diaphragm, giving it something to work against. Finally, it is much easier to be completely relaxed when you are lying down. Start the exercise with small breaths into your abdomen through your nose, then relax and let the air fall out of the lungs. Gradually increase the size of the breaths until they become slow and deep. Be careful not to hold the breath at the end of the inhalation; relax and let the air fall out. As previously described, breathing rate should be no more than 12 breaths per minute, but you should be able to work your way down to 6. Once you have achieved diaphragm breathing while lying down, transfer to standing upright in front of a mirror (as described) and start over.

Undertaking this process of restoring the pivotal role of the diaphragm in breathing is not essential before commencing IMT, but it should not be overlooked because it forms an important building block in the foundation phase of training. Treat it as a separate activity that runs in parallel with the first few weeks of IMT, and the two activities will reinforce one another.

Developing breath control is a generic skill that can and should be practiced, because it maximizes breathing efficiency and minimizes the distracting influence of breathing discomfort. What do I mean by this? First, developing efficient, diaphragm-focused breathing is vital, because this is the foundation of good breath control; once this becomes second nature, the second phase is much easier. The second phase involves developing breath control to overcome the natural desire to breathe as quickly as possible during periods when breathing demand is high and when breathing discomfort or distress is present. In other words, it involves preventing a situation where the tail wags the dog! Instead of allowing breathing to become rapid and shallow, voluntary breathing control imposes a deep, slow, calm, and efficient pattern. The only time that this can be practiced properly is in situations where breathing demand or distress is high (e.g., in the short breaks during repeated sprinting). Keeping breathing calm and relaxed under stressful conditions will minimize stress and anxiety and will enhance concentration. Breathing control can also provide a psychological advantage over opponents, who will be intimidated by the absence of any obvious signs of breathing discomfort.

Some exercises that you can do to develop breath control during exercise are provided in chapter 8.

Breathing Pattern During IMT

The guidance in this section relates to the generic aspects of IMT—that is, those aspects that apply to everyone. More detailed specific guidance for breathing patterns during functional training are provided for each exercise in chapter 11.

The first generic training principle is that IMT should involve the concerted action of as many inspiratory muscles as possible. At the present time, it is not known whether the adaptations that result in performance improvements are attributable to the diaphragm, the inspiratory accessory muscles of the rib cage, or both. Accordingly, during IMT, breathing movements should involve as much of the inspiratory musculature as possible.

Breath Volume   Although muscle is a very adaptable tissue, training adaptations are also highly specific to the nature of the training stimulus (see The Specificity Principle on page 82 of chapter 5). Adaptations elicited by IMT are specific to a number of characteristics of the training stimulus, including the lung volume at which training takes place. The practical implication of this is that IMT should be undertaken across the widest range of lung volumes possible—from the point at which the lungs are as empty as they can be to the point at which it is impossible to inhale any more. Failure to do this will lead to suboptimal adaptation at some lung volumes, which may have a performance impact if these lung volumes are called on during exercise. In addition, loading too heavily can also compromise the breath volume that can be achieved and the amount of work that can be undertaken during training, which will also impair the training response (see the sidebar on page 100). This impairment occurs because breath volume has a strong influence on the amount of work done per breath, and the training load is the most important determinant of the person's ability to inhale deeply. Functional weakening of the inspiratory muscles during inhalation means that if the load is too high, then the inspiratory muscles are not able to overcome the load at higher lung volumes (where the inspiratory muscles are weaker), despite maximal effort. The heavier the load, the more severely the breath is clipped.

This means that the training load must be set with these factors in mind. Figure 6.2 illustrates the interrelationships of inspiratory muscle strength, lung volume, and training load, as well as the effect of fatigue on the breath volume that can be achieved. Note that the breath volume is clipped progressively earlier in the breath with increasing loads.

Breathing Rate   To understand the advice in this section, you need to know a little about a property of muscle that is known as the force–velocity relationship. Essentially, this property dictates that the faster a muscle contracts, the lower the force it is able to generate (also see chapter 1). Think about how much more force can be exerted when pushing against a door that is closed versus a door that moves away when pushed. When the door is closed, the muscle does not shorten (static contraction), but when the door opens and moves away, the muscles exerting the force shorten (dynamic contraction). In addition, the faster the door moves away, the less force can be applied to it. Another example of the force–velocity relationship at work is how much less force a person can exert on the pedals when cycling in a low gear compared to a high gear.

We can exploit this property to optimize the training stimulus that the muscle receives. For example, let's assume that because of the force–velocity properties just described, as the rate of muscle contraction doubles, the strength of the muscle

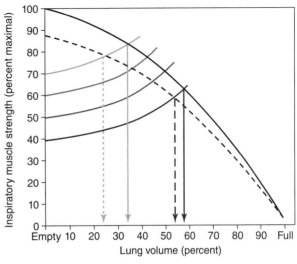

Figure 6.2 The interactions between inspiratory muscle strength (black line), various training loads (40, 50, 60, and 70 percent of maximal inspiratory muscle strength [shaded lines]), and the breath volume that can be achieved during training, as well as the effect of fatigue (dotted lines). For example, at 40 percent, it is possible to inhale to around 60 percent of lung volume, whereas at 70 percent it is only possible to inhale to around 35 percent of lung volume.

is halved, despite the same (maximal) effort being applied under both conditions. When muscles contract maximally at any speed, the number of muscle fibers that are recruited to the contraction is also maximized, despite the fact that faster contractions result in lower forces. Now let's look at the effect of doubling the rate of contraction slightly differently. When a muscle is contracting very slowly to move a load that requires half its maximal force-generating capacity, doubling the rate of contraction against the same load would require 100 percent of the muscle's force-generating capacity (because its ability to generate force would be halved). This means that close to 100 percent of the muscle fibers are recruited—for half the force. This can be turned to our advantage, because it means that it is possible to train at close to 100 percent of a muscle's force-generating capacity no matter what load is being applied, provided that the load is moved as fast as possible (i.e., with maximal effort). Under any given loading condition, fast muscle contractions recruit more muscle fibers than slow contractions. Therefore, maximal effort ensures maximum velocity and the recruitment of the greatest number of muscle fibers.

Muscle recruitment has an important impact on the response to training for two reasons. First, fibers that are not recruited will not be trained. So, if the velocity of contraction is slow, a load requiring half of a muscle's force-generating capacity will only require recruitment (and will only train) about half of its fibers. But if the same load is overcome as fast as possible, then close to 100 percent of the fibers will be recruited and trained. Second, maximizing recruitment is an important part of the neural adaptation to training, which also contributes to optimizing training

Why Loading Heavy Doesn't Deliver What You Expect

In a recently published study (McConnell & Griffiths, 2010), we examined the effects of various inspiratory loads on a range of variables, including the number of repetitions that could be tolerated, the volume of each breath during the training session, the amount of work completed during the session, and whether the session activated the inspiratory muscle metaboreflex (changing the threshold for activation of this reflex is one of the important mechanisms by which IMT improves performance). We studied well-trained young rowers who had not undergone any IMT previously. As expected, the number of breaths (reps) declined as the load increased (e.g., just 4 breaths at 90 percent of maximal inspiratory muscle strength and 84 breaths at 60 percent), and the volume of each breath declined with increasing load, as well as during each session (because of fatigue). The most surprising finding was the influence of heavy loads (greater than 70 percent) on the amount of work that was undertaken per breath (work is equivalent to the load multiplied by the breath volume). Because the volume of each breath was lower with heavy loads (figure 6.2), the amount of work done per breath was reduced markedly. This effect is completely counterintuitive, because during limb muscle training, heavier loads mean more work (that's because if you're maintaining good form, the range of movement doesn't change a great deal when moving from moderate to heavy loads). The detrimental effect of the reduction in breath volume on the training stimulus delivered to the inspiratory muscles was compounded by the reduction in the number of breaths at heavy loads. In other words, the total amount of work done by the inspiratory muscles is reduced markedly by increasing the load above 70 percent.

A further interesting finding was that the only training load to activate the inspiratory muscle metaboreflex was the 60 percent load, and this also happened to be the load closest to the 30-repetition maximum (RM) of our rowers. What do we conclude from all this? First, heavy loading does not deliver the increase in the intensity of the training stimulus that one might expect it to. Second, to prevent "work" from being jeopardized, the choice of load must be balanced carefully against the effect that it has on breath volume and RM (loading at 50 to 70 percent appears to thread this line most effectively). Third, if activating the metaboreflex during training is necessary in order to increase its threshold for activation, then the 30RM load delivers this.

outcomes. Training improves strength through two mechanisms: stimulating muscle fibers to grow and causing neural adaptations; the latter ensures the recruitment of all available fibers within a muscle, and that all muscles that contribute to a given movement are recruited.

For muscle fibers to be stimulated to grow (hypertrophy), they need to be subjected to mechanical stress, which requires the application of reasonably heavy loading.

This is why high-velocity, low-load training does not improve strength, no matter how much effort is applied at low training loads. The practical implications of this for IMT are that the training load must be at least moderate (50 percent of maximal strength), and the velocity of contraction (inhalation rate) must be as fast as possible.

Accordingly, IMT should be conducted with maximum effort; in other words, each inhalation should be executed as fast as possible. An inhalation should take 1 or 2 seconds and should be accompanied by a loud rushing sound as air is sucked through the valve of the training device at high velocity. Try to make this sound as loud as possible, because this indicates high flow rates. Be aware that the heavier the load, the slower the maximal flow rate that can be generated (and the smaller the lung volume; see figure 6.2 and the sidebar on the previous page). In contrast to the maximal nature of the inspiratory effort, exhalation should be passive and quiet, and it should require 3 or 4 seconds.

Because of the higher-than-normal breath volume and breathing frequency, some light-headedness may result from the hyperventilation. If this happens, pause at the end of exhalation and wait for the urge to breathe in again. More detailed guidance on hyperventilation is provided in the upcoming sections.

GETTING STARTED

The following sections describe the practicalities of setting the training load and completing an IMT workout. They also provide some guidance on how to structure the IMT around other training.

Setting the Training Load

The most important determinants of the outcome of any training regimen are the training intensity and frequency, because these factors define the size of the overloading stimulus to the muscles. Ironically, these are the two factors that cause people the greatest difficulty in terms of getting them right. The worst mistake is not overloading the inspiratory muscles sufficiently to elicit adaptation. But how do you know what intensity and frequency to use?

Setting the training load is actually much easier than people think, provided that a few underlying principles are understood. In chapter 1, we learned that the inspiratory muscles have evolved with an impressive ability to sustain physical work (high endurance), and that inspiratory muscle strength is dependent on lung volume (the muscles are strong when the lungs are empty, and they are weak when the lungs are full). These factors have important implications for optimizing the training regimen.

The high endurance capacity of the inspiratory muscles means that both the number of breaths (repetitions) and the frequency of training need to be higher than one would normally associate with limb weight training. For example, a typical strength training regimen for the biceps might involve three sets of eight arm curls, twice per week, but this regimen would not provide sufficient overload for the inspiratory muscles. In the foundation phase of IMT, a regimen consisting of 30 breaths, twice daily is required in order to elicit meaningful changes in inspiratory muscle function for healthy, active young people. The question then arises about the load setting for these 30 breaths. The load setting is a compromise between a number of factors, including the fact that the inspiratory muscles become much weaker as we inhale (see figure 6.2). This means that a load setting that was achievable at the onset of inspiration becomes unachievable partway through the breath, and the effect becomes more exaggerated as the inspiratory muscles fatigue, leading to breath clipping. If the loading is too heavy, this will have three consequences: Very few breaths can be achieved because the load cannot be overcome after the first few efforts; the inspiratory muscles only become trained over a small (low) range of lung volumes (this is detrimental because training specificity limits the benefits to these low lung volumes); and the amount of work undertaken by the inspiratory muscles is compromised. Both 1 and 2 have fairly obvious negative impacts on the quality of the training stimulus and the adaptations that it is able to stimulate, but the third point is less obvious and requires some further explanation. The practical repercussion of point 3 is that during heavy loading the amount of work done by the inspiratory muscles is lower than during moderate loading (see the sidebar on page 100). This means that heavy loading actually provides an inferior training stimulus, which limits its efficacy.

Research and experience have shown that the best load setting is one equivalent to 50 to 70 percent of the inspiratory muscle strength. This setting provides the widest range of benefits and the greatest level of comfort during training. But how do you know what setting this is on your breathing muscle trainer? It's simpler than you may think and can be achieved by applying the tried-and-trusted "rep max" principle from weight training. In other words, you find the load setting that allows you to achieve the number of reps that your training regimen requires. The trick with IMT is knowing how many reps (breaths) correspond to a load of 50 to 70 percent; once again, research provides the answer—the golden number is around 30 (also see the sidebar on page 100).

For the first training session, the best plan is to set the training load to the lowest setting on the training device and to complete 30 breaths, concentrating on developing good breathing technique (as described previously). If the first training session felt very easy, increase the load on the training device by one setting for the second training session of the day. With each training session, continue to increase the load until a setting is achieved that allows you to complete only 30 breaths (also see the upcoming section on repetition failure). Remember, the inspiratory phase *must* be executed with maximal effort (inhale as fast as possible against the load), but the expiratory phase should be slow and relaxed.

In chapter 11, guidance about the loads to be used during functional breathing training will be provided as light, moderate, or heavy. These correspond to the following repetition maximum settings:

Light: equivalent to the 50- to 100-repetition maximum

Moderate: equivalent to the 20- to 40-repetition maximum

Heavy: equivalent to the 10- to 20-repetition maximum

The breathing pattern during IMT (fast inhalation with maximal volume) can induce some dizziness due to hyperventilation and loss of carbon dioxide from the blood. This is harmless for the duration of a 30-breath workout, and it also seems to lessen in severity as training progresses. If the dizziness does become unpleasant at any time, simply pause at the end of the next exhalation and wait for the urge to

---

Top Tricks for Successful Foundation IMT

- Trick 1: Place the training device in a bag so that rebreathing can occur. This allows for fast sets with no dizziness.
- Trick 2: Ensure "failure" by increasing the load by half a turn on each successive breath after 30.
- Trick 3: Unload the inspiratory muscles during training by leaning forward and resting your hands on your knees or a chair back.
- Trick 4: After about 4 weeks of IMT, perform your training immediately after a whole-body training session three or four times per week (to introduce specificity).

---

breathe in. For maximal training overload, the training breaths should be completed as quickly as possible, but this has to be balanced against the dizziness. A trick that can be used to overcome the loss of carbon dioxide is to place the training device inside a bag that has a slit down one side (a grocery bag is ideal). When you exhale and inhale from the bag (rebreathing), the loss of carbon dioxide is largely abolished, and dizziness is prevented. This allows you to complete the breaths rapidly, maximizing the training benefits. (Also see the sidebar at the top of the page.)

When athletes are advised to undertake IMT twice per day, they often ask whether an even better result can be achieved by training three or even four times per day. The answer is emphatically no. Recovery is an important part of the training process, and the inspiratory muscles are already being subjected to a very challenging regimen of specific IMT twice per day, plus the work of breathing during other training. People should not be tempted to do IMT more than twice daily, and they should ensure that the two sessions are separated by at least 6 hours.

Repetition Failure

Although the target number of breaths is 30 (the 30RM), overload can be maximized by training beyond this threshold as soon as the inspiratory muscles are able to sustain the effort—in other words, if you get to 30 and feel as if you still have a few more breaths in you, you should go for it (see page 105 for advice on progressing the load). However, most people find it difficult to determine precisely when they have reached a point where they cannot continue (i.e., when they reach "failure"). As the training session progresses and fatigue sets in, each breath becomes progressively shallower than the previous one. This is a direct result of the fact that the inspiratory muscles are stronger at the start of the breath than at the end (see figure 6.2)—because of this, fatigue is expressed first at higher lung volumes, and successive breaths are "clipped" at a lower breath volume. Eventually, a point is reached where it may be possible to open the valve, but not possible to take a meaningful breath. This is very different from an exercise such as a biceps curl, where the biceps are weakest at the onset of the exercise, which means that failure is much easier to identify because the rep cannot be started.

So how is *repetition failure* defined for IMT? Once it's impossible to achieve a "satisfying breath," then it's time to stop. Another trick can also be used to ensure that failure is achieved on every training session; once 30 breaths have been completed, the load setting on the training device should be increased by half a turn with each successive breath (do this during the exhalation). This rapidly brings you to the point where the valve cannot even be opened—job done (don't forget to return the setting to the correct load for your next training session).

If your aim is to improve your exercise performance, the importance of training to failure for optimal results cannot be overstated. If training ceases before failure is achieved, then the training intensity has been suboptimal, and the training adaptations will be similarly suboptimal. As with any other kind of training, those people with the greatest commitment to achieving 30 breaths at the highest load possible—and who don't loaf by skipping sessions—always reap the best rewards in terms of the improvements that they achieve. Like most things in life, you reap what you sow.

Influence of Concurrent Training

If IMT is being undertaken concurrently with other training, some variation will likely be seen in the number of breaths that can be achieved before "failure" in the IMT sessions. This is because the inspiratory muscles will have different work histories, depending on the demands that have been placed on them by the other training that is being undertaken. Therefore, it is perfectly normal for an evening training session to involve fewer breaths to failure at a given load than a morning session. Accordingly, if an evening session has been especially challenging, you should *not* reduce the training load before the next session, because the inspiratory muscles will have largely recovered by the next morning. However, if you fail to complete 30 breaths for more than three training sessions, a small reduction in load should be made, because this may be a sign of overtraining of the inspiratory muscles. This kind of overtraining leads to severely impaired adaptation and a very poor overall result. If you suspect that there is any residual fatigue of the inspiratory muscles, take a day off from IMT.

However, undertaking IMT immediately after a whole-body training session can also be a very effective method of introducing specificity into your IMT. After a whole-body training session, your inspiratory muscles will be slightly fatigued. If IMT is undertaken when the inspiratory muscles are in this state, those muscles that have worked hardest during the preceding whole-body session will receive the greatest training stimulus. This approach is best introduced after about 4 weeks of foundation IMT, three or four times per week.

Just as whole-body training can influence the ability of the inspiratory muscles to tolerate IMT, so too can IMT influence the person's ability to perform whole-body training. Indeed, much of the evidence for an effect of inspiratory muscle fatigue on performance was based on prefatiguing the inspiratory muscles and noting a decrement in performance. The implications of this are clear for people engaged in concurrent training; they must be mindful of the interaction between the two forms of training. No athlete or coach would schedule a heavy squat session immediately before a cycle time trial—it's not rocket science, just common sense.

Foundation IMT Essentials

- Set the training load to the 30-repetition maximum (30RM) using a process of trial and error.
- Inhale against the load with maximum effort (as fast as possible).
- Breathe in AND out as far as possible during each breath.
- Train twice per day—morning and evening.
- Remember that repetition failure for the inspiratory muscles is an "inability to achieve a satisfying breath."
- Progress the training by keeping the load at your *new* 30RM to account for improvement (increase the load at least once per week).
- Train in a window between 25 and 35 breaths per session.
- Keep in mind that whole-body training may affect IMT because of residual fatigue, so evening IMT sessions may be more challenging than morning sessions—but don't reduce your training load.
- If you suspect that there is any residual fatigue of the inspiratory muscles, take a day off from IMT.
- Don't do IMT just before a big training session or competition.
- Keep an IMT diary.

PROGRESSING TRAINING

After training at a given load setting for a few days, you will find it progressively easier to achieve —and then to exceed—the 30-breath target. This is because the inspiratory muscles begin to adapt immediately to the training stimulus by increasing their strength and endurance. Therefore, to maintain the overloading stimulus, the load setting must be increased at least once per week during the first 6 weeks. Without these increases, continued adaptation will cease.

The increase in load should be sufficient to reduce the number of breaths that can be achieved before failure to between 25 and 30. On most training devices, this will be about one-quarter to one-half turn on the spring tensioner. Bringing the number of breaths down to 25 is acceptable, because within a few days, the maximum number of breaths will be back up to 30.

As a general rule, the training load should be increased by at least one-quarter turn each week for the first 6 weeks of training (i.e., during the foundation phase). Alternatively, small increases can be made as soon as the maximum number of breaths exceeds 33.

Keeping a training diary is a good way to keep track of the number of sessions completed, the increments in training load, the number of breaths completed, and how the session felt. Some training devices provide a training diary in their user manuals (e.g., POWERbreathe), but for people who don't have access to a template, figure 6.3 (page 106) provides a template that can be reproduced. Note that there is space for

Week number:	Monday		Tuesday		Wednesday		Thursday		Friday		Saturday		Sunday	
	Level	Reps	Level	Reps	Level	Reps	Level	Reps	Level	Reps	Level	Reps	Level	Reps
Morning														
Evening														
	Notes: How did your training feel, what other training did you do during the day, etc.?													
Monday														
Tuesday														
Wednesday														
Thursday														
Friday														
Saturday														
Sunday														

Figure 6.3 Training diary template.

From A. McConnell, 2011, *Breathe Strong, Perform Better* (Champaign, IL: Human Kinetics).

notes about how the training felt and other activities that were undertaken on the same day. This facilitates cross-referencing of circumstances that may be helpful for the athlete and coach in interpreting sudden up- or downturns in training quality.

When foundation training has been completed, you can switch to maintenance training, or training can be developed further using the functional training exercises in chapters 7 to 10.

Having reached the end of this section on progressing training, you may be saying to yourself, "What about periodization and varying the reps and sets?" However, there are good scientific reasons to believe that, for the breathing muscles, these factors are less important because of the mechanisms that underpin performance improvements after IMT. In a nutshell, the current research literature suggests that two main mechanisms operate to improve performance, irrespective of the type of activity:

1. Reduction in perception of breathing and whole-body effort (after IMT, any given intensity of exercise feels easier)

2. Preservation of limb blood flow because of an increase in the threshold for activation of a reflex (the metaboreflex) from the inspiratory muscles that would otherwise reduce limb blood flow (after IMT, blood flow to the limb muscles is maintained for longer periods)

Research also supports the effectiveness of the foundation training regimen—30 breaths at a load corresponding to the 30-repetition maximum (30RM), twice daily. This 30 × 2 regimen has been applied with great success across a wide range of sports, using time trials that vary in duration from a 100-meter front-crawl swim to a 40-kilometer cycle time trial. Performance in a test of repeated sprinting (speed endurance) has also been shown to improve using this regimen. Thus, 30RM × 2 appears to be a very versatile regimen that can be considered tried and trusted.

Undertaking IMT for longer than 6 weeks does not appear to yield further improvements in performance, suggesting that the response may be "all or nothing"—that is, once the benefits have been achieved, this represents the entire response. Furthermore, the benefits accrued from a single 6-week block of foundation training can be maintained if a maintenance program of IMT 2 days per week is adopted thereafter (see the section on maintenance training later in this chapter). In other words, the performance benefits of IMT can continue to be enjoyed by keeping the function of the inspiratory muscles "topped up" sufficiently to sustain the reduction in breathing effort and the increase in the threshold for metaboreflex activation.

Based on this evidence and the current understanding of the mechanisms underpinning the influence of IMT on performance—as well as the absence of any data indicating that alternative training regimens yield superior benefits—there is no good reason to adopt anything other than the 30RM × 2 loading regimen for foundation training.

Accordingly, after the initial 6 weeks of foundation IMT, the athlete should progress either to maintenance training or to a continuation of foundation training, interspersed with the sport-specific functional IMT.

However, at the risk of providing contradictory advice, one nuance to the previous recommendations needs to be considered—breathing intervals. As previously indicated, an excellent way to build specificity into IMT is to do the IMT immediately after a whole-body training session. Breathing intervals are an extension of this principle. In sports where interval training, drills, or circuits are used, IMT can be incorporated into the recovery phase between repetitions (use the 30RM load). A number of coaches and athletes from various sports have developed this idea independently, and they have reported that it makes an extremely positive impact on perception of breathing effort. One word of caution is required, however: The overloading of the inspiratory muscles between intervals will carry over into subsequent repetitions. Accordingly, breathing intervals should be restricted to specific breathing interval sessions and should not be applied to all sessions.

Remember: Breathing intervals and the functional exercises recommended in chapters 7 to 10 should only be attempted after completion of foundation IMT.

MONITORING PROGRESS

Athletes often want to know how they can determine if they are improving. There's a long and short answer to this. The short answer is that people can compare the training load at the start of their training with the load that can be tolerated by the end of the foundation phase. It's not unusual for this to be 5 or 6 load settings higher on a device with 10 load increments. However, this answer doesn't satisfy those people who want something more quantitative.

Most people don't have access to the laboratory equipment that research scientists use to measure the strength of research participants' breathing muscles. But is there another method? For the answer, we can again turn to the tried-and-trusted methods adopted by weightlifters. The concept of identifying a 1-repetition max

(1RM) to represent an individual's maximal performance in a specified lift has existed since time immemorial. To identify the 1RM in the gym, a bar is loaded with progressively higher weights, which the athlete lifts just once. Eventually, a weight is reached that cannot be lifted, making the preceding weight the 1RM. The same approach can be used to test the strength of the inspiratory muscles. However, care must be taken to ensure that the valve has genuinely opened, because the flow and volume of air at these very high loads are extremely small. Before the start of a 1RM test, the inspiratory muscles should be warmed up thoroughly, and loading should commence at the current training load. At least 30 seconds rest should be taken between efforts, and the load should be incremented by one-half to one level at first, decreasing to one-quarter to one-half level as the 1RM is approached. The test should be repeated on at least two occasions, quite close to each other (but on separate days), in order to ensure that a reliable estimate has been obtained.

For the latest information on equipment and techniques for breathing muscle assessment, please visit www.breathestrong.com.

MAINTENANCE TRAINING

At the completion of the foundation phase, many people are perfectly satisfied with the results that they have achieved, and they are content to enter a phase of maintenance training. Research has shown that training frequency can be reduced by as much as two thirds without any loss of functional benefits (Romer & McConnell, 2003). In other words, a person can switch from training twice daily to training once every other day. There is, of course, no reason that someone cannot switch directly from maintenance training into advanced functional training (see chapters 7 to 10), for example, to prepare for a specific competition or event.

For maintenance training, a good strategy is to combine it with another training session so that it remains part of a normal training routine. For example, tag an IMT session onto the end of another workout, such as a run. As mentioned previously, this has the added benefit of providing a degree of specificity, because the inspiratory muscles will already be slightly fatigued by the preceding workout, which means that they will receive the greatest relative training overload during IMT.

If training ceases completely, detraining will occur (see chapter 5), and there will be a reversal of the training-induced changes. In healthy, active young adults, about one-third of the improvement in strength is lost during a 9-week period of inspiratory muscle detraining, but after an additional 9 weeks, there appears to be no further decline (Romer & McConnell, 2003). Thus, it is possible to sustain about one-third of the strength gained from IMT for up to 18 weeks, but loss of endurance is more marked. These residual improvements are probably close to the threshold of what is required in order to elicit performance enhancement, so detraining is not advisable, especially considering that maintenance requires so little time.

INSPIRATORY MUSCLE WARM-UP AND STRETCHING

The concept of warming up is well established in sport and exercise. Not only does an appropriate warm-up help minimize the risk of injury, but it has also been shown to enhance performance at the level of both the muscle and the whole body. Around a decade ago, research showed that even a very strenuous functional whole-body warm-up failed to enhance the function of the inspiratory muscles—although the warm-up was successful in enhancing the function of limb muscles. This led to the development of a specific warm-up regimen for the inspiratory muscles; this warm-up regimen has been shown to enhance both inspiratory muscle function and whole-body exercise performance in both endurance (Volianitis, McConnell, Koutedakis, & Jones, 2001) and repeated-sprint activities (Tong & Fu, 2006; Lin et al., 2007). This quote from a professional international rugby player (after his conditioning coach had introduced the warm-up into his pregame and presubstitution preparation) encapsulates the benefits of the warm-up: "It's like a turbocharger for my breathing . . . I don't get lung burn during the first five minutes on the pitch, even if I've just been subbed and joined the game halfway through the second half when everything's going full tilt."

As with IMT, the warm-up isn't rocket science, but it's very effective and well worth the 3 or 4 minutes it requires. The warm-up can even be done while stretching or during other pretraining or precompetition routines. To execute the warm-up effectively, you need to find the appropriate loading intensity. This must be sufficiently intense to stimulate the response, but not so intense that it induces fatigue. Research has shown that the correct intensity is around 40 percent of maximal strength. To identify the correct setting, you need to know the characteristics of the spring that loads the valve in your training device. Armed with this knowledge, you can use your 30RM training load to estimate the warm-up load. Assuming that the training load is 50 to 60 percent (for a 30-breath regimen), you can look up what this corresponds to as a setting on your training device in order to calculate the setting that corresponds to 40 percent. The POWERbreathe training device has a chart that allows you to look up the correct warm-up setting based on your training setting (see table 6.1).

Table 6.1 Figuring Warm-Up Load Using 30RM Training Load

Current training load	Ideal warm-up load
10	8
9	7
8	6.5
7	5.5
6	5
5	4
4	3
3	2.5
2	1.5
1	1
0	0

Note: This method assumes that the training device has 10 load settings and that the training load is the 30RM.

Once the correct load has been identified, two sets of 30 breaths with 1 minute of rest in between should be completed no more than 10 minutes before a training session, competition, or match.

People often wonder whether a warm-up should be undertaken immediately before IMT. Because it is possible to sustain higher training loads if the IMT session is preceded by an inspiratory muscle warm-up, the answer is yes, but this doesn't mean that it's essential. Of course, if the IMT is undertaken immediately after a whole-body training session (which has some other advantages—see page 111), an inspiratory muscle warm-up is redundant, because the muscles are already warmed up.

The trunk and rib cage receive almost no attention when it comes to stretching; however, these areas include numerous muscles, their attachments, and associated connective tissue (e.g., the rib cage) that can potentially be a site of great resistance to inhalation. Any resistance to thoracic expansion increases the work of breathing and the associated perception of breathing effort. The stretches in figure 6.4 can be used to stretch the rib cage in order to free up rib expansion and reduce breathing effort. Each stretch should be sustained for around 30 seconds. You can also practice diaphragm breathing during the anterior stretch; the tension in the trunk muscles that is created during the stretch provides a useful resistance for the diaphragm to work against.

Figure 6.4 Breathing muscle stretches: *(a)* anterior stretch over Swiss ball and *(b)* lateral stretch over Swiss ball.

INSPIRATORY MUSCLE COOL-DOWN

Just as the warm-up is well established in conditioning science, so too is the notion of an active cool-down, or active recovery. The primary objective of an active cool-down is to clear metabolites from the muscles, particularly lactate. Essentially, when muscles work at a low to moderate intensity, the rate at which they consume lactate (for use as a fuel) exceeds the rate at which they produce it, making them net consumers. Therefore, rather than resting when your workout is complete, you should perform an active cool-down because this is the fastest and most efficient way to clear lactate.

Clearing metabolites at the end of a workout may help with the process of recovery and adaptation. During training that requires repeated high-intensity efforts, active recovery between efforts hastens lactate clearance and may therefore improve training quality by promoting the ability to tolerate higher-intensity or longer bouts of exercise. Hastening lactate removal may also be useful in sports with rolling substitutions (field hockey), penalty boxes (rugby), or short breaks (tennis, netball, basketball).

As we learned in chapter 1, the inspiratory muscles are highly aerobic, with a large blood supply, making them ideal candidates for lactate consumption during recovery. Recent research has found that breathing against a small inspiratory load (the lowest setting on most devices) immediately after exercise reduces blood lactate concentration by 16 percent. Unlike a whole-body active recovery, which takes around 5 minutes to speed up lactate clearance, inspiratory loading reduces lactate as soon as the exercise stops. The inspiratory loading also clears the lactate much more quickly. More important, when inspiratory loading is undertaken between two bouts of maximal cycling (a Wingate test), performance in the second cycle test is improved, compared to when a passive recovery takes place between the two cycle tests. Finally, research has also shown that trained inspiratory muscles are more effective consumers of lactate during both recovery and exercise.

Thus, low-intensity inspiratory loading, especially of trained inspiratory muscles, is a great tool for speeding lactate clearance and improving performance during repeated-sprint activities. In practical terms, the ideal load setting for cool-down is equivalent to the lowest setting on most training devices.

Chapter

7

Training for Exercise and Fitness

In this chapter, we consider how functional breathing training can be applied in four exercise and fitness contexts. First, we look at core training. Here, functional breathing training provides the missing link by recognizing the important contribution made by the breathing muscles to the core. Second, we consider how functional breathing training can help to optimize the weight loss that can be achieved during whole-body exercise. Third, the benefits of functional breathing training to a program of general fitness training are presented. Last, but not least, we consider how to combine breathing muscle training with weight training to maximize lifted weights and to minimize injury risk. This chapter also lists a selection of exercises that are recommended for each of the four categories (some of these exercises are also described in subsequent chapters where they have benefits to particular sports).

You need to ensure that you have good technique for all exercises before adding difficulty. Start by performing each exercise with nothing more than a focus on maintaining slow, deep diaphragmatic breathing throughout. Then add an external resistance to inhalation using a breathing muscle trainer (BMT) set on its minimum load. Gradually increase the load on the BMT over a period of a few weeks until it reaches the prescribed level for the exercise. Please also refer to the sidebar titled Tips for Bracing and Posture on page 114 for guidance regarding abdominal bracing and achieving a neutral spine position, as well as the sections on breath control, load setting, and thoracic stretching in chapter 6. In addition, don't forget to consider incorporating breathing intervals into interval training, drills, or circuits (see chapter 6); the breathing training can be introduced into the recovery phase, or it can be a separate station during a drill or circuit.

Before using these exercises, be sure to note the following principles:

- If possible, use a cable machine to provide resistance, rather than bands or cords (this is not essential). The resistance should be low to begin with, but it can be developed as the training progresses. Don't overdo the resistance, which

Tips for Bracing and Posture

Bracing

Many of the exercises in *Breathe Strong, Perform Better* involve an abdominal bracing maneuver. At the time of this writing, a fierce debate is raging about whether the rigidity implied by the term *bracing* is appropriate. Bracing requires cocontraction of muscles that bring about opposing movements. For example, cocontraction of the arm muscles involves simultaneous, forceful contraction of the elbow flexor (biceps) and extensor (triceps) such that the muscles are contracted but the arm neither flexes nor extends (i.e., there is a static contraction of both muscles). This same principle can be applied to the muscles of the abdomen such that they form a stiff, stabilizing corset around the midsection (also referred to as the inner unit). The muscle fibers in the multiple layers of the abdominal wall run obliquely across one another, like plywood, forming an extremely strong, yet flexible, cylinder.

Correct bracing requires some practice, and the best place to start is learning how to activate the main compressive muscle, the transversus abdominis. The failure to automatically activate the transversus abdominis is associated with low back pain, but learning how to activate this muscle voluntarily has been shown to restore its automatic function in stabilizing the spine. Reconnecting with the transversus abdominis can be achieved by practicing drawing in the abdominal wall by moving the belly button toward the spine. If you concentrate on maximizing the reduction in waist girth during this maneuver, the rectus abdominis and pelvic floor inevitably become involved. Once you can draw in successfully, you need to practice activating the transversus abdominis and accompanying abdominal muscles using a bracing contraction—one in which the trunk volume changes very little, yet the muscles are contracted.

Initially, you should practice this maneuver with maximal effort. Then, as you become accustomed to activating the muscles involved, you can reduce the intensity, and you will be able to feel (literally) the supportive corset that the maneuver creates around your midsection.

Keep in mind that the use of the term *bracing* in this book is not intended to imply the adoption of a rigid, inflexible trunk. Instead, it implies a focus on the core muscles as a seat of strength and stability. Moderate cocontraction of the abdominal stabilizing muscles (the corset) is what we are aiming to achieve, not inflexible rigidity of the abdominal compartment. The only exceptions to this are static exercises that specifically require trunk rigidity (e.g., the plank).

Breathing During Abdominal Bracing

Inhaling will feel more difficult during abdominal bracing because the downward movement of the diaphragm is opposed by the raised pressure and increased stiffness of the abdominal compartment. You will need to work hard to overcome this extra resistance without releasing the brace, but this resistance is providing a very potent training stimulus—not only to your diaphragm, but also to the muscles of the abdominal corset. This is because all of these muscles must work harder to maintain the brace as the diaphragm movement increases the pressure inside the abdominal compartment. In fact, when bracing is performed with maximal effort, this is an excellent exercise in its own right. You should practice diaphragm breathing during abdominal bracing in the seated or standing position before incorporating it into other exercises. For exercises that involve bracing, only add the BMT once you are able to force your diaphragm into the braced abdominal compartment without losing control of the brace.

Achieving a Neutral Spine

A neutral spine position is also referred to throughout *Breathe Strong, Perform Better;* this essentially describes a position in which the pelvis is level, with neither a forward nor backward tilt (see figure 7.1). Forward tilt accentuates lumbar lordosis, and backward tilt does the opposite. Both of these produce undesirable loading on the spine.

You can get a feel for this by standing with your back against a wall. If your heels, buttocks, and shoulder blades (upper portion, not the tips) are touching the wall, your pelvis should be in a neutral position.

Figure 7.1 Neutral spine position; the pelvis is level.

is intended primarily to create a postural challenge to your core, not to create a resistance training stimulus to your limbs.

- If using bands or cords, make sure that they are under tension at the start of the exercise (see the previous point for guidance on cable resistance).

- For exercises that incorporate abdominal bracing (see Tips for Bracing and Posture beginning on page 114), only add the BMT once you are able to force your diaphragm into the braced abdominal compartment.

Choose four or five exercises (an even mix of static and dynamic exercises) to incorporate into your schedule each week, and vary these from time to time, unless stated otherwise. This is probably best accomplished by designating one day as a "functional breathing training" day.

Executions of the exercises identified in this chapter are described in chapter 11; refer to the page numbers provided here.

CORE TRAINING ADJUNCT

As discussed in chapters 1 and 2, the breathing muscles are a vital component of the systems that enable a person to maintain an upright posture and to stabilize the body's core. These nonrespiratory functions are pivotal to performance and injury prevention in all sports. Competition between the nonrespiratory and respiratory functions of the trunk musculature can lead to overload. It can also compromise the effectiveness with which the breathing muscles contribute to their nonrespiratory functions.

This being the case, it seems obvious that specific training of the breathing muscles should be an integral component of core training, but breathing is often barely considered at all. In subsequent chapters, we will consider the competing nonrespiratory and respiratory demands in a functional way; in this section, a number of key exercises are offered for incorporation into a core conditioning routine. The objective is to train the core-stabilizing role of the breathing muscles. In this way, far from jeopardizing core stability, the respiratory function of the breathing muscles can be optimized to improve core stability.

Rationale

The trunk musculature is responsible for ensuring that we stay upright during movement. It is also responsible for creating the rigidity that is required to protect the spine and to provide a stable platform from which to generate forces using our limbs. Without the stable platform of the core, we are just "shooting a cannon from a canoe" (Tsatsouline, 2000)—with very similar results! Many experts in core conditioning fail to even acknowledge that the diaphragm is an important part of the core musculature, or at best, they pay it nothing more than lip service. This is surprising, because the diaphragm is one of only a handful of muscles that insert onto the spine, contributing directly to spinal stability and controlling spinal movements. Furthermore, the muscles of the rib cage are also an integral part of the complex system that controls trunk movements. These facts alone are sufficient justification for integrating breathing muscle conditioning within core conditioning.

An excellent test of whether the respiratory and nonrespiratory functions of the trunk muscles can be accommodated simultaneously is to force the muscles to perform both functions simultaneously. Using a test that combined high levels of ventilation with an isometric task intended to challenge the lumbar stabilization, McGill demonstrated that some people are unable to maintain the required trunk muscle cocontraction for lumbar stabilization during challenged breathing; instead of maintaining a constant level of muscle trunk activation during the task, these people demonstrated muscle activation that fluctuated in time with breathing (McGill, 2007, p. 209). This loss of cocontraction resulted in situations where spinal instability could arise, increasing injury risk.

Of course, one strategy to overcome the inability to stabilize and breathe at the same time is to hold your breath, and this is something that many people do during core-stabilizing exercises. This is undesirable for a number of reasons. One main reason is that it is completely unsustainable and may lead to premature termination of a task in order to breathe (thereby undermining the value of the training to the core muscles).

You can test how good you are at maintaining trunk stability in the face of a breathing requirement by seeing how effectively you can undertake deep, controlled breathing during the plank exercise; many people find this extremely challenging and are only able to maintain the plank either by holding their breath or by constraining breathing with short irregular breaths. If this sounds familiar, then this section is for you!

The diaphragm can be thought of as the lid on top of the "box" that forms the core. The inclusion of diaphragm training in core training finally makes core training complete.

Objectives

Here are the main objectives of undertaking breathing exercises during core-stabilizing training:

1. To enhance the ability to meet the demands of both tasks simultaneously

2. To incorporate breathing training into functional core training exercises in order to develop healthy, grooved patterns of muscle activation

3. To optimize core conditioning by incorporating the "lid of the core box," thereby making core conditioning truly comprehensive

Exercises

The inspiration (no pun intended) of Professor Stuart McGill (McGill, 2007) is acknowledged in the formulation of some of these exercises, which build upon the foundations of his research and practice. The following are a selection of conventional core training exercises to which inspiratory muscle training (IMT) has been added. The set of exercises comprises exercises to promote lumbopelvic stability, exercises that facilitate rotation movement, and exercises that build the ability to control rotational movements. See chapter 11 for a description of how to undertake each exercise.

Exercises for Core Training

WEIGHT LOSS TOOL

The inclusion of this section does not imply that training the breathing muscles will lead directly to weight loss. However, after IMT, exercise feels easier, endurance is increased, and recovery is faster—therefore, adding IMT to your routine will ultimately enable you to work harder and for longer periods, which will help you to achieve greater energy expenditure and weight loss. The usual caveats apply; weight loss can only be achieved if you control your calorie intake. In addition, IMT will only help you to expend more calories if you dip into the additional capacity that it provides and thus work harder or longer. If you carry on doing the same things at the same intensities, all that will happen is that the activities will feel easier. This is not a bad thing, but if you want to shed fat, then you need to work harder or longer, or (preferably) both.

Rationale

The latest position stand published by the American College of Sports Medicine regarding exercise for weight loss (Donnelly et al., 2009) indicates that significant weight loss can be achieved if you undertake more than 250 minutes of moderate-intensity exercise per week. This amounts to just over half an hour every day of the week, or 50 minutes on 5 days of the week. The ACSM also acknowledges that weight training can be a helpful adjunct to a weight loss program because it increases muscle mass (muscle uses energy even when you're asleep, so having more muscle increases total energy expenditure). However, ACSM concluded that weight training alone does not lead to weight loss. The implication of this guidance is that the likelihood of successful weight loss is greatest when using activity programs composed of workouts with continuous (over 30 minutes) moderate exercise.

For most (but not all) people who are exercising to lose weight, the presence of fat within the abdomen and on the rib cage increases the work of breathing. In addition, the breathing demands of weight-bearing activities such as walking and jogging are increased because a greater body mass requires more energy (and more breathing). It's therefore no surprise that overweight individuals have higher levels of breathing discomfort than their lean counterparts. This fact, combined with the greater risk of breathing muscle fatigue induced by the greater breathing demand, has a negative impact on the ability to achieve and sustain moderate-intensity exercise.

This section provides a number of exercises that are designed specifically to address the needs of people who want to use physical activity to lose body fat.

Objectives

Here are the two main objectives of incorporating breathing muscle training into a weight loss program:

1. To minimize breathing effort and the risk of breathing muscle fatigue during continuous exercise (which will cause breathing effort to increase). Research has shown that the key to minimizing breathing effort is maximizing breathing muscle strength, because there is a direct relationship between increases in strength and reductions in breathing effort.

2. To address the additional postural control (balance) demands of people who are overweight. Additional body mass, especially in the trunk, produces an extra challenge to the postural control and core-stabilizing systems; essentially, the larger mass has greater momentum and requires larger forces to reestablish stability. This can make dynamic activities such as walking, jogging, stair climbing, and exercising to music much more challenging. For this reason, specific exercises are recommended to enhance the ability of the breathing muscles to contribute effectively to postural control and core stabilization using context-specific movements, combined with breathing muscle training.

Remember, these exercises are intended to help make it easier and more comfortable to engage in the moderate-intensity dynamic exercise that burns calories; they will not contribute to significant weight loss on their own.

Exercises

The following exercises should be completed on separate days, at least once per week—for example, Dumbbell Running on Monday, Step-Up on Tuesday, Dynamic Walking Lunge on Thursday, and Resisted Front Raise on Friday. On one or two other days, normal foundation IMT should be completed at the 30RM load.

GENERAL FITNESS

People engaged in training for general fitness may think they don't have as much to gain from training their breathing muscles as a competitive athlete does, but they couldn't be more wrong. Again, you need to consider the fact that after IMT, exercise feels easier, endurance is increased, and recovery is faster. This means that adding IMT to your routine will ultimately enable you to work harder and for longer periods, thereby increasing fitness faster and to a greater extent. The ability to exercise harder also means that you could make your workouts shorter and still clock up the same number of miles or calories. The postural stabilizing benefits of the exercises outlined in this section will also improve spinal health and your ability to lift weights.

Rationale

Going faster or lifting heavier weights is not what motivates the majority of people who are physically active. Most people simply want to improve their cardiovascular health, reduce the risk of chronic illnesses (such as diabetes), maintain a healthy body mass, or keep fit and strong enough to engage in other physical activities such as playing tennis, sailing, hill walking, and so on. For these individuals, the priority for exercise is that it should optimize the balance between investment and reward, and between pain and gain. In other words, exercise should not be uncomfortable, should not take too long, and above all, should be effective. Adding breathing training to your regimen will help to achieve these priorities.

Objectives

The two main objectives for incorporating IMT into a general fitness program are as follows, and they must be achieved with maximum time efficiency:

1. To minimize breathing effort and the risk of breathing muscle fatigue during exercise (which will cause breathing effort to increase). The key to minimizing breathing effort is maximizing breathing muscle strength, because there is a direct relationship between increases in strength and reductions in breathing effort.

2. To improve core stability by ensuring that the diaphragm is not neglected during core conditioning. The benefits of this are twofold:
   - Enhancement of core stabilization to improve lifting and other activities that require a stable base from which to exert forces with the limbs

- Reduced risk of back injury due to competition between the respiratory and postural stabilizing roles of the breathing muscles

Exercises

Because time is of the essence, the following exercises have the advantage of providing multiple benefits.

Exercises for General Fitness

Swiss Ball Plank With Feet on Ball (page 174)

Dynamic Bird Dog (page 181)

Squat With Overhead Resistance (page 190)

Rotating Lift (page 199)

Dynamic Walking Lunge (page 203)

T Push-Up (page 209)

WEIGHT TRAINING ADJUNCT

For most people who weight train, the objective is to get bigger and stronger. Current research suggests that the way to build strength and muscle mass is to "lift heavy" (Fry, 2004). This being the case, the importance of a strong, stable core cannot be overstated. Without this platform, the ability to lift heavy weights is limited, and the risk of injury is increased. The analogy of "shooting a cannon from a canoe" (Tsatsouline, 2000) has been mentioned in previous sections, but it illustrates perfectly the limitations that the trunk places on a person's ability to "lift heavy"—and to do so safely. This section should also be used as a reference for exercises that incorporate breathing muscle training into a selection of fundamental sport movements or resistance exercises (the exercises in this section are also referred to in subsequent chapters).

Rationale

One of the great debates that still continues in weight training circles is whether a person should inhale or exhale during a particular phase of a given lift. For the purposes of stabilization and protection of the spine during heavy lifting, increasing intraabdominal pressure is essential (McGill, 2007). A person can increase this pressure by straining against a closed, or partially closed, glottis (also known as performing the Valsalva maneuver). People instinctively do this when lifting anything that is even moderately heavy—they inhale just before the effort, and they either hold or partially hold their breath as the object is lifted.

The heavier the load lifted, the greater the load on the spine, and the greater the requirement for spinal stabilizing actions. The key to spine stability is the ability to cocontract the spinal stabilizing muscles (abdominal brace) independently of breathing (McGill, 2007). Allowing the brace to be disrupted by breathing leads to instability, an increased risk of injury (McGill, 2007) and repetition failure. Perhaps more important, the diaphragm needs to be considered as an integral part of the stabilizing system. Failure to develop and maintain sufficient tension in the diaphragm will result in dissipation of intraabdominal pressure and a corresponding loss of this important stabilizing force. Thus, factors such as diaphragm weakness and fatigue may increase the risk of injury, as well as impair performance.

But what are the implications of all this for how a person should breathe during lifting? Essentially, as long as intraabdominal pressure is maintained and is not allowed to fluctuate or wane during lifting, then spinal stability is protected. The most common advice is that you should exhale during the effort phase of a lift (e.g., during the leg drive of a squat) and inhale during the recovery phase. But there is a fundamental misconception implicit within this advice. The misconception is that the spine is only loaded—and therefore only vulnerable—during the effort phase; however, the bar does not suddenly become weightless at the completion of the effort phase. The bar must be lowered, under control, in preparation for the next repetition. This is the phase during which inhalation takes place, and intraabdominal pressure can fall if the abdominal brace is not maintained. The problem is that it is difficult to inhale during abdominal bracing, so people generally relax the brace in order to inhale. The trick to safe lifting is to learn to brace and breathe simultaneously; if this can be achieved, then it actually doesn't matter whether you inhale or exhale during the effort phase—just do what feels comfortable and most stable. The exercises outlined in this section are designed to help people achieve this for the most popular heavy loading exercises involving large muscle groups.

Finally, a quick word about performance. We have focused on spinal stability from a safety perspective, but long before instability results in injury, it results in a loss of performance. The nervous system is very adept at detecting and responding to joint instability, and it has been shown to generate reflex inhibition of muscle contractile activity in the leg muscles of people with knee joint and ankle instability. This inhibition results in a loss of the muscle's force-generating capacity, which is manifested as weakness. In addition, the loss of stiffness within the structures that provide the stable platform from which the limbs generate force (i.e., the core) results in mechanical inefficiency that leads to some of the force generated being wasted within the core (remember the canoe analogy). Thus, increasing the ability to generate and maintain the muscle actions required to generate stability can also improve performance.

Objectives

Here are the key objectives for IMT in the context of weightlifting:

1. To ensure that the respiratory actions of the breathing muscles do not jeopardize stability during weightlifting or fundamental sport movements
2. To build a stable platform for heavy lifting

Exercises

The selection of exercises in this section comprises the main large muscle group exercises that are the staple of most weight training regimens (squatting, pushing, and pulling). Also included are exercises that build the ability to control trunk rotation during loaded movements of the arms.

Exercises for Weight Training

Brace and Breathe (page 167)

Bent-Leg Deadlift (page 186)

Barbell Overhead Step-Up (page 188)

Barbell Single-Leg Squat (page 189)

Squat With Overhead Resistance (page 190)

Cable Push Pull (page 196)

Wood Chop and Lift (page 198)

Standing Split-Stance Cable Chest Press (page 207)

Standing Split-Stance Shoulder Press (page 208)

Standing Single-Arm, Single-Leg Cable Row (page 211)

Chapter

8

Training for Endurance Sports

The basic requirements of major endurance sports are similar. Thus, the recommended exercises identified in this chapter include some repetition of exercises between sports (particularly running, cycling, and rowing). But on the whole, the set of exercises for each sport has been devised with the specific requirements of that sport in mind. Before using any of these exercises, be sure to note the following important principles:

- If possible, use a cable machine to provide resistance, rather than bands or cords (this is not essential). The resistance should be low to begin with, but it can be developed as the training progresses. Don't overdo the resistance, which is intended primarily to create a postural challenge to your core, not to create a resistance training stimulus to your limbs.

- If using bands or cords, ensure that they are under tension at the start of the exercise (see the previous point for guidance on cable resistance).

- For exercises that incorporate abdominal bracing (see the sidebar entitled Tips for Bracing and Posture in chapter 7 on page 114), only add the breathing muscle trainer (BMT) once you are able to force your diaphragm into the braced abdominal compartment.

You need to ensure that you have good technique for all exercises before adding difficulty. Start by performing each exercise with nothing more than a focus on maintaining slow, deep diaphragmatic breathing throughout. Then add an external resistance to inhalation using a BMT set on its minimum load. Gradually increase the load on the BMT over a period of a few weeks until it reaches the prescribed level for the exercise. Please also refer to the sidebar on page 114 of chapter 7 for guidance regarding abdominal bracing and achieving a neutral spine position, as well as the sections on breath control, load setting, and thoracic stretching in chapter 6. In addition, don't forget to consider incorporating breathing intervals into interval training, drills, or circuits (see chapter 6). The breathing training can be introduced into the recovery phase, or it can be a separate station during a drill or circuit.

Choose about five exercises to incorporate into your schedule each week, and vary these from time to time. This is probably best accomplished by designating one day as a "functional breathing training" day.

Executions of the exercises identified in this chapter are described in chapter 11; refer to the page numbers provided here.

RUNNING

In addition to functional breathing exercises, this section provides advice on developing the all-important breath control that many runners lack. This is a vital and valuable skill, because it puts you in the driving seat, instead of your breathing.

Developing Breath Control

Here's an "on-the-run" exercise that's similar to a popular breath control exercise undertaken by swimmers to improve their stroke-to-breathing rate. Practicing this exercise will help you develop a controlled, efficient breathing pattern during runs. The best time to practice this exercise is during a steady phase of the run when you are running at a constant cadence; the exercise doesn't need to be done for more than a minute or two at a time, so it should be possible to practice this exercise several times during a typical run.

The idea is to extend inspiratory and expiratory time for as long as you can (i.e., for a fixed number of strides) so that you breathe as infrequently as you can tolerate. Typically, most people find a 2:1 stride-to-breath ratio to be the most comfortable during a steady run (see chapter 1). Start by extending the duration of both inspiratory and expiratory time roughly equally (to 3:1 or even 4:1), but once you're accustomed to this, you can mix it up by shortening one phase and extending the other phase disproportionately. This exercise will help you to develop breath control and discipline.

Rationale

In chapter 2, the challenges that running poses to the breathing muscles were considered. Running is a state of almost continuous instability that requires the entire trunk musculature to work hard—not only to ensure that the body remains upright, but also to ensure that the sacroiliac joints (SIJ) and the spine function properly and to protect the spine from damage. Tender ribs and a tender abdomen the day after a run (especially over uneven terrain) are a sign that the postural stabilizers of the trunk have been challenged. If you watch inexperienced runners, especially when they are tired, you'll see that one of the most noticeable deficits in their style is that their trunk and hips buckle and flex as they run. You will also notice that their shoulders roll from side to side with each stride during the enforced counter-rotation of the upper and lower halves of their body. When this happens, propulsive forces are dissipated (visualize the forces leaking away like water from a cracked glass), and the efficiency of movement is reduced, making the runner slower. The goal is to maintain trunk stiffness, stand tall, and minimize shoulder rotation as you run. These things take time to develop, and even experienced runners can find it difficult to maintain them when fatigued. This is also a time when the breathing muscles are fatigued and the breathing requirement is elevated. Failing to maintain a stiff, tall trunk with minimal shoulder rotation is bad for movement efficiency and bad for injury risk, and it can only be avoided through specific training of the muscles involved.

As an integral part of the core-stabilizing and postural control systems, the breathing muscles should be trained in contexts that mimic the challenges posed during running. Failure to do so increases the risk of injury due to the competing demands of breathing and postural stabilization. It also impairs performance by reducing the runner's ability to maintain a stable core from which to generate leg power. Failure to do this type of training also increases the risk of developing stitch pain.

Objectives

Here are the two key objectives of running-specific inspiratory muscle training (IMT):

1. To enhance the core and pelvic stabilization role of the diaphragm and other inspiratory muscles in order to optimize running efficiency
2. To enhance the ability of the breathing and stabilizing musculature to work together effectively during the varied challenges posed by running (changes in pace, terrain, incline, direction, and so on)

Exercises

Fredericson and Moore's excellent recommendations published in the IAAF's *New Studies in Athletics* are gratefully acknowledged (Fredericson & Moore, 2005). These have been developed and embellished with an emphasis on contexts that challenge the core-stabilizing and respiratory roles of the trunk musculature simultaneously.

Exercises for Running

Plank (page 168)

Side Bridge (page 169)

Bridge (page 170)

Bridge With Bent Knees (page 171)

Swiss Ball Squat Thrust (page 175)

Swiss Ball Plank With Elbows on Ball (page 177)

Gluteal Bridge With Shoulders on Ball (page 179)

Dynamic Bird Dog (page 181)

Full-Range Hip Extension and Flexion (page 182)

Raised Alternating Crunch (page 192)

Kneeling Lateral Rotation (page 194)

Raised Bicycle (page 206)

Dynamic Weighted Walking Lunge (page 210)

Upright Crunch (page 214)

Dumbbell Running on Balance Cushion (page 215)

CYCLING

In addition to functional breathing exercises, this section provides advice on developing breath control. This is a vital and valuable skill, because it puts you in the driving seat, instead of your breathing.

Developing Breath Control

Here's an "on-your-bike" exercise that's similar to a popular breath control exercise undertaken by swimmers to improve their stroke-to-breathing rate. Practicing this will help you develop a controlled, efficient breathing pattern. The best time to practice this exercise is during a phase of the ride when the cadence is relatively constant; the exercise doesn't need to be done for more than a minute or two at a time, so it should be possible to practice this exercise several times during a typical ride.

The idea is to extend inspiratory and expiratory time for as long as you can (i.e., for a fixed number of pedal revolutions) so that you breathe as infrequently as you can tolerate. Start by extending the duration of both inspiratory and expiratory time roughly equally, but once you're accustomed to this, you can mix it up by shortening one phase and extending the other phase disproportionately.

Table 8.1 provides some guidance on the relationship between pedal cadence and breathing frequency for various breathing control exercises. Depending on how hard you are working, different breathing frequencies will feel more or less challenging for a given cadence. As a general rule, during light to moderate exercise, breathing frequency needs to be below 20 breaths per minute (bpm) for it to feel challenging; during moderate to heavy exercise, frequency needs to be below 30; during heavy to very heavy exercise, frequency needs to be below 45. The object of the exercise is to breathe less frequently than you normally would, which will help you to develop your breath control.

An example of how to use this table is as follows. Let's say that you're exercising at an intensity that is moderate to heavy, and that your pedal cadence is 90 rpm. Bearing in mind that your comfortable breathing frequency at this cadence will be 30 bpm or higher, in order to challenge yourself, your breathing frequency needs to be less than 30 bpm. Use the table to identify the pedal-to-breath ratio that results in a breathing frequency of less than 30 bpm. In our example, this corresponds to breathing every four pedal revolutions, giving a breathing frequency of 22 bpm at 90 rpm.

Table 8.1 Pedal Cadence and Breathing Frequency

Pedal cadence (rpm)	Breathing frequency (bpm) when breathing every *two* revs	Breathing frequency (bpm) when breathing every *three* revs	Breathing frequency (bpm) when breathing every *four* revs
60	30	20	15
70	35	23	17
80	40	27	20
90	45	30	22
100	50	33	25

Rationale

In chapter 2, we considered the interrelationship of cycle exercise and core stability; evidence was presented that adequate stabilization is necessary not only for reducing the risk of injury, but also for optimizing the mechanical efficiency of pedaling. Because the breathing muscles, especially the diaphragm, form such an important part of the core-stabilizing system, training these muscles in a cycling-specific context is a logical addition to any cyclist's training regimen.

Furthermore, the use of aerodynamic body positions that minimize frontal area—and hence minimize aerodynamic drag—has unintended consequences for respiratory muscle mechanics that may impair performance. When a cyclist is in the crouched body position, the abdominal organs are forced upward so that they rest more forcefully against the diaphragm. This impedes the movement of the diaphragm and increases inspiratory muscle work, which not only increases breathing effort, but also leads to the use of inefficient breathing patterns (rapid and shallow) and an increased risk of inspiratory muscle fatigue. Fortunately, these impediments can be overcome by undertaking breathing training in cycle-specific postures.

Objectives

Here are the three key objectives of cycling-specific IMT:

1. To enhance the core and pelvic stabilization role of the diaphragm in order to optimize pedaling efficiency
2. To enhance the ability of the respiratory and stabilizing musculature to work together effectively during the varied challenges posed by cycling (climbing, surging, sprinting, time trials, and so on)
3. To enhance the ability of the breathing muscles to tolerate and overcome the restrictions imposed by crouched body positions

Exercises

When doing research for this section of *Breathe Strong, Perform Better,* I was surprised to find a dearth of information and guidance about cycling-specific core-stabilizing exercises. Although I found one excellent book on general muscular training for cycling (Sovndal, 2009), this book did not incorporate any specific consideration of the role of the breathing muscles. The following recommendations seek to fill this gap with a range of exercises that address both core stability and cycling-specific breathing muscle training.

Exercises for Cycling

Plank (page 168)

Swiss Ball Plank With Feet on Ball (page 174)

Swiss Ball Pike (page 176)

Swiss Ball Plank With Elbows on Ball (page 177)

Ski Squats With Alternate Leg Raise (page 184)

(continued)

Exercises for Cycling (continued)
Swiss Ball Side Crunch (page 193)
Raised Bicycle (page 206)
Ab Crush (page 212)
Aerobars (page 216)
Standing One-Leg Cycle (page 217)
Ride 'Em Cowboy (page 218)
Big Gear Climb (page 219)

SWIMMING

I am very grateful for the guidance and insight provided by Dan Bullock (www. swim4tri.com) in the formulation of this section. Coach Bullock is a prominent swim and triathlon coach based in the United Kingdom.

In addition to the posture-specific exercises outlined in this section, the sidebar on page 132 provides Coach Bullock's account of a set of exercises that he "road tested" and found to be very effective.

Open-water swimmers should also see the multisport section (beginning on page 133) for guidance on techniques that can be used to overcome the influence of wet suits on breathing (see chapter 1 for background information).

Rationale

In swimming, the name of the game is to maximize the efficiency of the transfer of propulsive force from the limbs to forward movement through an extremely dense environment, where hydrodynamic drag is the swimmer's biggest enemy. Because of the controversy surrounding the use of certain swimsuits during the summer of 2009 (banned in 2010), we've heard a great deal about the huge advantages that certain swimsuits can bring in terms of minimizing hydrodynamic drag and increasing buoyancy. The importance of buoyancy and body position cannot be overstated, and these factors are well understood by most swimmers; however, what many swimmers may not understand is the contribution that the air in the lungs and core stability make to buoyancy and body position. To experience the effect of lung inflation for yourself, lie on your back in the pool with your feet anchored at the poolside at surface level. Inhale and exhale as deeply as possible, concentrating on keeping your body flat. Notice how you rise and sink as you inhale and exhale. The size of the movement is directly proportional to the volume of air that is moved into and out of your lungs. See figure 8.1, which illustrates the influence of lung volume on body position.

Filling the lungs rapidly and maintaining a high lung volume minimize disruption to body alignment and maximize buoyancy, both of which reduce drag. Now that the buoyancy-giving suits have been banned, swimmers need to look elsewhere, and optimizing their breathing is an obvious source of buoyancy that is probably underused.

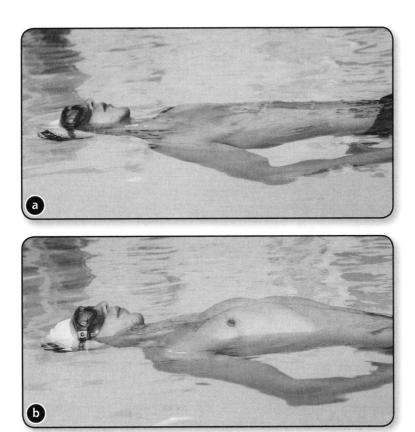

Figure 8.1 The influence of lung volume on body position: *(a)* lungs empty; *(b)* lungs full.

Furthermore, when swimmers increase their ability to maintain a stable core from which to generate propulsive forces with the limbs, this not only optimizes force transmission, but also minimizes disruption to body alignment. The vital role of the trunk muscles in stabilization demands that they function simultaneously as stabilizers and breathing muscles. The exercises in this section are designed to optimize the positive contribution that conditioning of the breathing muscles can make to maximizing buoyancy, minimizing drag, and providing a stable platform from which to generate forward movement through the water—*without* compromising breathing.

Objectives

Here are the three main objectives of swimming-specific IMT:

1. To train the inspiratory muscles to overcome external (hydrostatic) impedance of thoracic expansion
2. To train the breathing muscles to be capable of achieving rapid, deep inhalations in supine positions
3. To enhance the ability of the breathing muscles to function both as contributors to propulsive force and as thoracic and pelvic stabilizers

Coach Dan Bullock's Early-Season Swim Set

My first experience of the huge difference that specific IMT can make to breath control came during a swim training camp I was running. I had been sent a breathing muscle trainer (BMT) for evaluation and decided to use the camp to give it a good "road test." As I became more familiar with IMT, I quickly noticed some great improvements that were not just due to the general benefits of the more intensive training I was doing over the course of the week. I've run these camps many times before, and although my swim fitness usually improves over the course of the week, what I noticed this time was unusual—I really thought that the IMT helped accelerate my fitness and breath-holding capacity.

People I spoke to about IMT mentioned that it was useful, but they said that they found it difficult to find the time to incorporate it into a daily routine (I'm not sure why, given that it only takes about 5 minutes a day). I thought about this and came up with the idea of using the BMT during the rest period between swim sets (I discovered later that "great minds think alike" and that many coaches in different sports have hit on the same idea). Here's one of my swim sets for that week; I used a BMT in the breaks between swim repetitions:

10 × 200-second front crawl—recover with 15 deep breaths on the BMT between each 200

10 × 100-second front crawl—recover with 10 deep breaths on the BMT between each 100

10 × 50-second front crawl—recover with 5 deep breaths on the BMT between each 50

My yardstick for the benefits of this set was my ability to fly kick off the wall, which is a real lung buster, but we all want to make the best use of the 15-meter rule by swimming as far as possible underwater (it certainly works for Mr. Phelps!). I started the week on three kicks, and I ended it on five. This improvement in my ability to fly kick off the wall was more rapid than I've ever experienced before. After this experience, I was completely sold on IMT.

—Coach Dan Bullock

To help meet objective 1, the exercises in this section should be undertaken with a wide elastic exercise band tensioned around the lower ribs, just below the sternum (see figure 8.2). This is the region of the thorax that expands to the greatest extent because of the movement of the diaphragm and the action of the rib cage muscles during inhalation. This region is therefore the area that experiences the greatest impedance from hydrostatic pressure acting on the thorax during immersion. Restricting thoracic expansion simulates the effect of hydrostatic pressure on the thorax.

To ease the transition from foundation training to the swim-specific exercises, you should undertake foundation IMT with the addition of the elastic thoracic restriction for the final 1 or 2 weeks. When commencing the swim-specific exercises, do so using just the thoracic restriction; once you are accustomed to this, add the BMT.

Exercises

The following exercises are recommended for swimmers. Add specificity to all of these exercises by wrapping the lower rib cage with a wide elastic band (figure 8.2).

Figure 8.2 Position a wide elastic band around the lower ribs, just below the sternum.

Exercises for Swimming

Swiss Ball Side Rotation (page 191)

Cable Push Pull (page 196)

Cross Band Rotation (page 197)

Wood Chop and Lift (page 198)

Rotating Lift (page 199)

Trickle and Blast (page 220)

Swiss Ball Hyperextension (page 221)

Swiss Ball Crawl (page 222)

Plank With Arm Extension (page 223)

MULTISPORT

Multisport athletes should choose exercises that they find most relevant from those in the running, cycling, and swimming sections. In addition, some supplementary advice is provided on the following page that addresses specific challenges faced by the multisport athlete.

Rationale

As far as challenges to breathing are concerned, the unique features of multisport training and competition are as follows:

- The influence of equipment and environment (e.g., wet suits and open water)
- The requirement to move from one exercise modality to another as quickly and efficiently as possible (e.g., cycle to run)
- The transition between phases (races can be "lost in transition")
- The nutritional demands of prolonged activity (i.e., eating or drinking and breathing simultaneously are a challenge)

Like any other part of an athlete's preparation, these challenges need to be prepared for and rehearsed during training. The following sections provide guidance on how to achieve this.

Objectives

The objectives of training for multisport events are to address the four issues raised in the rationale section and to provide exercises and rehearsal strategies that minimize any negative impact that breathing may have on these issues.

Strategies to Minimize Breathing Discomfort

This section offers some guidance on minimizing the negative impact that breathing-related factors can have on your performance.

Equipment and Environmental Issues

In the previous section on cycling, the influence of the aero position in cycling was covered; if you plan to use aerobars, you should include the exercises suggested in that section as part of your training. The other piece of equipment that produces problems for breathing is the wet suit. Ideally, a wet suit should be as tight as is tolerable in order to minimize the volume of water that is trapped between the skin and the suit. An unwanted side effect of a tight wet suit is that it squeezes your chest and abdomen, adding to the compression already created by the surrounding water. Arm movements exacerbate the compression. Elastic resistance bands can be wrapped around the thorax and over the shoulders to simulate the restrictions imposed by a wet suit (see the compressed shrug and breathe exercise on page 234 of chapter 11). Undertaking IMT with this additional elastic resistance will build breathing strength and endurance, making it easier to overcome the restrictions imposed by wearing a wet suit. The resistance created by a wet suit is simulated most accurately by undertaking some breathing training while wearing a wet suit, but don't suit up specifically to do your breathing training; instead, add some breathing training onto a session during which you are already wearing your wet suit. You can either do some of the exercises previously described, do some breathing intervals, or just do some foundation IMT.

An aspect related to the wet suit is the challenge of the open-water swim. Breathing-related factors that must be considered include the anxiety-related increase in breathing rate, the influence of being buffeted or swam over by other competitors, the effect of waves on your ability to breathe on your preferred side (or at all!), and the need to sight efficiently (breaking your rhythm). All of these factors can lead to panic and the loss of breathing rhythm. No specific exercises are suggested here, but the best advice is to practice and rehearse for the things that concern you most. Also, be reassured by the knowledge that specific breathing training will help you to master your breath control during the swim—and that this alone will make a huge difference to your confidence (see the case study in the sidebar on page 136 for an example of this).

Multiple Exercise Modalities

The cycle-run (CR) transition is the one cited most often by multisport athletes as posing the biggest psychological and physiological barrier, but it's far from being all in the mind. Athletes' most common complaint is the feeling that breathing discomfort is increased, as well as a feeling of "heavy legs" during the initial stages of the run phase. Brick sessions (consecutive bouts of running and cycling) are a mainstay of multisport training. These sessions also offer an opportunity to build breathing resilience for the transition by punctuating the brick session with bouts of IMT (similar to the breathing intervals).

Some intriguing physiological changes occur during the CR transition. For example, running economy is reduced by anywhere from 2 to 12 percent during the early part of the run phase (when compared to running economy in the "fresh" state), and ventilation and breathing discomfort are also elevated. In other words, when running is preceded by cycling, the oxygen uptake requirement of running increases. The precise reasons for this are uncertain; however, postevent decrements in lung function, along with the presence of inspiratory muscle fatigue, suggest that the reduction in running economy may be associated with the impaired breathing function.

The pattern of changes in breathing muscle fatigue during a triathlon is also interesting, because it is not as one might predict. Research on swimmers has shown that front-crawl swimming is associated with the highest magnitude of inspiratory muscle fatigue (IMF) yet recorded—a 29 percent deficit in strength after a 200-meter swim at 90 to 95 percent of race pace. In light of this, we might predict that IMF would be present after the swim phase of the triathlon and that it would become progressively more severe after the cycle and run phases. However, there appears to be little or no IMF after the swim phase. In contrast, quite severe IMF is present after the cycle and run phases (about 25 percent), but surprisingly, no worsening of fatigue occurs between the cycle and run phases. In other words, cycling induces fatigue that is not exacerbated by subsequent running. In addition, there is no evidence of expiratory muscle fatigue.

The absence of IMF after the swim phase is likely because of the triathletes' pacing strategy—and not an indication that triathletes are more resistant than swimmers to the IMF induced by swimming. Most triathletes pace themselves during the swim, knowing that not pushing too hard during this phase results in a better overall performance.

It's not clear why inspiratory muscle fatigue does not worsen during the run; however, this might indicate that there is a critical level of fatigue that the system will not allow to be exceeded—and that this level is reached during the cycle. The

Triathlon Case Study

Lisa was an age-group triathlete who was relatively new to the sport, but who had enjoyed early success over the sprint and Olympic distances. Lisa achieved wins in her age group (35 to 39) in almost every event she entered in her first season, including the London Triathlon, the largest triathlon in Europe. This success spurred Lisa on to attempt the ultimate triathlon challenge—an Ironman. The event she chose was Taupo in New Zealand, and her specific preparation took place over a 9-month period.

Swimming had always been Lisa's weakest discipline, and over the Ironman distance of 3.8 kilometers, a bad swim could leave her with a lot of ground to make up. Lisa's swimming coach had identified her breathing as being a major weakness in terms of her swimming stroke, leading to poor stroke mechanics and poor body position. He gave her a range of drills to work on, but despite diligent application of the drills and hours spent in the pool, Lisa could not complete a full set of drills without running out of breath; she had hit a seemingly insurmountable plateau in terms of her swim speed. This weakness was also confirmed by Lisa herself, who said that she dreaded the swim in every race because she not only felt slow, but also felt severely limited by her breathing. She said that she was occasionally frightened by the inability to breathe freely. Needless to say, this was having a very poor impact on her confidence and enjoyment.

With 3 months to go before the Ironman, we began Lisa's IMT with a 4-week period of foundation training (see chapter 6). This was supplemented by a couple of sessions in which we concentrated on developing good breathing technique. It was clear from the latter that Lisa was not an efficient breather, but experience had shown me that some breathing drills and the IMT would resolve this. In addition to using the IMT, Lisa also began to include an inspiratory muscle warm-up in her training.

At the completion of the foundation training, Lisa's inspiratory muscle strength had increased by 28 percent, and she reported that her swim drills had finally begun to improve. She also felt less troubled by her breathing during brick sessions, which had previously been very challenging, especially in the couple of minutes after the transition from cycle to run. In addition, Lisa reported that the warm-up had improved her ability to get up to speed more quickly, especially during her swim sessions. As part of her buildup for the Ironman, Lisa competed in a half marathon, slicing 4 minutes from her personal best.

We agreed to take Lisa's IMT to the next level by introducing some functional training techniques that included elements for all three disciplines. After a further 4 weeks of functional IMT, Lisa's inspiratory muscle strength improved by an additional 8 percent, and she reported that her transition from cycle to run seemed effortless by comparison with what she experienced before the IMT. Thanks to the advanced aerobar IMT exercise, Lisa also felt much more comfortable when pushing hard while staying tucked in the aerobars. In addition, Lisa was far more able to achieve and sustain short bursts of acceleration during her long rides and runs, which was confirmed by her coach based on her heart rate recordings. Finally, and most important, Lisa was beginning to enjoy her swim sessions, thanks to her newfound breathing control and improved stroke mechanics.

During the final 4 weeks before the race, we stepped down the frequency of the training from daily to every other day, and Lisa undertook these sessions immediately after her whole-body training. This introduced another element of specificity, because the IMT was being undertaken when the inspiratory muscles were already fatigued from the whole-body training. Finally, Lisa stopped the IMT 4 days before race day.

When race day finally arrived, Lisa was physically prepared, but more important, she felt mentally prepared because she knew that she'd left no stone unturned in her preparation—and that she had finally achieved a state of mastery over her breathing. Lisa finished sixth in her age group, narrowly missing qualification for the World Championships in Kona—not bad for someone who took part in her first competitive triathlon less than 2 years earlier at the age of 36. Her next goal is to qualify for Kona in the 40 to 44 age group!

implications of this are that run performance may be limited by the "unwillingness" of the system to permit any further inspiratory muscle fatigue. Exactly how the body knows this is unclear, but it may be related to an increase in breathing effort or the influence of the inspiratory muscle metaboreflex on leg blood flow.

Don't Get Lost in Transition

The swim leaves many athletes feeling "spaced out," disoriented, and anxious, especially in cold conditions where athletes may even become slightly hypothermic during the swim. This is not the ideal frame of mind for transitioning to a cycle. Similarly, the frenzy of moving from cycle to run can leave athletes in a state of blind panic if they are not well rehearsed. As with every other aspect of racing, rehearsal and practice are vital, but there is something else you can do to help you to keep your head. Breathing control is a well-known technique for reducing anxiety and promoting concentration. But breathing control doesn't have to be limited to a resting, meditative state; it can also be helpful during activities that require clear, calm thinking during a physically demanding task. A number of years ago, I conducted a small pilot study to examine the influence of IMT on decision making during periods of high breathing demand. After IMT, people showed an improvement in decision making under identical conditions of physical stress. In addition, IMT also promotes deep, slow, controlled breathing. Add these benefits together—and combine them with a conscious awareness of the need to maintain deep, calm, controlled breathing—and you have the recipe for the perfect transition. If you just let your breathing happen, with everything else you need to think about, your breathing will be rapid, shallow, and panicky. When rehearsing your transition, you must also rehearse your breathing during transition. Remember, practice makes permanent.

Eating and Drinking on the Move

Not only does eating and drinking interfere with normal breathing, but the act of getting the food or drink to your mouth also spoils your rhythm and disturbs your postural stability. Feeding yourself while cycling or running requires arm movements to retrieve food from pockets or bottles from frame cages; you may even have to grab goodies from a feed station as you pass. These disruptions to breathing, rhythm, and stability need to be rehearsed and practiced during training. One thing is guaranteed—having some IMT under your belt, especially some of the cycle- and run-specific exercises, will make all of these disturbances a lot easier to train for. You should practice for the postural challenges of eating and drinking on the move by forcing yourself to break your rhythm during a run or cycle and simulating the movements of eating and drinking.

ROWING

I am very grateful for the guidance and insight provided by Eddie Fletcher (www.fletchersportscience.co.uk) in the formulation of this section. Coach Fletcher is a prominent multisport and indoor rowing coach based in the United Kingdom.

Like swimmers, rowers must synchronize breathing with propulsive movements in order to maximize performance and minimize injury. Unless breathing can be maintained under conscious control, there is a danger that it will take over and dominate the rhythm of the propulsive movement. This makes breathing training particularly important for rowers.

Rationale

In chapter 2, we considered the challenges that rowing poses for the breathing muscles. Rowers, especially experienced rowers, show a high degree of entrainment between their breathing and the rowing stroke, which implies that this synchrony is advantageous. This linkage between stroke rate and breathing pushes the breathing muscles to their limits. During a 2,000-meter race, athletes commonly try to maintain the 2:1 breathing pattern; they breathe out during the initial part of the drive (when the blade is in the water), inhale as they reach the end of the drive, breathe out again as they begin to come forward, and take a small breath just before the catch. At both of the inhalation points, the breathing muscles are compromised to some extent by their action as trunk stabilizers (end of the drive) or by compression of the abdominal wall (the catch). These impairments can be minimized through specific training.

The muscles of the trunk have a number of important roles during rowing: contributing to the transmission of propulsive force, maintaining structural stability of the spine, ribs and other bony structures, and last but not least, breathing. However, these roles may become contradictory from time to time, which may have a negative impact on both performance and injury risk. The exercises in this section seek to address these issues and are applicable to sweep rowers, scullers, and indoor rowers.

> ## Inspiratory Muscle Fatigue Makes Your Drive Weaker
>
> In an unpublished study, we found that static force-generating capacity in the catch position for rowing was impaired in the presence of inspiratory muscle fatigue. This implies an important role for the inspiratory muscles (most likely the diaphragm) in transmitting force (up to 900 newtons) through the trunk. To paraphrase a quote that has been used previously in *Breathe Strong, Perform Better,* without the stable platform of the core, we are just "shooting a cannon from a canoe" (Tsatsouline, 2000).

Objectives

Here are the two key objectives of rowing-specific IMT:

1. To enhance the trunk-stabilizing role of the diaphragm and inspiratory accessory muscles in order to optimize rowing efficiency and reduce risk of injury.
2. To enhance the ability of the respiratory and stabilizing musculature to work together effectively during the challenges posed by rowing (e.g., breathing effectively at the catch and finish)

Exercises

The following exercises are recommended for rowers.

Exercises for Rowing

Plank (page 168)

Swiss Ball Plank With Feet on Ball (page 174)

Swiss Ball Pike (page 176)

Swiss Ball Side Rotation (page 191)

Swiss Ball Side Crunch (page 193)

Cable Push Pull (page 196)

Rotating Lift (page 199)

Ab Crush (page 212)

Swiss Ball Hip Extension (page 224)

Swiss Ball Lateral Rotation (page 225)

Sculling Sit-Up (page 226)

Seated Row (page 227)

SLIDING SPORTS

In this section, the focus is on the most popular winter sports (alpine and Nordic skiing, snowboarding, ice skating), as well as spin-off sports (roller skiing and skating). In chapter 2, we considered how the postural control demands of these sliding sports can interact with breathing to create challenges for both. We also considered the effects of altitude on the breathing requirements of physical activity.

Rationale

Loss of postural control spells disaster in sliding sports, because it often results in a fall. Competition between the postural control and breathing roles of the breathing muscles can jeopardize postural control in situations where breathing demand is high (a particular problem at altitude). Accordingly, using specific functional training to improve the ability of the breathing muscles to cope with this dual demand will lower the risk of overload—and therefore lower the risk of losing one's balance. In addition, specific training of the breathing muscles will enhance enjoyment of the activity by reducing unpleasant breathing sensations. For people with a performance objective, the functional exercises outlined in this section will also improve their ability to maintain aerodynamic postures for longer periods without breathing discomfort (e.g., banish the need to stand up in order to relieve breathlessness).

Objectives

Here are the three key objectives of undertaking IMT that are specific to sliding sports:

1. To enhance the ability to meet the demands of postural control and breathing simultaneously (reducing fall risk)
2. To enhance the core and pelvic stabilization role of the diaphragm in order to optimize the efficiency of force production during skating
3. To minimize breathlessness due to aerodynamic postures and altitude

Exercises

The following exercises are recommended for sliding sports.

Exercises for Sliding Sports

Plank (page 168)

Ski Squats With Alternate Leg Raise (page 184)

Swiss Ball Side Rotation (page 191)

Balance Squats (page 228)

Balance Squats With a Twist (page 229)

Skater Leg Drives (page 230)

Single-Leg Balance With Opposing Arm and Leg Resistance (page 231)

HIKING AND MOUNTAINEERING

Hiking and mountaineering might not traditionally be thought of as endurance sports, but they go on for days, sometimes weeks, in a harsh environment that is unique in its ability to push breathing to its limits. In fact, you can think of an expedition to high altitude as being an ultraendurance event for the breathing muscles!

Rationale

In chapter 2, we discussed the reasons for the enormous increase in the perception of breathing effort when people ascend to high altitude. In addition to contending with this challenge, hikers and mountaineers must also cope with the challenges imposed by carrying heavy backpacks. These challenges are twofold: Backpacks move the center of gravity backward, and this must be corrected by using active forward flexion of the trunk; the straps of backpacks restrict thoracic and abdominal movements, increasing the work of breathing and impairing lung function.

The combined influence of an increased breathing requirement and the challenges of wearing a backpack induce profound inspiratory muscle fatigue. Furthermore, the steep, uneven terrain and the effects of loading on the upper body can increase the risk of falling and injury. Accordingly, the breathing muscles should be trained using exercises specifically designed to simulate these conditions of overload. These exercises will not only reduce the risk of injury, but also enhance the comfort and enjoyment of the hike.

Objectives

Here are the three key objectives of IMT that are specific to mountaineering and hiking:

1. To minimize the influence of backpacks on breathing effort and postural control
2. To enhance the core and pelvic stabilization role of the diaphragm in order to optimize postural control and spinal stability
3. To enhance the ability of the respiratory and stabilizing musculature to work together effectively during the varied challenges posed by external loading and uneven terrain—while facing a severely increased ventilatory demand

Exercises

If you are training for a specific expedition and you have a backpack that you plan to use for it (or you have a backpack that you use routinely), you should consider adding further specificity to these exercises by wearing the pack (preferably loaded) when you undertake your breathing muscle training.

Exercises for Hiking and Mountaineering

Plank (page 168)

Dumbbell Running (page 200)

Step-Up (page 202)

Dynamic Weighted Walking Lunge (page 210)

Backpack Shrug and Breathe (page 232)

Step-Down (page 233)

Chapter

9

Training for Team Sports

Although the sports discussed in this chapter are very different from each other, they also have three important things in common: They all involve repeated, high-intensity efforts that drive breathing to its limits; they all require the contribution of the upper body and the core-stabilizing system (e.g., fending off opponents, changing direction quickly, passing objects to teammates); and they all require tactical decision making at a time when the distraction from breathing discomfort is high. The exercises that are suggested in this chapter not only recognize these commonalities (reflected in the generic exercises) but also recognize the need for specificity to the sport in question (reflected in the sport-specific exercises). The exercises also emphasize the importance of the trunk musculature for injury prevention in sports where collisions, falls, and sudden rotational movements of the trunk can jeopardize spinal stability.

Because of the similarities between these repeated-sprint sports, a number of the suggested exercises are generic, and these are listed at the beginning of this chapter. In addition to these, the sections dealing with each type of sport also contain a small number of specific exercises. Before using any of these exercises, be sure to note the following important principles:

- If possible, use a cable machine to provide resistance, rather than bands or cords (this is not essential). The resistance should be low to begin with, but it can be developed as the training progresses. Don't overdo the resistance, which is intended primarily to create a postural challenge, not to create a resistance training stimulus to your limbs.

- If using bands or cords, ensure that they are under tension at the start of the exercise (see the previous point for guidance on cable resistance).

- For exercises that incorporate abdominal bracing (see Tips for Bracing and Posture in chapter 7), only add the BMT once you are able to force your diaphragm into the braced abdominal compartment.

You need to ensure that you have good technique for all exercises before adding difficulty. Start by performing each exercise with nothing more than a focus on maintaining slow, deep diaphragmatic breathing throughout. Then add an external resistance to inhalation using a breathing muscle trainer (BMT) set on its minimum load. Gradually increase the load on the BMT over a period of a few weeks until it reaches the prescribed level for the exercise. Please also refer to the sidebar titled Tips for Bracing and Posture in chapter 7 on page 114 for guidance regarding abdominal bracing and achieving a neutral spine position, as well as the sections on breath control, load setting, and thoracic stretching in chapter 6. In addition, don't forget to consider incorporating breathing intervals into interval training, drills, or circuits (see chapter 6). The breathing training can be introduced into the recovery phase, or it can be a separate station during a drill or circuit.

Choose about five exercises to incorporate into your training each week, and vary these from time to time. This is probably best accomplished by designating one day as a "functional breathing training" day.

Executions of the exercises identified in this chapter are described in chapter 11; refer to the page numbers provided here.

GENERIC FUNCTIONAL EXERCISES FOR TEAM SPORTS

The following exercises will develop the trunk and stabilizing musculature in ways that are beneficial to all team sports. For these exercises, the focus is on developing lumbopelvic stability and rotational strength. These exercises are drawn primarily from the lumbopelvic stabilizing exercises in the core training section of chapter 7, as well as the weight training section of that chapter. If alternative exercises from these sections of chapter 7 are more applicable to your sport, or if they address specific weaknesses, feel free to draw from those also.

The breathing muscles are an integral part of the kinetic chain that connects the upper and lower body. Thus, in sports that require the involvement and coordination of the upper and lower body, athletes need to train the muscles that provide the link between the two. The exercises in this section focus on developing a strong, stable core (providing the foundation for movement), as well as developing strength and coordination of the muscles responsible for controlling trunk movements and those linking the trunk and legs.

Generic Functional Exercises

Plank (page 168)

Side Bridge (page 169)

Bridge (page 170)

Bridge With Bent Knees (page 171)

Swiss Ball Squat Thrust (page 175)

Dynamic Bird Dog (page 181)

Full-Range Hip Extension and Flexion (page 182)

Barbell Overhead Step-Up (page 188)

Barbell Single-Leg Squat (page 189)

Squat With Overhead Resistance (page 190)

Swiss Ball Side Rotation (page 191)

Raised Alternating Crunch (page 192)

Swiss Ball Side Crunch (page 193)

Kneeling Lateral Rotation (page 194)

Cable Push Pull (page 196)

Wood Chop and Lift (page 198)

Rotating Lift (page 199)

T Push-Up (page 209)

Dynamic Weighted Walking Lunge (page 210)

FOOTBALL

The exercises contained within the rugby football section may also be of interest to football players, because the two sports have some similarities.

Rationale

A typical lineman weighing 340 pounds (154 kg) delivers over 1,800 pounds (816 kg) of force per second during a collision. The shoulder pad ensemble worn by players to protect them from these collisions is an obvious source of thoracic restriction, especially if it includes rib protection. The equipment needs to be tight fitting in order to function effectively and to keep it from interfering with movement, but this comes at a cost to breathing efficiency and comfort. Furthermore, players also wear mouth guards, and these add to the impairment of breathing and increase the discomfort. The combination of these impediments to breathing and the high intensity of the plays results in brief periods during which the demands on the breathing muscles are extremely high.

Although protective equipment minimizes injury risk, it cannot eliminate the risk completely. This is where "prehabilitation" of the systems that protect the body from injury, especially the spine, has a role to play. In chapter 1, the role of the breathing muscles in the core-stabilizing system was described; we learned that the diaphragm and other breathing muscles are a vital component of the system that protects the spine. The core has also been identified as a contributor to running performance via its influence on the production of leg power. Integration of inspiratory muscle training (IMT) into a general core conditioning program is described in chapter 7. In this section, football-specific exercises are identified that address the effects of protective equipment and the need for optimized core conditioning. They also help players develop the ability to breathe efficiently during activities that involve the trunk.

Objectives

Here are the three key objectives of football-specific IMT:

1. To minimize the influence of protective equipment on breathing effort
2. To enhance the core and pelvic stabilization role of the diaphragm in order to optimize spinal stability and running efficiency
3. To enhance the ability of the respiratory and stabilizing musculature to work together effectively during the varied challenges posed by the game

Exercises

Don't forget the generic functional exercises for team sports provided at the beginning of this chapter. Also, consider doing the exercises while wearing your normal protective equipment (possibly secured a little more tightly than normal).

Exercises for Football

The Dominator (page 187)

Compressed Shrug and Breathe (page 234)

Lineman Stance (page 235)

SOCCER

Soccer is famously described as a game of two halves. In contrast to the duality of the game itself, the musculature that contributes to the varied demands of soccer must function as a single kinetic unit. This section provides guidance on achieving just that.

Rationale

The breathing challenges associated with soccer include a surprisingly large contribution from the trunk muscles, which are engaged during the large amount of contact that takes place between opponents in the modern game. Much of the contact with opponents occurs while the players are running at high speed; during this time, the players are also required to change direction rapidly to obtain or maintain possession. These activities are difficult enough in isolation, but they often occur simultaneously and during periods when breathing requirements are extremely high. The involvement of the trunk musculature in these activities places huge demands on the breathing muscles. These muscles must not only meet the requirements of breathing, but must also contribute to overcoming opponents, maintaining postural control, and protecting the spine. With this kind of overload, it's easy to see that something has to give. At best, the result of this overload will be an increase in breathing effort and an acceleration of breathing muscle fatigue; at worst, it may be an injury due to loss of balance or spinal stability.

This is where "prehabilitation" of the systems that protect the body from injury, especially the spine, has a role to play. In chapter 1, the role of the breathing muscles in the core-stabilizing system was described; we learned that the diaphragm and other breathing muscles are a vital component of the system that protects the spine. The core has also been identified as a contributor to running performance via its influence on the production of leg power. Integration of IMT into a general core conditioning program is described in chapter 7. Later in this section, some soccer-specific exercises are identified. These exercises address the need for optimized core conditioning, and they help players develop the ability to breathe efficiently during activities that involve the trunk.

Objectives

Here are the two key objectives of soccer-specific IMT:

1. To enhance the core and pelvic stabilization role of the diaphragm in order to optimize spinal stability and running efficiency
2. To enhance the ability of the respiratory and stabilizing musculature to work together effectively during the varied challenges posed by the game

Exercises

Don't forget the generic functional exercises for team sports provided at the beginning of this chapter.

Exercises for Soccer

Ski Squats With Alternate Leg Raise (page 184)

Palloff Press (page 195)

Single-Leg Squat Kick (page 204)

Single-Leg Resisted Knee Raise and Twist (page 236)

BASKETBALL AND NETBALL

I am indebted to Coach Arthur Horne, strength and conditioning coach at Northeastern University at Boston, for his guidance and extremely insightful contributions to the contents of this section. The exercises described in this section were developed in collaboration with Coach Horne.

Rationale

Like soccer, basketball and netball involve a surprisingly large contribution from the trunk muscles, which are engaged during contact with opponents (less so in netball) and during vigorous movements to protect the ball from the opposition. Things are arguably more challenging in basketball and netball because the ball is controlled by the hands and because the trunk is frequently in a forward-flexed position (especially in basketball). Although basketball is theoretically a noncontact sport, players are also required to engage in a surprising amount of tussling to maintain advantageous playing positions; this is very challenging for the trunk musculature. The trunk is also heavily involved in passing the ball, both directly (via the use of trunk muscles to contribute to the throw) and indirectly (via the involvement of the diaphragm and other trunk muscles as contributors to core stabilization). As is the case in other team sports, the competing demands of postural control, spinal stabilization, and breathing conspire to overload the breathing muscles. This exacerbates breathing discomfort, impairs the role of the trunk in tactical maneuvering, and increases the risk of injury.

This is where "prehabilitation" of the systems that protect the body from injury, especially the spine, has a role to play. In chapter 1, the role of the breathing muscles in the core-stabilizing system was described; we learned that the diaphragm and other breathing muscles are a vital component of the system that protects the spine. The core has also been identified as a contributor to running performance via its influence on the production of leg power. Integration of IMT into a general core conditioning program is described in chapter 7. In this section, some functional exercises that are specific to basketball and netball are identified. These exercises address the need for optimized core conditioning, and they help players develop the ability to breathe efficiently during activities that involve the trunk.

Objectives

Here are the three key objectives of IMT that is specific to basketball or netball:

1. To enhance the core and pelvic stabilization role of the diaphragm in order to optimize spinal stability and running efficiency

2. To enhance the ability of the respiratory and stabilizing musculature to work together effectively during the varied challenges posed by the game

3. To optimize the role of the trunk in passing the ball and maintaining advantageous playing positions

Exercises

Don't forget the generic functional exercises for team sports provided at the beginning of this chapter.

Exercises for Basketball and Netball

Palloff Press (page 195)

Jump to It (page 213)

Single-Leg Hip to Shoulder Lift (page 237)

Kneeling Diagonal Lift (page 238)

Standing Partner Antirotation (page 239)

Medicine Ball Pivot Series (page 240)

Ski Squats With Alternate Leg Raise and Medicine Ball Rip (page 242)

Bounce and Breathe (page 243)

ICE HOCKEY AND ROLLER HOCKEY

I am indebted to Coach Dan Boothby, director of strength and conditioning at Northeastern University at Boston, for his guidance and extremely insightful contributions to the contents of this section. The exercises described in this section were developed in collaboration with Coach Boothby. Also see Coach Boothby's Top Tips for Hockey Players.

Because hockey involves a good deal of striking the puck on ice, you might also want to refer to the guidance provided in chapter 10 for striking sports, as well as that for sliding sports in chapter 8.

Coach Boothby's Top Tips for Hockey Players

The following breathing-related topics have been highlighted by Coach Boothby as areas for specific focus by hockey athletes.

Stabilization

One of the most important skills that an athlete can possess is the ability to sustain a braced posture while maintaining the demand for breathing. You should practice deep, diaphragm-led breathing during drills and during the exercises described here, because this will enable you to maximize tidal volume* no matter how tough the going gets. At specific times during a game, the trunk muscles will be required suddenly to engage in stabilizing actions, including when passing, shooting, or making contact with other players either on open ice or against the boards. Developing the ability to accommodate stabilizing and breathing simultaneously will decrease the risk of lumbar injury during contact, shooting, and skating.

Impulse

Players must be able to transfer energy through the core in order to pass and shoot, which requires the ability to quickly contract and relax the stabilizing muscles. This skill is vital to on-ice performance, requiring anticipatory skills and the ability to activate the stabilizing musculature precisely and "on cue." This is not as easy as it sounds, because the trunk muscles will be engaged constantly in breathing, which must be accommodated within the periodic demand to provide a stabilizing role. You can practice this during drills and during some of the exercises described in this chapter.

Breathing Recovery

A typical hockey shift is predominantly anaerobic and lasts an average of 40 seconds. The aerobic portion of the sport is the time spent on the bench. Hockey players have consistently been able to log more minutes on the ice when they practice deep breathing techniques during the recovery between shifts (Ray Borque [Boston Bruins], personal communication). Also see the section on cool-downs using a BMT in chapter 6.

*A little known additional benefit of deep inhalation is that, by making the pressure within the chest more negative, it "sucks" blood back toward the heart, which helps to sustain a high cardiac output.

Rationale

In ice hockey, the trunk muscles are subjected to a multitude of challenges, including the effects of protective equipment, maintenance of balance, forward flexion, full contact with opponents and boards, use of the arms to manipulate the stick during passing and possession, rapid changes of speed and direction, and high breathing demand. It's easy to see how the trunk muscles could become overloaded under such conditions. As described for other sports in this chapter, these competing demands conspire to overload the breathing muscles. This exacerbates breathing discomfort, impairs the role of the trunk in tactical maneuvering, and increases the risk of injury.

This is where "prehabilitation" of the systems that protect the body from injury, especially the spine, has a role to play. In chapter 1, the role of the breathing muscles in the core-stabilizing system was described; we learned that the diaphragm and other breathing muscles are a vital component of the system that protects the spine. Integration of IMT into a general core conditioning program is described in chapter 7. In this section, some exercises that are specific to ice hockey are identified. These exercises address the need for optimized core conditioning, and they help players develop the ability to breathe efficiently during activities that involve the trunk.

Objectives

Here are the four key objectives of IMT that is specific to ice and roller hockey:

1. To minimize the influence of protective equipment on breathing effort
2. To enhance the core and pelvic stabilization role of the diaphragm in order to optimize spinal stability and skating efficiency
3. To enhance the ability of the respiratory and stabilizing musculature to work together effectively during the varied challenges posed by the game
4. To optimize the role of the trunk in stick control and puck striking

Exercises

Don't forget the generic functional exercises for team sports provided at the beginning of this chapter. Also, consider doing the exercises while wearing your normal protective equipment (possibly secured a little more tightly than normal).

Exercises for Ice Hockey and Roller Hockey

Ski Squats With Alternate Leg Raise (page 184)

Cross Band Rotation (page 197)

Skater Leg Drives (page 230)

Compressed Shrug and Breathe (page 234)

Point Plank (page 244)

Single-Leg Russian Deadlift With Press (page 245)

Stride Grid (page 246)

FIELD HOCKEY

Because field hockey involves a good deal of striking of the ball, you might also want to refer to the guidance provided in chapter 10 for striking sports.

Rationale

Field hockey challenges the trunk muscles in very similar ways to ice hockey, but without the challenges of protective equipment, clashes with opponents, and maintaining balance on a narrow strip of metal. Thus, in field hockey, the trunk muscles are subjected to the effects of forward flexion, use of the arms to manipulate the stick during passing and possession, rapid changes of speed and direction, and high breathing demand. The stick is much shorter in field hockey, leading to a more forward-flexed position and a greater demand on the trunk muscles. Although the intensity of play is not quite as high as in ice hockey, the opportunities for recovery occur less frequently in field hockey, so the breathing muscles can still become overloaded. As described for other sports in this chapter, the competing demands placed on the breathing muscles conspire to overload them. This exacerbates breathing discomfort, impairs the role of the trunk in tactical maneuvering, and increases the risk of injury.

This is where "prehabilitation" of the systems that protect the body from injury, especially the spine, has a role to play. In chapter 1, the role of the breathing muscles in the core-stabilizing system was described; we learned that the diaphragm and other breathing muscles are a vital component of the system that protects the spine. Integration of IMT into a general core conditioning program is described in chapter 7. In this section, some exercises that are specific to field hockey are identified. These exercises address the need for optimized core conditioning, and they help players develop the ability to breathe efficiently during activities that involve the trunk.

Objectives

Here are the three key objectives of IMT that is specific to field hockey:

1. To enhance the core and pelvic stabilization role of the diaphragm in order to optimize spinal stability and running efficiency
2. To enhance the ability of the respiratory and stabilizing musculature to work together effectively during the varied challenges posed by the game
3. To optimize the role of the trunk in stick control and ball striking

Exercises

Don't forget the generic functional exercises for team sports provided at the beginning of this chapter.

Exercises for Field Hockey

Ski Squats With Alternate Leg Raise (page 184)

Single-Leg Squat Kick (page 204)

Single-Leg Balance With Opposing Arm and Leg Resistance (page 231)

Single-Leg Box Squat (page 247)

RUGBY FOOTBALL

I am indebted to Dr. Paul Gamble for his input to this section (as well as to other sections in this chapter). Dr. Gamble is the national strength and conditioning lead for Scottish Squash and was formerly the head strength and conditioning coach for the London Irish Rugby Football Club. He is also the author of the book *Strength and Conditioning for Team Sports: Sport-Specific Physical Preparation for High Performance* (Gamble, 2010).

Rugby Case Study

Ben played rugby union in the English Premiership. Playing at the position of lock, Ben was among the tallest and most athletic players. As a lock, he had roles in most aspects of the game, including winning the ball at restarts and line-outs, supporting the front row of the scrum, and taking an active role in rucks and mauls. This multitude of roles places a huge demand on locks, who are required to show great anaerobic endurance, as well as strength and power.

At 260 pounds (118 kg) and almost 6 feet 6 inches (2 m) tall, Ben's huge frame had a correspondingly large breathing requirement, and this was an aspect of his fitness that he was always unhappy with. During training and matches, Ben always felt as though he was limited by his ability to breathe, and he never thought he had sufficient time to recover. The higher the standard of rugby that he achieved, the more difficult it became, because the intensity and the demands of the game increased correspondingly.

Ben first encountered IMT as a junior international, but initially, he only used it as part of his prematch warm-up (which he'd found extremely helpful, especially when subbed into a match that had already gained momentum). The strength and conditioning coach at Ben's club then made the decision to implement IMT across the entire squad, incorporating it into their routine as part of a circuit drill.

Within a couple of weeks, Ben began to notice some changes; his breathing felt more relaxed, and he didn't feel the sickening sense of suffocation that had dogged his playing career to date. After an additional 4 weeks, Ben recovered more quickly between bursts of play, and a fitness test (the yo-yo anaerobic endurance test) showed that he had improved more than anyone else on the squad since the previous test, which had been done in the preseason. Indeed, the entire squad was reporting similar experiences to Ben's.

During a training cycle in which the focus was on developing core strength, the coach began to incorporate IMT into static core exercises such as planking and bridging. Ben now found that his ability to function effectively in the scrum and in rucks and mauls was transformed. Previously, he had habitually held his breath during these efforts, but after practicing the IMT during static core work, he found that he had the strength and control to be able to breathe steadily without compromising his ability to perform his role in the play; in addition, Ben's ability to transfer immediately from a scrum, ruck, or maul into open play was also improved—gone was the feeling that he just wanted to stop and catch his breath, and with this came an increase in the pace and intensity of Ben's game.

Rationale

Both codes of the modern game of rugby football (union and league) are among the most physically demanding of all sports. The combined duration, intensity, and diversity of activity during a game of rugby football place unprecedented demands on the trunk muscles. The trunk muscles are subjected to a multitude of challenges, including the effects of rapid changes in running speed and direction; carrying and passing the ball with the hands; full contact with opponents during tackling; participation in rucks, mauls, and scrums (union only); and high breathing demand. As in all of the sports covered in this chapter, the competing demands placed on the breathing muscles conspire to overload them, impairing the role of the trunk muscles in the activities just listed. At best, this results in a heightened sense of breathing effort and an impaired contribution of the trunk muscles to crucial aspects of the game, such as passing, rucks, mauls, and scrums. At worst, the resulting overload heightens the risk of injury.

This is where "prehabilitation" of the systems that protect the body from injury, especially the spine, has a role to play. In chapter 1, the role of the breathing muscles in the core-stabilizing system was described; we learned that the diaphragm and other breathing muscles are a vital component of the system that protects the spine. The core has also been identified as a contributor to running performance via its influence on the production of leg power. Integration of IMT into a general core conditioning program is described in chapter 7. In this section, some rugby-specific exercises are identified. These exercises address the need for optimized core conditioning, and they help players develop the ability to breathe efficiently during activities that involve the trunk. Also see the sidebar on the previous page.

Objectives

Here are the three key objectives of rugby-specific IMT:

1. To enhance the core and pelvic stabilization role of the diaphragm in order to optimize spinal stability and running efficiency
2. To enhance the ability of the respiratory and stabilizing musculature to work together effectively during the varied challenges posed by the game
3. To optimize the role of the trunk in passing the ball

Exercises

Don't forget the generic functional exercises for team sports provided at the beginning of this chapter.

Exercises for Rugby Football

Brace and Breathe (page 167)

Swiss Ball Plank With Elbows on Ball (page 177)

The Dominator (page 187)

Jump to It (page 213)

Alternate Arm Cable Fly (page 248)

Single-Arm Standing Cable Press (page 249)

Ball Snatch (page 250)

Chapter

10

Training for Racket, Striking, and Throwing Sports

This chapter deals with sports that require the participants to use an implement to strike a projectile—such as a racket (e.g., tennis, squash, badminton), club (e.g., golf), or bat (e.g., baseball, softball, cricket)—as well as those sports that involve throwing a ball (pitching and bowling) or implement (track and field). In the case of racket sports, the player is required to direct the ball within the bounds of the court using a range of strokes. Matches are fast paced, requiring speed, agility, and skill. With the exception of the service, strokes are made while the player is in motion. In contrast, in sports such as golf or baseball, the player is able to square up to the ball or pitcher and is stationary as the ball is struck. These two scenarios create very different demands on the breathing muscles. In racket sports, the trunk musculature is involved simultaneously in breathing, postural control, core stabilization, and contributing to racket motion. In a sport such as golf or baseball, the breathing function of the trunk muscles is suspended temporarily in order to concentrate trunk muscle activity on swinging the club (during a drive) or bat as fast as possible through an optimal movement path.

As discussed in chapter 1, the breathing muscles, in particular the diaphragm, play a vital role in postural control and core stabilization. In chapter 2, the concept was developed further by considering the role of the trunk musculature in providing a solid foundation from which to generate arm or bat speed. Without the stable platform of the core, we are just "shooting a cannon from a canoe" (Tsatsouline, 2000)—with very similar results! The exercises suggested in this chapter recognize two common denominators among the various sports that fall under the category of racket, striking, and throwing sports: the involvement of the trunk musculature in providing a stable platform and in protecting the spine; the contribution of the entire trunk musculature to the task of accelerating a racket, club, bat, or arm. The exercises also emphasize the importance of movement and situational specificity. This type of specificity is important in training the trunk muscles to achieve sport-specific performance outcomes as well as in injury prevention.

In any sport that involves striking or throwing an object, the participants need to achieve the correct rhythm. Athletes cannot develop the correct movement rhythm without incorporating the correct breathing rhythm. Human beings appear to have an implicit understanding of this and have a hardwired anticipatory activation of key stabilizing muscles, including the diaphragm, when lifting or encountering postural challenges. It has also been shown that for lifting tasks, the volume and timing of the preceding breath are determined by the size of the load being lifted (a heavier load initiates a larger inhalation immediately before lifting). Therefore, to set up the stroke or throw, you must prepare your breathing so that it flows as part of the natural rhythm of your movement. One way to ensure that this becomes a subconscious element of your repertoire is to practice it over and over again. Accordingly, a starting point for good breathing technique in striking sports is to make breathing part of a rhythmic drill, such as hitting a ball against a wall. Every time you practice the movement, practice the breathing that accompanies it. But what's the correct breathing rhythm? Unfortunately, there is no hard data, but based on the pure mechanics of hitting and throwing, a person should inhale so that this phase is completed just before the start of the stroke or throw, and this should be followed seamlessly (no breath holding on the inhale) by a controlled exhale during the stroke or throw (also see the sidebar titled The Tennis Grunt on the next page). Ideally, the point of contact or release should occur at the transition from inhale to exhale, where lung volume is at its peak and trunk stiffness should be greatest. Remember, practice may not make perfect, but it does make permanent.

Because of the similarity between the racket, striking, and throwing sports, a number of generic exercises are common to all three types of sport, and these are listed at the beginning of this chapter. In addition to these, the sections dealing with each type of sport also contain a small number of specific exercises. Before using any of these exercises, be sure to note the following important principles:

1. If possible, use a cable machine to provide resistance, rather than bands or cords (this is not essential). The resistance should be low to begin with, but it can be developed as the training progresses. Don't overdo the resistance, which is intended primarily to create a postural challenge, not to create a resistance training stimulus to your limbs.

2. If using bands or cords, ensure that these are under tension at the start of the exercise (see the previous point for guidance on cable resistance).

3. Remember that the movement patterns required by racket sports, baseball, golf, throwing, pitching, and so on, are extremely complex and need to be executed precisely to achieve proper form. These require coaching by experts. The exercises in this chapter are *not* intended to teach these movement patterns; rather, they are intended to provide postural challenges that simulate those encountered during the sports in question. In doing so, the exercises

The Tennis Grunt

Almost every year in June (around Wimbledon), I'm contacted by a journalist from some news media or another asking me for my comments on the supposed benefits of the grunt that has become a common part of the modern game of tennis, especially among women. Every year I say that I cannot comment because I have not undertaken any research that would enable me to throw any light onto the benefits (or otherwise) of the grunt. However, in writing *Breathe Strong, Perform Better,* I indulged my curiosity and set about trawling the sport science and coaching literature for some data. Given the amount of media attention that the phenomenon has attracted, I was surprised to find not one single research paper on the topic. That left me with no alternative but to apply my knowledge and to speculate . . .

Disregarding the hype and suggestions that the grunt is merely a cheating tactic to put off opponents, I focused on whether there might be a physiological rationale for grunting. Forceful exhalation during strenuous efforts such as lifting weights is considered normal. Furthermore, research has shown that during lifting tasks, the volume and timing of the preceding breath are determined by the size of the load being lifted (a heavier load means a larger inhalation immediately before lifting). This has been ascribed to the role of breathing in raising intraabdominal pressure, which in turn increases spinal stability (see chapter 1). However, I doubt that this is the whole story, because it disregards the potential importance of intrathoracic pressure in maintaining a stiff thorax, which is also important if the load is in the hands. The expiratory muscles generate much greater intrathoracic pressures when the lungs are fuller, so it's easy to see a link between breath volume and intrathoracic pressure. But why the need for a grunt? Let's say you have just taken a really deep breath to help stiffen your trunk so that you can transmit as much force as possible to a ball; your next problem is when and how to release the breath. Because the contact with the ball is so fleeting (unlike the effort of a bench press), it makes sense to release the air as soon as possible so that you can get on with the business of breathing. However, if you just exhale, you suddenly lose trunk stiffness and any control you had over it, because the length of the muscles that were maintaining the stiffness (the expiratory muscles) has suddenly changed, making them much weaker. This may throw you off balance and break your all-important rhythm. In addition, some people have suggested that a smooth exhale as you strike the ball generates a more relaxed stroke (Ranney, 2008).

One way to "brake" the exhalation of air and to release the pressure in a controlled way without precipitating unwanted tension in the upper body is to use your larynx, or voice box (singers generate huge intrathoracic pressures by doing just this). By narrowing this opening to your lungs, you slow down the rate of airflow from them, while maintaining stiffness in your trunk. Braking exhalation to optimize trunk control may be the function of the grunt. Why doesn't Roger Federer feel the need to grunt, while Nadal, Sharapova, and the Williams sisters do? It may simply be that Mr. Federer is able to produce a controlled exhalation without making any sound. Perhaps the other players can too, but they choose the grunt for psychological reasons (affecting themselves and their opponents).

require the activation of the trunk muscles that contribute to different *parts* of a given movement, not the entire movement. By combining these exercises, it is possible to train all of the muscles that are engaged in the entire movement. Doing so in isolation minimizes the chances of ruining your natural stroke.

4. Even though you have a dominant side, always undertake the exercises on both sides. Not doing so will accentuate existing imbalance and increase the risk of injury.

5. For exercises that incorporate abdominal bracing (see the sidebar titled Tips for Bracing and Posture in chapter 7 on page 114), only add the BMT once you are able to force your diaphragm into the braced abdominal compartment.

You need to ensure that you have good technique for all exercises before adding difficulty. Start by performing each exercise with nothing more than a focus on maintaining slow, deep diaphragmatic breathing throughout. Then add an external resistance to inhalation using a breathing muscle trainer (BMT) set on its minimum load. Gradually increase the load on the BMT over a period of a few weeks until it reaches the prescribed level for the exercise. Please also refer to the sidebar on page 114 of chapter 7 for guidance regarding abdominal bracing and achieving a neutral spine position, as well as the sections on breath control, load setting, and thoracic stretching in chapter 6. In addition, don't forget to consider incorporating breathing intervals into interval training, drills, or circuits (see chapter 6). The breathing training can be introduced into the recovery phase, or it can be a separate station during a drill or circuit.

Choose about five exercises to incorporate into your training each week, and vary these from time to time. This is probably best accomplished by designating one day as a "functional breathing training" day.

I am indebted to Dr. Paul Gamble for his input to this chapter. Dr. Gamble is the national strength and conditioning lead for Scottish Squash and was formerly the head strength and conditioning coach for the London Irish Rugby Football Club. He is also the author of the book *Strength and Conditioning for Team Sports: Sport-Specific Physical Preparation for High Performance* (Gamble, 2010).

Executions of the exercises identified in this chapter are described in chapter 11; refer to the page numbers provided here.

GENERIC FUNCTIONAL EXERCISES FOR RACKET, STRIKING, AND THROWING SPORTS

The following exercises will develop the trunk musculature in ways that are beneficial to all three types of sports. The breathing muscles are an integral part of the kinetic chain that connects the upper and lower body. For sports that require the involvement and coordination of the upper and lower body, athletes need to train the muscles that provide the link between the two. The exercises in this section focus on developing a strong, stable core (providing the foundation for arm movements), as well as developing strength and coordination of the muscles responsible for creating and controlling rotational movements of the trunk and arms.

Generic Functional Exercises

Plank (page 168)

Side Bridge (page 169)

Dynamic Bird Dog (page 181)

Raised Alternating Crunch (page 192)

Swiss Ball Side Crunch (page 193)

Cable Push Pull (page 196)

Cross Band Rotation (page 197)

Wood Chop and Lift (page 198)

Overhead Extension and Flexion (page 205)

T Push-Up (page 209)

Rotating Chest Press (page 263)

Assisted Crossover Lunge (page 264)

Resisted Crossover Lunge (page 265)

RACKET SPORTS

Racket sports are those in which opposing players hit an object back and forth between them on a court (e.g., tennis, table tennis, squash, badminton, racquetball).

Rationale

Unlike the striking sports considered in the next section, racket sports are played with high physical intensity, placing simultaneous demands on the players' trunk muscles for postural control, stabilization, breathing, and the precise movement of a racket. The frequent and extreme forward flexion movements required of players in racket sports make low back problems one of the most common injuries in these sports. This should be no great surprise, given that research suggests that the breathing function predominates in situations where conflicting demands are placed on the breathing muscles. This underscores the importance of ensuring that the trunk musculature is conditioned specifically to cope with the competing demands that are placed on it. In addition, the contribution of the trunk musculature to developing racket speed should not be underestimated; after all, twisting and flexing movements of the trunk are brought about by muscles that also function as important breathing muscles (rib cage and abdominal wall). For the rib cage muscles (intercostal muscles), sports involving forceful twisting movements are associated with an increased risk of thoracic muscle strains and tears. As with other muscle injuries of this kind, the risk of injury can be minimized by strengthening the muscles involved by overloading them in a controlled way during training. Also see the sidebar on page 160.

Tennis Case Study

Rebecca was a junior tennis player who competed at national level in the United Kingdom. At only 15, she had enjoyed a good deal of success, but she had begun to experience bouts of extreme breathlessness during training and competitions. Initially, Rebecca was diagnosed with exercise-induced asthma, but when medication failed to resolve the problem, she was sent for further assessment in a specialist laboratory—which is where I met her.

Further testing revealed that Rebecca's lung function was indeed normal, but when her breathing was examined during exercise, the source of the problem revealed itself. Rebecca had a very inefficient breathing pattern, relying heavily on increasing the breathing rate as ventilatory demand increased. We immediately started Rebecca on a 4-week program of foundation inspiratory muscle training (IMT). This was supplemented by short running sessions each week during which she concentrated on trying to increase breathing volume. Rebecca also began to use a breathing drill during hitting practice in order to help get some rhythm into her stroke. In addition, Rebecca began to include an inspiratory muscle warm-up in her training.

After 4 weeks on the foundation program, Rebecca's inspiratory muscle strength had increased by 32 percent, and her breathing pattern had improved such that tidal (breath) volume increased by an average of 22 percent (making it normal). Her breathing discomfort rating was reduced by 34 percent. I then had Rebecca embark on some of the functional breathing training exercises featured in this chapter. After an additional 4 weeks of functional training, Rebecca's coach reported that all aspects of her game were much improved, and that she seemed to be able to hit the ball harder and to maintain focus and momentum during rallies. This also gave her the ability to dictate the pace of the game, which she had previously been forced to try to slow down so that she could catch her breath. As a result of these improvements, Rebecca moved up the junior rankings later that season. Most important, Rebecca was enjoying her game much more, and she thought that her newfound "breathing power" (as she put it) had liberated her from the doubts and worries that had distracted her before the IMT.

Objectives

Here are the three key objectives of racket-specific breathing muscle training:

1. To enhance the core and pelvic stabilization role of the inspiratory muscles in order to optimize core stability (for injury prevention and racket speed)
2. To enhance the ability of the breathing and stabilizing musculature to work together effectively during the varied challenges posed by the sport (changing speed and direction, lunging, returning, serving, and so on)
3. To enhance the ability of the trunk musculature to contribute to arm speed, as well as minimize the risk of rib muscle injuries

Exercises

Don't forget the generic functional exercises for racket, striking, and throwing sports provided at the beginning of this chapter.

Exercises for Racket Sports

Dynamic Weighted Walking Lunge (page 210)

Jump to It (page 213)

Clockwise Weighted Lunge (page 251)

Slide Board Lunge (page 252)

Racket Lunge (page 253)

Standing Racket Swing (page 254)

Split Squat With Racket Swing (page 255)

Overhead Racket Swing (page 256)

Resisted Lateral Raise (page 257)

Single-Leg Balance With Resisted Shoulder Flexion (page 258)

STRIKING SPORTS

Striking sports include those where the participants are stationary and either strike a stationary ball (e.g., golf) or hit a ball that is moving toward them (e.g., baseball, softball, cricket).

Rationale

Although the role of the trunk musculature in breathing can be suspended briefly in order to focus on striking the ball as hard (e.g., tee shot) or precisely (e.g., putting) as possible, this does not mean that there is nothing to be gained by training the breathing muscles in this context. Participants must also be sure not to overlook the importance of breathing as part of the rhythm of the stroke (as described earlier). Overloading the trunk muscles by forcing them to perform breathing-related activities is an excellent way to provide a training stimulus to these muscles. Indeed, breathing-related actions are the only way that a muscle such as the diaphragm can be trained specifically. When a person undertakes this overload during functional movements, the training can be optimized, and the muscle activation patterns will become grooved (see chapter 2).

As is the case for racket sports, the contribution of the trunk musculature to the task of developing club or bat speed is important in striking sports, and breathing muscles have a part to play in this. Unfortunately, this involvement also means that striking sports are associated with the same increased risk of thoracic muscle strains and tears. As with other muscle injuries of this kind, the risk of injury can be minimized by strengthening the muscles involved.

Objectives

Here are the two key objectives of striking-specific inspiratory muscle training (IMT):

1. To enhance the core and pelvic stabilization role of the inspiratory muscles in order to optimize core stability (for injury prevention and bat or club speed)

2. To enhance the ability of the trunk musculature to contribute to bat or club speed, as well as minimize the risk of rib muscle injuries

Exercises

Don't forget the generic functional exercises for racket, striking, and throwing sports provided at the beginning of this chapter.

Exercises for Striking Sports

Rotating Lift (page 199)

Front Arm Extension (page 259)

Lunge and Swing (page 260)

THROWING SPORTS

Throwing sports include some of the striking sports (e.g., baseball, softball, cricket) but also include the throwing events in track and field.

Rationale

As with striking a ball, the role of the trunk musculature in breathing can be suspended briefly in order to focus on throwing the object as fast or far as possible, but this does not mean that there is nothing to be gained by training the breathing muscles in this context. Overloading the trunk muscles by forcing them to perform breathing-related activities is an excellent way to provide a training stimulus to these muscles. Indeed, breathing-related actions are the only way that a muscle such as the diaphragm can be trained specifically. When a person undertakes this overload during functional movements, the training can be optimized, and the muscle activation patterns will become grooved (see chapter 2).

Similar to swinging a racket, club, or bat, throwing involves a major contribution from the trunk musculature in order to develop arm speed, and the breathing muscles have a part to play in this (see the earlier description). Unfortunately, this involvement also means that throwing sports are associated with the same increased risk of thoracic muscle strains and tears. However, the risk of injury can be minimized by strengthening the muscles involved. Also see the sidebar on the next page.

Making the Most of Diaphragm Breathing

Anxiety and tension are the archenemies of any sport that requires skill and coordination. Deep, relaxed diaphragm breathing has been shown to have an almost mystical power to induce relaxation, and there is even evidence that it reduces blood pressure—so this is founded in physiology, not mumbo jumbo! You can harness this power to help keep a cool head and to promote relaxation in times of physiological and psychological stress. The key to harnessing the relaxing power of diaphragm breathing is to keep it deep and slow. For example, during racket sports, take any pause in play as an opportunity to practice "deep and slow," such as between points and especially during changeovers. In sports such as golf, or before a throw or pitch in baseball, prepare yourself with a few deep and slow breaths—as many as you can perform without disrupting the game. While breathing, mentally rehearse your stroke or throw and visualize success.

Objectives

Here are the two key objectives of throwing-specific IMT:

1. To enhance the core and pelvic stabilization role of the inspiratory muscles in order to optimize core stability (for injury prevention and arm speed)
2. To enhance the ability of the trunk musculature to contribute to arm speed, as well as minimize the risk of rib muscle injuries

Exercises

Don't forget the generic functional exercises for racket, striking, and throwing sports provided at the beginning of this chapter.

Exercises for Throwing Sports

One-Leg Overhead Cable Pulls (page 261)
Standing Cable Chest Press With Lunge (page 262)

Chapter

11

Exercises for Breathing Muscle Training

In this chapter, you will find specific instructions for each of the exercises listed in chapters 7 to 10, as well as a description of the benefits of the exercise. The benefits are summarized in two ways: First, where relevant, the main muscles and muscle groups involved are identified; second, any activity-specific benefits of the exercise are highlighted. For example, the plank is a great generic exercise for a wide range of activities, but the challenges associated with some activities make the plank especially effective for those activities. For instance, in rowing, a stiff trunk and pelvic stability are vital assets that are enhanced by the generic benefits of the plank exercise; by combining the plank exercise with breathing muscle training, rowers can improve their ability to breathe effectively without jeopardizing trunk stiffness and pelvic stability, thereby imparting some activity-specific benefits. The result is that the plank exercise will help to reduce the risk of low back injury, optimize the transmission of force from foot stretcher to blade, and improve breathing efficiency for rowers.

The exercises in this chapter have been divided into two main categories—those that are applicable to more than one sport or activity (generic) and those that are specific to a particular sport or activity. The generic functional exercise category is further divided into broad subcategories based on specific benefits (this categorization is pragmatic and should not be interpreted as a strict classification of the exercises concerned):

- Trunk strength and lumbopelvic stability
- Trunk rotation and antirotation
- Postural control
- Combined rotational and postural challenge

Your starting point for using this chapter should be the section relating to the activity that you are training for. For example, if you are a swimmer, you should review the swimming section of chapter 8. In that section, you will find some background information and a list of all the recommended exercises for swimmers, along with the page number in this chapter where you can find the information for each exercise. Please do not restrict yourself to the recommended exercises; feel free to browse and select additions or alternatives, especially if your sport crosses boundaries, such as trail running. In this case, reviewing the exercises for running as well as hiking and mountaineering would be helpful. However you choose to use this section, please ensure that you select exercises that have specificity to your application—for example, exercises devised for striking sports are of limited benefit to a mountaineer.

BRACE AND BREATHE

Benefits: This exercise is deceptively difficult when executed properly. Breathing into a braced abdominal compartment is like trying to depress the barrel of a blocked syringe; movement of the diaphragm is opposed by the rigid (pressurized) abdominal compartment. However, the effect of the diaphragm movement is to increase internal pressure and stability. For this reason, Brace and Breathe should be considered as a fundamental building block for any activity that requires strenuous bracing (e.g., heavy weightlifting, scrimmaging in rugby football). Without the ability to brace and breathe simultaneously, the spine is vulnerable, and the platform provided by the core is unstable. This exercise is also an excellent method of training all of the muscles that form the "box" structure that comprises the core, including the diaphragm.

IMT loading level: none

Duration: 60 seconds

Sets: 3 sets separated by 30 to 60 seconds of rest (1 standing, 1 sitting, 1 lying)

Procedure: This exercise does not require a BMT, but you must be proficient at diaphragm breathing to do this exercise effectively (see the section on developing an efficient breathing technique in chapter 6 on page 95). The principles are identical whether the exercise is performed standing, sitting, or lying. First brace the abdominal corset muscles by cocontracting the trunk (see the sidebar titled Tips for Bracing and Posture on page 114); effort should be maximal. Next, inhale as deeply as you can, using your diaphragm, without allowing the brace to relax. Relaxation will be evident if your abdomen bulges outward; rest your hands over your abdomen to confirm that the brace is "hard" and that movement is minimized. Inhale slowly (4 seconds in, 4 seconds out [you may need to increase the length of the inspiratory phase once you are able to take deeper breaths]) and focus on pushing your diaphragm into the braced abdominal compartment. Do NOT breathe with your rib cage, because this bypasses the diaphragm (place one hand on your chest and one on your abdomen to feel for movement). This is a tough exercise, but it gets results when you do it right.

PLANK

Benefits: This is a bread-and-butter core exercise for developing trunk strength and lumbopelvic stability. It engages the entire trunk and pelvic stabilizing musculature, including the rectus abdominis, the obliques, the transversus abdominis, and the deep pelvic stabilizers. Breathing muscles not only contribute to trunk stability, but must also function as breathing muscles during stabilization, which is an ability that requires specific training. This exercise is a great way to build your inner strength. It will also help you develop the ability to maintain pelvic stability in the face of large posturally challenging movements of the legs, such as those that occur during running, cycling, and skating. The stable platform of the core also enhances force transmission by the legs and arms, and it is therefore relevant to all sports. Combining this stabilizing exercise with a breathing challenge ensures that you can perform both functions without compromise to either.

IMT loading level: moderate

Duration: 30 to 60 seconds

Sets: 3 sets during static version; 2 or 3 sets per side during variations with limb movements

Procedure: Facing the floor with your BMT in your mouth, rest on your elbows and toes (place your feet as close together as you can), maintaining a straight body line (*a*). Once you are in position, brace the abdominal corset muscles (maximally) and inhale forcefully through your BMT before exhaling slowly and fully for about 4 seconds (breathing rate should be around 12 per minute).

Variations: To add difficulty, do any of the following: Raise one straight leg off the floor and move it toward the ceiling, bring one knee forward to the side of your body toward the same elbow as if climbing a rock face (*b*), or bring one knee in and underneath your body toward the opposite elbow. Inhale in time with the leg movements.

SIDE BRIDGE

Benefits: This is another bread-and-butter core exercise for developing trunk strength and lumbopelvic stability. It engages the trunk and pelvic stabilizing musculature, including the obliques, the transversus abdominis, the deep pelvic stabilizers, and the back extensors. Superimposing the requirement for increased breathing effort onto this exercise helps ensure that the challenge of keeping the trunk stiff doesn't lead to a failure to maintain deep, controlled breathing (see the plank exercise for information on the benefits of a stable core).

IMT loading level: moderate

Duration: 30 to 60 seconds

Sets: 2 or 3 sets per side

Procedure: Place your feet together and then balance on one hand, with your hips facing forward and your feet on top of one another. Once stable, brace the abdominal corset muscles (maximally) and inhale forcefully through your BMT before exhaling slowly and fully for about 4 seconds (breathing rate should be around 12 per minute). Make sure you maintain a completely straight body line and do not flex at the hip or abdomen.

Variations: To add difficulty, raise your top arm and leg during the inhalation phase of the exercise.

BRIDGE

Benefits: This exercise involves the deep lumbopelvic stabilizers, the rectus abdominis, the transversus abdominis, the back extensors, the gluteals, and the hamstrings. It helps develop balance between the muscles of the front and back of the body. When undertaken with a leg lift, the exercise challenges the ability to maintain pelvic alignment (if your unsupported hip drops toward the floor, your deep stabilizers are weak). This is a great exercise for developing stiffness in the core, which helps optimize the leg drive during running and helps minimize the loss of efficiency due to trunk flexion. Superimposing the requirement for increased breathing effort onto this exercise also helps ensure that the challenge of keeping the trunk and pelvis stiff doesn't lead to a failure to maintain deep, controlled breathing.

IMT loading level: moderate

Duration: 10 repetitions

Sets: 2 sets

Procedure: Lie on your back and prop yourself either on your elbows (most difficult; a) or on your hands (easiest; b) with your weight on your heels and a straight body line. With your BMT in your mouth, brace the abdominal corset muscles (maximally) and raise a straight leg as high as you can (you will need to work hard not to sag in the middle or tilt to one side). As you raise your leg, inhale forcefully through your BMT before exhaling slowly as you lower it. Then repeat using the opposite leg. Swap breathing phases between sets so that you exhale as you lift your leg.

BRIDGE WITH BENT KNEES

Benefits: Like the bridge exercise, this exercise involves the deep lumbopelvic stabilizers, the rectus abdominis, the transversus abdominis, the back extensors, the gluteals, and the hamstrings. Although it's not quite as challenging as its straight-leg counterpart, this exercise still helps to generate balance between the muscles of the front and back of the body, and it challenges pelvic stability. This exercise will help ensure that you can use a higher knee lift during running without causing overrotation of the hips and a loss of efficiency. Adding the breathing challenge will ensure that a high breathing demand does not jeopardize this ability.

IMT loading level: moderate

Duration: 10 repetitions

Sets: 2 sets

Procedure: Lie on your back and prop yourself on your elbows, with your knees bent, your weight on your heels, and your trunk parallel with the floor (a). With your BMT in your mouth, brace the abdominal corset muscles (maximally) and raise your foot off the floor until your leg is fully extended (b); you will need to work hard not to sag in the middle. As you raise your leg, inhale forcefully through your BMT before exhaling slowly as you lower it. Then repeat using the opposite leg. Swap breathing phases between sets so that you exhale as you lift your leg.

STRAIGHT LEG RAISE

Benefits: This is a good exercise for challenging the rectus abdominis, transversus abdominis, hip flexors, and back muscles. As with other static exercises, this one challenges the ability to maintain lumbopelvic stability without suspending breathing.

IMT loading level: moderate

External resistance: ankle weights

Duration: 30 to 60 seconds

Sets: 2 or 3 sets

Procedure: Lie on your back with your BMT in your mouth and with your arms at your sides. Push your back toward the floor, concentrating on maintaining a neutral spine (it may help to place your fingers under the small of your back). Raise your feet about 6 to 8 inches (15 to 20 cm) off the floor and brace your abdominal corset muscles (maximally). Once in position, inhale forcefully through the BMT before exhaling slowly and fully for about 4 seconds (breathing rate should be around 12 per minute).

Variations: To add difficulty, extend duration, add ankle weights, or move your legs in a continuous scissor action, breathing steadily throughout.

BRACED CURL-UP

Benefits: This is a good exercise for challenging all of the key trunk-stiffening muscles, especially the rectus abdominis and transversus abdominis. During this exercise, the rectus abdominis and other expiratory muscles pull the ribs downward in an expiratory movement. Developing the ability to inhale under these conditions will enhance the ability to breathe during situations when the body movements and breathing are out of phase in terms of the actions required of the breathing muscles—that is, inhaling during activation of expiratory muscles and vice versa.

IMT loading level: moderate

Duration: 60 to 90 seconds

Sets: 3 to 6 sets

Procedure: Lie on your back with your knees bent slightly, your back pressed into the floor (it may help to place your fingers under the small of your back), and your BMT in your mouth. Brace your abdominal corset muscles (maximally). Curl up and raise your shoulders off the floor (3 to 4 inches [8 to 10 cm]), curling into the brace and keeping your neck position neutral (don't allow your chin to rest on your chest). While in the up position, take three to six rapid but deep and force-ful inhalations through the BMT. Maintain the up position for long enough to complete the required number of breath reps. Make sure you maintain the brace during the up phase. Then relax, release the brace, and rest your shoulders on the floor for no more than 2 or 3 seconds before repeating (15 to 30 seconds up, 2 or 3 seconds down).

Variations: To add difficulty, take your feet off the floor and pulse them up and down a few inches. Here are two other alternatives: Keep one leg extended, either resting on the floor or raised 2 to 3 inches (swap legs between sets); extend one leg and the opposite arm, raising them off the floor in time with your inhalations (swap limbs between sets).

SWISS BALL PLANK WITH FEET ON BALL

Benefits: This is a slightly more advanced version of the plank (see the plank exercise to learn the muscles involved); a postural control dimension is added to the exercise so that trunk stabilization has to be maintained under conditions of instability. This is especially challenging for the breathing muscles, which must not only contend with their role in maintaining trunk stiffness, but must also contend with variations in muscle activation patterns that are created by instability. Because the lower body is the unstable section, the emphasis is on the pelvic stabilizers. This exercise is especially beneficial for athletes in sports where trunk stiffness and core stability must be maintained in the face of instability. For example, the exercise can help athletes meet the need to maintain a dynamic, balanced, but fixed position during events such as cycling time trials and rowing (on water).

IMT loading level: moderate

Duration: 30 to 60 seconds

Sets: 2 or 3 sets

Procedure: Assume a press-up position with your ankles resting on a Swiss ball and with your BMT in your mouth; brace your abdominal corset muscles (moderately) and make sure that you have a completely straight body line, with your spine in a neutral position. Once in position, inhale forcefully through the BMT before exhaling slowly and fully for about 4 seconds (breathing rate should be around 12 per minute).

Variations: To add difficulty, move the ankles closer together, or gently rotate the ball sideways, controlling its movement with your trunk muscles.

SWISS BALL SQUAT THRUST

Benefits: This exercise is a variation of the Swiss Ball Plank With Feet on Ball and includes all of the demands of that exercise, plus the added challenge of hip flexion. It involves the lumbopelvic stabilizers, the rectus abdominis, the transversus abdominis, the obliques, and the back muscles. The Swiss ball adds a postural control challenge and tests your ability to control the upper and lower body (independently) during trunk flexion. Superimposing the requirement for increased breathing effort onto this exercise also helps ensure that this challenge doesn't lead to a failure to maintain deep, controlled breathing.

IMT loading level: moderate

Duration: 10 to 15 repetitions

Sets: 2 sets

Procedure: Assume a press-up position with your ankles resting on a Swiss ball and with your BMT in your mouth; brace your abdominal corset muscles (moderately) and ensure that you have a completely straight body line and your spine is in a neutral position (a). Once in position, lift your pelvis up and bend your knees, rolling the ball toward your hands (b). As you do so, inhale forcefully through the BMT, exhaling as you roll the ball back to the start position. Swap breathing phases on the second set.

GENERIC FUNCTIONAL EXERCISES

SWISS BALL PIKE

Benefits: This exercise is another variation of the Swiss Ball Plank With Feet on Ball and includes all of the demands of that exercise, plus the added challenge of hip flexion. It involves the rectus abdominis, transversus abdominis, obliques, hip flexors, quadriceps, and triceps. This exercise develops the strength, endurance, and coordination of the trunk and hip flexor musculature. In sports such as cycling, these muscles are vital for climbing and sprinting. In rowing, they play an important role at the start of a race, where blade forces are highest and the emphasis is on accelerating the boat as quickly as possible. The addition of the breathing challenge to the exercise ensures that trunk stability and hip flexor strength do not come at the cost of breathing.

IMT loading level: moderate

Duration: 10 to 15 repetitions

Sets: 2 sets

Procedure: Assume a press-up position with your shins resting on a Swiss ball and with your BMT in your mouth; brace your abdominal corset muscles (moderately), making sure that you have a straight body line and that your spine is in a neutral position (a). Once in position, lift your pelvis upward and roll the ball toward your hands, keeping your legs straight (b). As you do this, inhale forcefully through the BMT, exhaling slowly and fully as you return to the start position. Swap breathing cycles on the second set (exhale as you move your pelvis up).

SWISS BALL PLANK WITH ELBOWS ON BALL

Benefits: This is another variation of the plank (see the plank exercise to learn the muscles involved) that adds a postural control dimension to the exercise so that trunk stabilization has to be maintained under conditions of instability. The breathing muscles must not only contend with their role in maintaining trunk stiffness, but must also contend with variations in muscle activation patterns that are created by instability. Because the upper body is the unstable section, the trunk stabilizers make a larger contribution to the task of maintaining stability. This exercise helps you develop control over the linkage between movements of the upper body and the "seat of power" in the lower body. When you are pushing hard with the lower-body force producers, power delivery is compromised if this linkage is allowed to flex so that what's happening below your waist destabilizes your trunk. This exercise therefore has relevance to cycling, as well as to sports that involve running. The exercise is also helpful in a sport such as rugby; during a scrum or maul, players need to maintain trunk stability while the object they are pushing against is moving. This exercise enhances the ability to breathe freely while maintaining trunk stability when the body weight is resting on an unstable platform.

IMT loading level: moderate

Duration: 30 to 60 seconds

Sets: 2 or 3 sets

Procedure: Rest your elbows on the top of the Swiss ball and take the weight on your toes (feet slightly apart), adopting a straight body line. Your BMT should be in your mouth. Be careful to keep your hip position neutral and not to round your shoulders. Once in position, inhale forcefully through the BMT before exhaling slowly and fully for about 4 seconds (breathing rate should be around 12 per minute).

Variations: To add difficulty, move the feet closer together, or gently rotate the ball sideways, controlling its movement with your trunk muscles. You can also lift one foot off the floor.

GLUTEAL BRIDGE WITH SHOULDERS ON FLOOR

Benefits: This is a good exercise for challenging the gluteals, hamstrings, and back muscles, as well as the deep pelvic stabilizers. If your pelvis tilts toward the floor when you take the weight off one foot, your deep stabilizers are weak. This exercise challenges the ability to breathe effectively during full hip extension.

IMT loading level: moderate

Duration: 30 to 60 seconds

Sets: 2 or 3 sets

Procedure: Lie on the floor with your knees bent and with your BMT in your mouth. Raise your hips toward the ceiling, activating your gluteals while maintaining a straight body line through the knees, hips, and trunk (this requires maintenance of full hip extension). Once your weight is on your shoulders and heels, inhale forcefully through the BMT before exhaling slowly and fully for about 4 seconds (breathing rate should be around 12 per minute).

Variations: To add difficulty, raise one foot off the floor and straighten it in line with the rest of your body; hold for 5 seconds. Alternate the raised leg for the duration of the exercise. Be careful to maintain a straight body line and to keep the hips level. Inhale in time with each leg lift.

GLUTEAL BRIDGE WITH SHOULDERS ON BALL

Benefits: This core development exercise produces a particular challenge for lumbo-pelvic stability, and it involves the gluteals, the rectus abdominis, the transversus abdominis, the obliques, the back muscles, and the thigh muscles. The instability created by the ball will help "groove" the correct activation patterns of the pelvic stabilizer muscles, as well as develop their strength (see the plank exercise for information on the benefits of a stable core). This is especially challenging for the breathing muscles, which must not only contend with their role in maintaining trunk stiffness, but must also contend with variations in muscle activation patterns that are created by instability.

IMT loading level: moderate

Duration: 30 to 60 seconds

Sets: 2 or 3 sets

Procedure: Lie on your back with your shoulders and head resting on a Swiss ball, your feet on the ground (hip-width apart), and your BMT in your mouth. Raise your hips, activating your gluteals, and brace your abdominal corset muscles (moderately) to adopt a straight body line through the knees, hips, and trunk. Once in position, inhale forcefully through the BMT before exhaling slowly and fully for about 4 seconds (breathing rate should be around 12 per minute).

Variations: To add difficulty, raise one foot off the floor and straighten it in line with the rest of your body; hold for 5 seconds. Alternate the raised leg for the duration of the exercise. Be careful to maintain a straight body line and to keep the hips level. Inhale in time with each leg lift.

SWISS BALL BRIDGE

Benefits: This exercise adds a postural instability dimension to the standard bridge exercise (see the bridge exercise to learn the muscles involved). As with other Swiss ball exercises in this section, this exercise promotes the development of "grooved" activation patterns that will permit the automatic activation of pelvic stabilizing activity in the face of an increased breathing demand.

IMT loading level: moderate

Duration: 30 to 60 seconds

Sets: 2 or 3 sets

Procedure: Lie on your back with your heels on the top of the Swiss ball (feet slightly apart), adopting a straight body line, with your BMT in your mouth. Brace your abdominal corset muscles (moderately). Once in position, inhale forcefully through the BMT before exhaling slowly and fully for about 4 seconds (breathing rate should be around 12 per minute). Make sure that you maintain a straight body line through the heels, hips, and trunk—but be careful not to push the hips up too high by arching your back.

Variations: To add difficulty, move the feet closer together, or gently rotate the ball sideways, controlling its movement with your pelvic and trunk muscles.

DYNAMIC BIRD DOG

Benefits: This exercise is a bread-and-butter exercise for promoting healthy, "grooved" muscle activation patterns, while ensuring that this can be combined (automatically) with breathing. It involves the deep pelvic stabilizers and the extensors of the hip and lumbar spine, as well as the transversus abdominis. This exercise places a particular emphasis on developing lumbopelvic stability.

IMT loading level: moderate

External resistance: wrist and ankle weights

Duration: 10 to 20 repetitions

Sets: 2 sets (1 for each side)

Procedure: Go into a kneeling position with your hands on the floor and with your BMT in your mouth. Once you are in position, brace the abdominal corset muscles (moderately), ensuring that you maintain a neutral spine. Lift your left hand and right knee off the floor and extend your arm and leg until both are horizontal. As you swing your arm and leg toward the horizontal position, inhale against your BMT. Pause for 1 or 2 seconds and commence a slow, controlled exhale as you bring your hand and knee back toward the floor (swap breathing phases between sets). Do not allow your hand and knee to touch the floor; instead, bring them together under your body, and then immediately return your arm and leg to the horizontal position and inhale. Make sure that your back remains flat and that your shoulders and hips remain level. Complete the required number of reps as a continuous set before swapping sides. Swap breathing phases halfway through the set so that you exhale as your limbs are lifted to horizontal.

Variations: To add difficulty, wrist and ankle weights can be used. You can also pause in the extended position to "draw" a square in the air with your hand and foot, inhaling against your BMT as you do this.

FULL-RANGE HIP EXTENSION AND FLEXION

Benefits: This exercise is a variation of the Dynamic Bird Dog. It challenges postural control and involves the thoracic and abdominal flexors, the hamstrings, and the extensors of the lumbar spine and hip. The exercise combines the need for coordinated activation of the deep muscles that stabilize the lumbopelvic complex (including the gluteals) with the additional challenge of a unilateral destabilizing force originating at the hip. Because it helps to develop and maintain good form during sprinting and uphill running, this exercise is good for all activities that involve running.

IMT loading level: moderate

External resistance: ankle weights

Duration: 10 to 20 repetitions

Sets: 2 sets (1 on each side)

Procedure: Assume a kneeling position with your hands on the floor and your BMT in your mouth (*a*). Once you are in position, brace the abdominal corset muscles (moderately), ensuring that you maintain a neutral spine. Keeping your knee flexed, move your left foot toward the ceiling swiftly (but controlled), extending as far as you can at the hip (*b*). As you extend your leg upward, inhale against your BMT (tighten your gluteals and brace your core). Pause for 1 or 2 seconds in the extended position before commencing a slow, controlled exhale as you bring your knee back toward the floor. Do not allow your knee to touch the floor; instead, bring it as far forward as you can, under your body, crunching your abdominal muscles as you do so (don't allow your shoulders to tilt or drop) (*c*). Pause for 1 or 2 seconds in the flexed position before extending again. Concentrate on keeping your hips and shoulders level at all times. Swap breathing phases halfway through the set.

Variations: To add difficulty, ankle weights can be used. You can also kneel on a balance cushion.

DYNAMIC SUPERMAN

Benefits: This exercise is primarily for the back extensors, but it also challenges the gluteals and shoulder flexors. Inhalation is challenged by the stiffening of the trunk induced by the trunk extensor activity combined with the abdominal compression of resting on the abdomen.

IMT loading level: moderate

External resistance: wrist and ankle weights

Duration: 30 to 60 repetitions

Sets: 2 or 3 sets

Procedure: Lie facedown on the floor with your arms extended in front of you and with your BMT in your mouth. Raise and lower your opposite arm and leg (e.g., right arm with left leg), lifting your trunk slightly with each repetition. Inhale forcefully through your BMT on the up phase (swap between sets to inhale on the down phase). As soon as you have reached the top of the movement, immediately lower your arm and leg and start raising the opposite limbs. At first, place the resting limbs on the floor (try not to rest too heavily). Then, as you become more adept, let the resting limbs just hover above the floor.

Variations: To add difficulty, use wrist and ankle weights. As an alternative, you can pulse the same limbs for 30 seconds before swapping sides.

SKI SQUATS WITH ALTERNATE LEG RAISE

Benefits: This exercise involves the lumbopelvic stabilizers, quadriceps, gluteals, and hip flexors. It will help you develop the ability to keep the hips level, and it puts emphasis on the development of strength in the lumbopelvic stabilizers. In a sport such as cycling, this helps the athlete maintain a balanced, aerodynamic body position when surging in the saddle. In sliding sports, where weight is transferred from one leg to the other, improving pelvic stability will enhance postural control, as well as increase the efficiency of the leg drive. In soccer, pelvic stability will enhance kicking performance. The added breathing challenge helps ensure that forceful breathing does not jeopardize pelvic stability.

IMT loading level: moderate

Duration: 30 to 60 seconds

Sets: 2 or 3 sets

Procedure: Assume the ski squat position with your back resting against a wall and your thighs as close to horizontal as you can manage (a). With your BMT in your mouth, adopt a neutral spine alignment. Once you are in position, brace the abdominal corset muscles (moderately) and extend one knee so that your weight is on the opposite leg (b); as you do this, inhale forcefully through your BMT before exhaling slowly and fully for about 3 seconds as you return to the start position (breathing rate should be around 15 per minute). Be careful not to allow your hip to drop to the unsupported side. Repeat with the opposite leg, alternating for as many reps as you can manage. Swap breathing phases between sets.

Variations: To add difficulty, deepen the squat, place a Swiss ball between your back and the wall, or stand on a balance cushion. You can also do repeats on the same leg and then swap legs on the next set.

LYING LATERAL LEG SWEEP

Benefits: This exercise challenges the ability to control trunk rotation during pelvic rotation. It is a good exercise for challenging the rectus abdominis and the obliques, as well as the deep pelvic stabilizers. The strong involvement of the rectus abdominis also impedes inhalation (see the braced curl-up exercise). This exercise will benefit activities requiring the ability to control trunk and pelvic counter-rotation, such as running and racket sports.

IMT loading level: moderate

External resistance: ankle weights

Duration: 10 to 15 repetitions

Sets: 2 sets

Procedure: Lie on your back with your arms out to the sides and with your BMT in your mouth. Lift your legs into the air so that they are at 90 degrees to your body; keep your legs straight and your spine in a neutral position (*a*). Move your legs over to one side, keeping your upper back and shoulders on the floor (*b*); go as far as you can without losing control. Inhale forcefully through your BMT as you lower your legs. Once you've gone as far as you can, pause momentarily before pulling your legs up to vertical, exhaling as you do; then move your legs over to the opposite side, inhaling again (swap breathing phases between sets, exhaling when lowering the legs and inhaling when raising them). Once you return to the upright position for the second time, you have completed one repetition.

Variations: To add difficulty, use ankle weights.

BENT-LEG DEADLIFT

Benefits: This exercise has been described as "the best core exercise of them all," because it is such a great challenge to the entire lumbopelvic stabilizing system, as well as to the trunk (from ankles to shoulders). It involves the hamstrings, gluteals, deep lumbopelvic stabilizers, quadriceps, rib cage, and back muscles. This exercise is a staple of weight training, but it carries a high risk of injury if not performed with good style. A common fault is losing the flat-back posture, and this can occur if the drive to breathe overwhelms the ability to maintain the braced position. By using a manageable weight and imposing a breathing challenge simultaneously, you can train to accommodate the dual demands that these challenges impose.

IMT loading level: light to moderate

External resistance: dumbbells or bar (15RM load)

Duration: 10 repetitions

Sets: 2 sets separated by 30 to 60 seconds of rest

Procedure: Standing upright with your feet shoulder-width apart and your BMT in your mouth, bend down and grasp the weight on either side of your knees (knees bent slightly) (a). Once you are in position, brace the abdominal corset muscles (moderately). As you drive upward, inhale forcefully through your BMT throughout the drive (exhale as you lower the weight) (b). Alternate this pattern between sets so that you exhale as you lift and inhale as you lower the weight. Concentrate on not allowing the brace to release during either phase of breathing. Also concentrate on maintaining good lifting form and extending fully at the hip.

THE DOMINATOR

Benefits: This exercise has much in common with the Bent-Leg Deadlift, and it is a great exercise for developing your ability to overcome opponents in full-contact sports (pick them up and throw them down). It involves the hamstrings, gluteals, deep lumbopelvic stabilizers, quadriceps, rib cage, and back muscles, as well as the biceps. This exercise promotes activation of the entire trunk musculature, as well as the legs. It also challenges your ability to maintain postural control while being pulled off balance. By adding a breathing challenge, you can work on optimizing the functional (postural) link between the upper and lower body, as well as the ability to breathe effectively during physically strenuous tasks involving the entire trunk.

IMT loading level: moderate

External resistance: weight bar bearing 22 to 44 pounds (10 to 20 kg) on the top of the bar (you can use another small disk weight to help anchor the base of the bar on the floor), or a "Dominator" machine (www.getstrength.com)

Duration: 15 to 20 repetitions

Sets: 2 sets

Procedure: Stand with your feet slightly more than shoulder-width apart and with the loaded bar positioned vertically at arm's length (a). With your BMT in your mouth, your spine in a neutral position, and your abdominal corset muscles braced (moderately), allow the top of the bar to move sideways, toward the floor (b). Do not oppose the weight by sitting back against it; instead, try to stand as upright as possible. Controlling the fall of the bar, inhale forcefully through your BMT. Exhale as you wrestle the bar to the upright position once more. Repeat the maneuver without pausing in the upright position, but allow the bar to fall at a slightly different angle. On the second set, swap breathing phases so that you inhale as you wrestle the bar upright and exhale as you control its descent.

Variations: You can add difficulty by increasing the amount of weight on the bar and standing more upright.

Add weight here.

187

BARBELL OVERHEAD STEP-UP

Benefits: This exercise combines the need for lumbopelvic and thoracic stabilization with a demand for postural control. It involves the quadriceps, gluteals, deep lumbopelvic stabilizers, and back. It is a great compound exercise that has generic applicability to a wide range of sporting contexts, but especially to weightlifting and team sports.

IMT loading level: light to moderate

External resistance: barbell or dumbbells (15RM load), step or box

Duration: 15 repetitions

Sets: 2 sets separated by 30 to 60 seconds of rest

Procedure: Standing upright with your feet shoulder-width apart and your BMT in your mouth, brace the abdominal corset muscles (moderately). Press the weight above your head and begin stepping (a). Step up with your left leg and stand on this leg briefly on the step, keeping your right leg unweighted (b). Then step down, leading with your right leg, and return to the start position standing on both feet in front of the step. Alternate the lead stepping leg with each repetition, and step at a comfortable but challenging pace. Inhale forcefully through your BMT as you step up (swap the breathing phase between sets so that you are inhaling as you step down).

Variations: Increase the size of the weight or the height of the step.

BARBELL SINGLE-LEG SQUAT

Benefits: This lumbopelvic stabilizing exercise helps improve postural control, and it involves the quadriceps, gluteals, deep lumbopelvic stabilizers, and back. The single-leg stance creates a huge tipping force across the pelvis, which must remain balanced. This is another great compound exercise that can start with body weight and progress to lifting a barbell. Ensure that you have good form before adding a barbell. The addition of the breathing challenge enhances the ability to stabilize the pelvis in the face of a high breathing demand. This is a good exercise for sports that involve lunging or going up hills.

IMT loading level: light to moderate

External resistance: barbell, step or box

Duration: 10 repetitions

Sets: 2 sets

Procedure: Standing upright with your feet shoulder-width apart, your BMT in your mouth, and the barbell on your shoulders or upper back, brace the abdominal corset muscles (moderately). Assume a split stance with your rear foot resting on a stable step or box (a). Squat on your front leg until your thigh is parallel with the floor (it may take some time to achieve this depth, but this should be your aim) (b). Inhale forcefully through your BMT as you squat (swap breathing phases halfway through the set so that you are inhaling as you stand). Swap leading legs between sets.

Variations: Increase the depth of the squat and the size of the weight.

SQUAT WITH OVERHEAD RESISTANCE

Benefits: This is a surprising little exercise that is more challenging than it appears, involving the quadriceps, gluteals, lumbopelvic stabilizers, upper back, shoulders, and chest. The exercise also challenges postural control. By combining a body weight squat with an additional challenge to the trunk (from the overhead resistance) and a breathing challenge, you end up with something much more challenging than a conventional squat. Think of this exercise as one that will enhance your ability to coordinate and control multiple actions involving large muscle groups.

IMT loading level: light to moderate

Duration: 30 to 60 seconds (30 seconds for a beginner; 60 seconds for an expert)

Sets: 4 sets separated by 30 to 60 seconds of rest

Procedure: Standing upright with your feet shoulder-width apart and your BMT in your mouth, place your hands above your head with one palm resting on the back of the other hand. Once you are in position, brace the abdominal corset muscles (moderately) and press your hands together, ensuring that the brace and the hand pressure are maintained throughout the squat exercise. The squat should be to a knee angle of about 130 degrees (roughly a half squat); squat at a comfortable but challenging pace, concentrating on maintaining hand pressure and squat style. Squat down while inhaling forcefully through your BMT (exhale as you stand up). You can alternate this pattern between sets so that you exhale into the squat and inhale as you stand. Halfway through each set, swap hands so that the opposite hand is in front.

Variations: In addition to increasing duration, you can make the exercise more challenging by increasing cadence, squeezing a weight between your hands, or standing on a large balance cushion or a Bosu.

SWISS BALL SIDE ROTATION

Benefits: This trunk rotation and flexion exercise involves the rectus abdominis, transversus abdominis, obliques, and back and rib cage muscles. It is great for developing the ability to separate movements of the upper and lower body, without sacrificing the need to breathe in the process. It requires the shoulders to remain static while a rotational movement takes place below the waist. You start this exercise in the same posture as for the Swiss Ball Plank With Feet on Ball (see the benefits on page 174) before moving into a rotational crunch. This exercise is beneficial for people in sports that involve counter-rotation of the upper body; in this context, the core must control the extent of the rotation while maintaining a solid foundation for force production (e.g., during the "mule kick" of a skater's leg drive). Similarly, in striking and throwing sports, the transfer of force from the ground must be made in a controlled and efficient way via the hips and trunk (e.g., the baseball swing). Sports such as sweep rowing also require the coordinated but separate control of the upper and lower body. Like many exercises that involve the trunk, this one is associated with some chest compression, so combining it with a breathing exercise that requires forceful inhalation helps you build the ability to inhale during movements that compress the chest.

IMT loading level: moderate

Duration: 15 to 20 repetitions

Sets: 2 sets (1 on each side)

Procedure: Assume a press-up position with your shins resting on a Swiss ball (feet apart) and with your BMT in your mouth; make sure you have a completely straight body line (*a*). Once stable, and keeping your feet on the ball, draw your left knee toward your right elbow (keep your knees together, your arms straight, and your shoulders level), and inhale forcefully through the BMT before returning to the start position, exhaling as you do so (swap breathing phases halfway through the set) (*b*). After completing the desired number of reps on one side, swap sides.

GENERIC FUNCTIONAL EXERCISES

RAISED ALTERNATING CRUNCH

Benefits: This is a trunk rotation and flexion exercise that develops the ability to separate the upper and lower body. Although it has some common ground with the Swiss Ball Side Rotation, the rotation takes place in the upper body, and with greater activation of trunk flexors; because the trunk is not loaded, this exercise is also less demanding from a strength perspective (see the benefits for the Swiss Ball Side Rotation on page 191).

IMT loading level: moderate

Duration: 15 to 20 repetitions

Sets: 2 sets

Procedure: Sit on the floor with your hips flexed slightly, your knees bent, your feet off the floor, your hands behind your head (elbows in line with your shoulders), and your BMT in your mouth. Brace your abdominal corset muscles (moderately) and move your left elbow toward your right knee, keeping both feet off the floor, your elbows in line with your shoulders, and your spine in a neutral position (you should be balancing on your gluteals). As you bring your elbow and knee together, inhale forcefully through the BMT; exhale as you return to the start position and then crunch in the opposite direction. Swap breathing phases between sets.

SWISS BALL SIDE CRUNCH

Benefits: This lateral trunk flexion exercise involves not only the oblique muscles, but also those of the rib cage. Developing these muscles is beneficial to athletes in any sport that involves twisting or flexing the trunk (e.g., at the catch in sweep rowing, or during the tennis serve). These muscles also play a role in stabilizing the trunk during less obvious activities such as when cycling out of the saddle. Strengthening the rib cage muscles will also help to protect the rib cage from injury (e.g., rib stress fractures and muscle tears) in sports that place great stress on the rib cage, such as rowing and striking or throwing sports. This exercise essentially compresses the rib cage, so combining it with a breathing exercise that requires forceful inhalation will help you build the ability to inhale during movements that compress the chest.

IMT loading level: moderate

External resistance: disk weight or dumbbell

Duration: 15 to 20 repetitions

Sets: 2 sets (1 on each side)

Procedure: Position your hip sideways on the ball, and brace your feet against a wall (one slightly in front of the other); your BMT should be in your mouth. Make sure you have as straight a body line as possible from ankles to shoulder (*a*). Place the hand of your lower arm to your temple and the other hand on your hip, then flex your upper body toward the wall, inhaling forcefully through your BMT as you crunch (*b*). Exhale as you return to the start position (swap breathing phases halfway through each set).

Variations: To add difficulty, clasp a small disk weight or dumbbell to your chest.

KNEELING LATERAL ROTATION

Benefits: This exercise involves the rectus abdominis, transversus abdominis, obliques, and back and rib cage muscles. The obliques are responsible for controlling the counter-rotation of the shoulders during running. Too much rotation will generate instability and inefficiency. When runners are breathing heavily, it is not unusual to see their shoulders rolling more than normal. This is caused by the conflict between breathing and postural control (breathing is in charge). This exercise will help you develop the ability to control trunk movement, even when breathing demand is high. For striking and throwing sports, the exercise develops the strength of the muscles responsible for producing trunk rotation.

IMT loading level: moderate

External resistance: cable pulley machine or elastic resistance band or cord

Duration: 15 to 20 repetitions

Sets: 2 sets (1 on each side)

Procedure: Kneel facing side on to the resistance source with your BMT in your mouth, your spine in neutral, your abdominal corset muscles braced (moderately), and your shoulders turned toward the anchor point of the resistance. Your hips should remain facing forward (a). Rotate your upper body away from the anchor point, inhaling forcefully through your BMT as you do so (b). Halfway through the set, swap breathing phases so that you exhale as you rotate away from the anchor point. On the second set, place the resistance on the opposite side of your body and repeat. You can add difficulty by increasing the resistance or kneeling on an unstable surface and keeping your toes off the floor.

PALLOFF PRESS

Benefits: In every team sport, there are times during the game where you must battle to prevent an opponent from dislodging you from possession or from an advantageous playing position (e.g., the post position in basketball). This requires the ability to resist rotational forces that disrupt your center of gravity. The Palloff Press exercise requires you to resist a rotational force and helps you develop the ability to breathe effectively in a posturally challenging position. It's tougher than it looks; watch out for asymmetry when you swap sides, and work to correct this.

IMT loading level: moderate

External resistance: cable pulley machine or elastic resistance band or cord

Duration: 10 to 15 repetitions (each rep is held for 3 to 5 seconds at the end position)

Sets: 2 to 4 sets (1 or 2 on each side)

Procedure: Assume a bilateral one-quarter squat position facing sideways to either a cable column or the anchor point of an elastic resistance band. With tension on the band, or weight through a cable column, hold the band or handle at midsternum level with both hands (a). With your BMT in your mouth, your spine in a neutral position, and your abdominal corset muscles braced (moderately), extend the handle directly forward in a straight line while resisting the rotational force that is being applied to your outstretched arms (b). As you extend your arms forward, inhale forcefully through your BMT, and hold this end position for 3 to 5 seconds. Exhale as you bring your hands back toward your chest. Without pausing, repeat the maneuver, swapping breathing phases halfway through the set so that you exhale as you extend your hands forward. If you have difficulty engaging and maintaining the abdominal corset brace, begin this exercise in a tall kneeling position.

CABLE PUSH PULL

Benefits: This is an excellent trunk antirotation exercise. To do this exercise well, you must activate the entire trunk stabilizing and antirotation musculature (deep pelvic stabilizers, transversus abdominis, obliques, back muscles, and rib cage muscles). The objective is to resist the rotational forces that are applied to the trunk so that complete alignment is maintained throughout. There should be no rotation at the hips or shoulders. For this exercise to be effective, you need to maintain a neutral spine position and resist rotation through the lumbar spine. An impulse component can be added by bracing and holding at each end of the range of movement while exhaling. Just because there is no rotation, don't think there's nothing beneficial happening; the exercise trains the ability to control the independent rotating segments of your trunk (hips, lumbar spine, thorax). This will enable you to isolate and control these independently during activities such as the rowing stroke, front-crawl swimming, fending off opponents in team sports, and striking or throwing (see also Swiss Ball Lateral Rotation).

IMT loading level: moderate

External resistance: double cable pulley machine

Duration: 10 to 15 repetitions

Sets: 2 or 3 in each direction

Procedure: Stand in the middle of the cable machine, with the columns to each side of you, and hold the handles in each hand. Turn 90 degrees and stand with your feet shoulder-width apart and with your knees bent slightly (a). With your BMT in your mouth, your spine in a neutral position, and your abdominal corset muscles braced (moderately), push and pull simultaneously (b), controlling the rotational force using your trunk muscles. During this concentric push–pull phase, inhale forcefully through your BMT, exhaling during the eccentric phase as you recover to the start position; swap breathing phases halfway through the set so that you exhale on the concentric push–pull phase. This exercise is very challenging, and you should only introduce the BMT once you are able to maintain the brace throughout the exercise, while executing deep, diaphragm-led inhalations.

CROSS BAND ROTATION

Benefits: This trunk rotation exercise targets the thoracic rotators and the obliques, while also emphasizing stability and control of the lumbar spine, which should not rotate. Undertaking this exercise with an added breathing challenge ensures that when the rib cage muscles are engaged in trunk rotation, they are also capable of contributing to breathing. The exercise should be preceded by unresisted trunk rotations to develop range of motion.

IMT loading level: moderate

External resistance: cable pulley machine or elastic resistance band or cord

Duration: 15 to 20 repetitions

Sets: 1 or 2 sets on each side

Procedure: Hold the end of the resistance and stand sideways to the anchor point with your arm across your chest (*a*). Brace the abdominal corset muscles (moderately) and rotate through the *thoracic* region of the trunk (only), keeping the hips and lumbar spine in line (*b*). Hold at the maximum range of movement for a moment, before returning (under control) to the start position. Emphasis should be placed on maintaining the brace, rotating through the thorax, and sustaining lumbar stability (do not rotate in the lumbar region). During the stretch, focus on regular, deep diaphragm breathing that is not in phase with the movement.

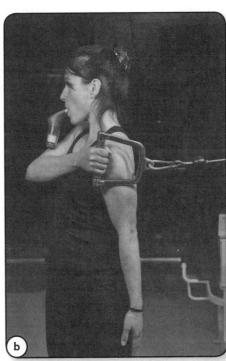

WOOD CHOP AND LIFT

Benefits: The two diagonal movement arcs of the chop and the lift require arm movements through the full range of pulling (chop) and lifting. However, this is a trunk stabilization exercise, not an arm exercise. In these very strict versions of the exercise, the arms are transferring force diagonally via a *stable* trunk. By bringing breathing into the mix, this exercise optimizes the contribution of the breathing muscles to trunk stabilization. Perform the chop exercise and the lift exercise separately using a high and low resistance, respectively. Several stance options may be used; the least challenging is standing with feet shoulder-width apart, and the most challenging is a split squat (you can also kneel). Where possible, use the stance that befits your sport—for example, feet side by side for golf or a split stance for tennis (tennis players can also use the side-by-side stance).

IMT loading level: moderate

External resistance: cable pulley machine with a rope or bar attachment (the bar needs to be attached to the pulley at the end, not the middle)

Duration: 10 to 20 repetitions

Sets: 2 sets (1 on each side)

Procedure for chop: Stand sideways to the resistance (*a*). Make sure your hips are fully extended, your BMT is in your mouth, your spine is in a neutral position, and your abdominal corset muscles are braced (moderately). Pull the cable down and across your body, keeping it close to your body (*b*). Your shoulders should barely rotate (if at all). As you bring your arms down, inhale forcefully through your BMT, exhaling as you return to the start position (swap breathing phases halfway through the set). Swap sides between sets.

Procedure for lift: Stand sideways to the resistance (*c*). Make sure your hips are fully extended, your BMT is in your mouth, your spine is in a neutral position, and your abdominal corset muscles are braced (moderately). Push the cable up and across your body, keeping it close to your body (*d*). Your shoulders should barely rotate (if at all). As you bring your arms up, inhale forcefully through your BMT, exhaling as you return to the start position (swap breathing phases halfway through the set). Swap sides between sets.

ROTATING LIFT

Benefits: This is a great compound exercise with multiple benefits. The exercise requires an extension and rotation movement that links the force generators of the lower body (ankle, knee, and hip) to those of the upper body. This exercise will help to optimize the passage of forces through this kinetic chain, developing stability and power. Because almost all sports require the transfer of forces through the entire body (e.g., a tennis serve, a rowing stroke, fending off an opposing player, or front-crawl swimming), this exercise will be of benefit to most athletes. By combining the movement with a breathing challenge, this exercise ensures that the efficient transfer of force through the kinetic chain is not disrupted by breathing.

IMT loading level: moderate

External resistance: loading plate, medicine ball, or dumbbell

Duration: 10 to 15 repetitions

Sets: 2 sets (1 on each side)

Procedure: Stand with your feet shoulder-width apart and with your BMT in your mouth. Hold the weight in both hands. Making sure your spine is in a neutral position, brace your abdominal corset muscles (moderately). To start the exercise, move to a squatting position with the weight to one side of your knees (a). Then move to a fully extended position, rotating your hips, turning your shoulders through almost 180 degrees, and extending your arms overhead (b). As you rotate the hips, drive with the leg where the weight started the movement—that is, if the squat started with the weight to the left of the left leg, drive with the left leg. Return to the same squatting position and repeat for the required number of reps. You should inhale forcefully through the BMT as you drive upward, and you should exhale as you recoil to the squat, swapping breathing phases halfway through the set. Swap sides between sets.

Variations: To add difficulty, increase the magnitude of the resistance.

DUMBBELL RUNNING

Benefits: This exercise involves the entire trunk musculature, deltoids, and biceps. It challenges the ability of the postural control system to maintain an upright posture. Most people find that they become much more breathless during walking and running activities than they do during cycling. This is because the postural control system is required to make continuous adjustments to posture during walking or running, which brings the breathing function of these muscles into conflict with their postural function. This exercise will help you develop the ability to cope with external destabilizing forces that can cause loss of balance and breathlessness during activities such as jogging, power walking, and hiking on uneven terrain.

IMT loading level: light to moderate

External resistance: dumbbells (light)

Duration: 30 to 60 seconds (30 seconds for a beginner; 60 seconds for an expert)

Sets: 2 sets (1 on each leg) separated by 30 to 60 seconds of rest

Procedure: Stand upright on one leg with your BMT in your mouth and with a dumbbell in each hand. Make sure your spine is in a neutral position, and brace the abdominal corset muscles (moderately). Then pump your arms back and forth as you would if you were sprinting. Do this using a cadence that you find challenging but comfortable (enough to throw you slightly off balance). At the same time, inhale forcefully through your BMT so that you complete 5 to 6 deep breaths in 30 seconds (10 to 12 in 60 seconds). Try to breathe *out of synch* with your arm movements.

Variations: To add difficulty, stand on a balance cushion or Bosu.

RESISTED FRONT RAISE

Benefits: This exercise involves the trunk musculature and deltoids, and it is a good exercise for improving postural control. Flinging your arms away from the body requires immediate, anticipatory activity of the diaphragm and tranversus abdominis; without this, you would simply lose your balance and fall over. Luckily, you don't need to think about this process, because it happens automatically. However, in situations where breathing demand is high, there is a direct conflict between the requirements for breathing and the requirements for postural control—and breathing always wins (see chapter 1). This exercise will help you develop the ability to meet both of those demands comfortably, without compromising either. The benefits will be translated into a myriad of everyday activities where the demands of postural control and breathing are high (e.g., walking on uneven ground).

IMT loading level: light to moderate

External resistance: dumbbell, medicine ball, disk weight, or resistance cord (weight should be moderate)

Duration: 30 to 60 seconds (30 seconds for a beginner; 60 seconds for an expert)

Sets: 2 to 4 sets separated by 30 to 60 seconds of rest

Procedure: With your BMT in your mouth, stand upright and hold your resistance device (e.g., disk weight) in both hands (a). Make sure your spine is in a neutral position, and brace the abdominal corset muscles (moderately); then swing your arms forward and upward, finishing with them above your head (b). Do this with a cadence that you find challenging but comfortable (enough to throw you slightly off balance). As you raise your arms, inhale forcefully through your BMT, and exhale as you lower your arms (swap breathing phases between sets so that you are inhaling as you lower your arms).

Variations: In addition to increasing duration, or the weight of the resistance, you can make the exercise more challenging by increasing cadence, using a balance cushion, or adopting a split stance (one foot in front of the other, shoulder-width apart). You must maintain complete control of the weight at ALL times.

STEP-UP

Benefits: This exercise involves the lumbopelvic stabilizers, quadriceps, gluteals, and calf muscles. Stepping is an activity that causes many people to become out of breath. This is not only because stepping is metabolically hard work, but also because it requires the breathing muscles to be engaged simultaneously in active postural control. This exercise will help you develop the ability to deal with these dual demands. After mastering this exercise, you'll see a flight of stairs or a steep scramble in a whole new (positive) light! Furthermore, when hikers and mountaineers are ascending steep slopes, they can have a tendency to topple backward, especially if carrying a heavy pack and when breathing demand is high. This exercise will help you develop the ability to cope with the destabilizing forces during large vertical movements when breathing demand is high.

IMT loading level: light to moderate

Step height: 6 to 12 inches (15 to 30 cm) (6 inches for a beginner; 12 inches for an expert)

Duration: 30 to 60 seconds (30 seconds for a beginner; 60 seconds for an expert)

Sets: 2 to 4 sets separated by 30 to 60 seconds of rest

Procedure: Stand upright with your hands by your sides or crossed on your chest (try not to use your arms to assist your balance). With your BMT in your mouth and with your spine in a neutral position, brace the abdominal corset muscles (moderately), then begin stepping (a). Step up with your left leg and stand on this leg briefly on the step (b), keeping your right leg unweighted (c). Then step down, leading with your right leg, and return to the start position standing on both feet in front of the step. Alternate the lead stepping leg with each repetition, and step at a comfortable but challenging pace. Inhale forcefully through your BMT as you step up (swap breathing phases between sets so you are inhaling as you step down).

Variations: In addition to increasing duration or step height, you can make the exercise more challenging by increasing cadence, using hand weights, using a balance cushion (only if you are confident that you will not fall), or adding a weighted backpack.

DYNAMIC WALKING LUNGE

Benefits: This exercise involves the quadriceps, gluteals, lumbopelvic stabilizers, and trunk musculature. This is another exercise that challenges the ability to maintain postural control, and it will help you develop the capacity to breathe effectively during movements that require forceful activation of large muscle groups. This combines an exercise for the lower body, a challenge to postural stability and control, and a breathing exercise in order to maximize the benefits from a single activity.

IMT loading level: light to moderate

External resistance: weight, dumbbell or medicine ball (light to moderate)

Duration: 30 to 60 seconds (30 seconds for a beginner; 60 seconds for an expert)

Sets: 2 to 4 sets separated by 30 to 60 seconds of rest

Procedure: Standing upright with your feet together and your BMT in your mouth, place your hands on your hips (or hold a small weight at arm's length to add difficulty). Make sure your spine is in a neutral position, and brace the abdominal corset muscles (moderately); then step forward and drop down into the lunge as deeply as is comfortable (active phase) before standing upright again with feet together (recovery phase). Next, step forward with the opposite leg (you will effectively be walking forward with large, deep steps, punctuated by standing). Alternate the leading leg with each repetition, and step at a comfortable but challenging pace. Each time you drop downward, inhale forcefully through your BMT, and exhale during the recovery phase (swap breathing phases between sets).

Variations: In addition to increasing duration, you can make the exercise more challenging by increasing cadence, increasing depth of the lunge, lunging laterally as well as to the front, using hand weights or a medicine ball, or stepping onto a large balance cushion or Bosu (on the spot).

SINGLE-LEG SQUAT KICK

Benefits: In various team sports (e.g., soccer, rugby, hockey), you need to be ready to pass or shoot whenever the opportunity presents itself, which may occur when you are in a posture that is far from ideal. This exercise involves the quadriceps, gluteals, lumbopelvic stabilizers, and hip flexors; it promotes balance and coordination during a kicking motion. It also helps you develop the ability to breathe effectively in a posturally challenging position.

IMT loading level: moderate

Duration: 15 to 20 repetitions

Sets: 2 sets (1 on each side)

Procedure: Assume a single-leg squat position with your opposite arm outstretched (a). With your BMT in your mouth, your spine in a neutral position, and your abdominal corset muscles braced (moderately), bring your non-weight-bearing foot up to meet your hand (b). As you do so, inhale forcefully through your BMT, exhaling as you bring your foot back to tap the ground next to your other foot. Without pausing, repeat the maneuver, swapping breathing phases halfway through the set so that you exhale as you lift your foot toward your hand.

Variations: To add difficulty, increase the depth of the squat, or increase instability by standing on a balance cushion.

OVERHEAD EXTENSION AND FLEXION

Benefits: This exercise primarily engages the trunk musculature, but it also involves the shoulder extensors and flexors. Rapid overhead arm movements are very challenging to the systems that maintain an upright posture, and these movements demand precise, complex activation of the core muscles. This exercise will help you develop the ability to maintain balance in situations where it is challenged by destabilizing overhead arm movements.

IMT loading level: moderate

External resistance: 2 elastic resistance bands or cords attached to either end of a pole and anchored to the same point (this point must be strong enough to hold your full weight)

Duration: 60 seconds

Sets: 2 sets

Procedure: Stand inside the triangle created by the pole and resistance bands (or cords), facing the pole. Hold the pole with your hands shoulder-width apart and your arms straight. Lean forward slightly, until the bands are under tension and taking your weight (a). Stand with your BMT in your mouth, your spine in a neutral position, and your abdominal corset muscles braced (moderately). Rotate your arms through 90 degrees so that they are directly above your head, and pulse them up and down (through 90 degrees) about once per second (b). During the pulsations, inhale forcefully through your BMT before exhaling slowly and fully for about 4 seconds (breathing rate should be around 12 per minute; concentrate on keeping it smooth and regular). Make sure you maintain a completely straight body line and do not flex at the hip.

GENERIC FUNCTIONAL EXERCISES

GENERIC FUNCTIONAL EXERCISES

RAISED BICYCLE

Benefits: This exercise involves the rectus abdominis, transversus abdominis, and hip flexors. The exercise challenges postural control during alternating hip flexion and extension. Superimposing the requirement for increased breathing effort onto this exercise ensures that this challenge doesn't lead to a failure to maintain deep, controlled breathing.

IMT loading level: moderate

Duration: 15 to 20 repetitions

Sets: 2 sets

Procedure: Sit on the floor with your hips flexed slightly, your knees bent, both feet off the floor, and your hands on the floor resting just behind you. Your BMT should be in your mouth. Brace your abdominal corset muscles (moderately) and cycle your legs as though pedaling (you should be balancing on your gluteals). Breathing should be continuous, not in time with your pedaling cadence. Inhale forcefully and deeply through the BMT, and then exhale slowly and fully for about 4 seconds (breathing rate should be around 12 per minute).

STANDING SPLIT-STANCE CABLE CHEST PRESS

Benefits: This exercise is good for postural control, and it involves the trunk muscu-lature, chest, and triceps muscles. The chest press requires the ability to transform the thorax into a stable platform, but doing so places huge demands on the ability of the trunk muscles to carry out their breathing function (the muscle actions tend to compress the rib cage). This exercise will help develop the coordinated action of the trunk stabilization and control musculature during the bench press movement. By undertaking this exercise in an unstable standing position and with a breathing challenge, you will improve your ability to coordinate the stabilizing and breathing actions of the trunk during an exercise that compresses the rib cage. This transforms the exercise into a core exercise that is highly functional.

IMT loading level: light to moderate

External resistance: double cable machine (15RM load)

Duration: 10 repetitions

Sets: 2 sets separated by 30 to 60 seconds of rest

Procedure: Stand with your back to the double cable machine, with one foot about 12 inches (30 cm) in front of the other; your feet should be approximately shoulder-width apart, with your knees slightly bent (a). With your BMT in your mouth, hold both cables in your hands. Once you are in position, brace the abdominal corset muscles (moderately). As you press the cables away from you (b), inhale forcefully through your BMT throughout the movement (exhale as you return to the start position). Swap breathing phases between sets so that you exhale as you press. Concentrate on not allowing the brace to release during either phase of breathing. Also concentrate on maintaining good form.

Variations: You can add difficulty by using only one arm at a time (the opposite arm from the front foot—this creates an additional rotational postural challenge), as well as combining the press phase with a lunge.

GENERIC FUNCTIONAL EXERCISES

STANDING SPLIT-STANCE SHOULDER PRESS

Benefits: This exercise is good for postural control, and it involves the trunk musculature, shoulders, and triceps. As with the chest press, the shoulder press requires the ability to transform the thorax into a stable platform. This places huge demands on the ability of the trunk muscles to carry out their breathing function, because this action stiffens the trunk (making inhalation more challenging). This exercise will help develop the coordinated action of the trunk stabilization and control musculature during the shoulder press movement. As described for the previous chest press exercise, the unstable standing position and the breathing challenge will improve your ability to coordinate the stabilizing and breathing actions of the trunk. This transforms the exercise into a core exercise that is highly functional.

IMT loading level: light to moderate

External resistance: dumbbells or bar (10 to 15RM load)

Duration: 10 repetitions

Sets: 2 sets separated by 30 to 60 seconds of rest

Procedure: Stand with one foot about 12 inches (30 cm) in front of the other; your feet should be approximately shoulder-width apart, with your knees bent slightly, your BMT in your mouth, and the weight at shoulder level (a). Once you are in position, brace the abdominal corset muscles (moderately), and ensure that your spine is in a neutral position. As you press the weight over your head (b), inhale forcefully through your BMT (exhale as you lower the weight to your shoulders). Alternate this pattern between sets so that you exhale as you press the weight and inhale as you lower the weight. Concentrate on not allowing the brace to release during either phase of breathing. Also concentrate on maintaining good lifting form and a neutral spine.

Variations: You can add postural difficulty to this exercise by placing your feet in a narrower stance (less than shoulder width, or heel to toe). You may also do single-arm presses, which add to the postural challenge.

T PUSH-UP

Benefits: This is a great multi-benefit exercise that develops trunk strength, lumbo-pelvic stability, and rotational strength and postural control. In the first phase of the movement, the exercise engages the entire trunk and pelvic stabilizing musculature, including the rectus abdominis, the obliques, the transversus abdominis, and the deep pelvic stabilizers, as well as the pectorals. Then, in the second phase, the trunk must be actively rotated and balanced without losing stiffness or postural control. Adding a breathing muscle challenge to the movements helps you develop the ability to maintain stiffness, stability, and balance in situations where breathing demand is high. By combining a core exercise (plank) with a push-up, trunk rotation, *and* a breathing challenge, you definitely get more "bang for your buck."

IMT loading level: moderate

Duration: 5 to 10 repetitions

Sets: 1 set

Procedure: Go into the push-up position (arms extended) with your feet together and hands shoulder-width apart; your BMT should be in your mouth. Brace the abdominal corset muscles (maximally), then lower yourself until your chest is a fist width from the floor, exhaling as you do so (a). As you push back up, lift your left arm up and rotate your body to the right (clockwise) until your body forms a T shape (b). As you lift and rotate, inhale against the load on the BMT. Hold briefly and exhale before returning to the push-up start position, then inhale again. Begin again, this time lifting the right arm and rotating to the left (counterclockwise).

DYNAMIC WEIGHTED WALKING LUNGE

Benefits: This exercise involves the quadriceps, gluteals, and trunk musculature—in particular, the obliques. The postural control system strives to maintain control of the center of gravity by counteracting rotational forces using the oblique muscles. If the obliques are weak or fatigued, rotation goes unchecked, and the risk of falling is increased. This is another good exercise for controlling shoulder rotation in an unstable stance, as well as for developing the ability to breathe deeply and in a controlled way, no matter how difficult the postural challenge.

IMT loading level: light to moderate

External resistance: dumbbell or medicine ball (up to 11 pounds [5 kg])

Duration: 30 to 60 seconds

Sets: 2 sets

Procedure: Standing upright with your feet together and your BMT in your mouth, hold a weight or medicine ball at arm's length (a). Make sure your spine is in a neutral position, brace your abdominal corset muscles (moderately), and step forward into a lunge (drop as deeply as is comfortable). At the lowest point of the lunge, rotate your shoulders to the same side as the leading leg (b). Step forward with the opposite leg, rotating your shoulders toward this leg (you will effectively be walking forward with large, deep steps). Step at a comfortable but challenging pace, concentrating on control, not speed. Inhale forcefully through your BMT when stepping forward with your right leg, and exhale when stepping with your left (swap breathing phases between sets).

Variations: In addition to increasing duration, you can make the exercise more challenging by increasing cadence, increasing depth of the lunge, lunging laterally as well as to the front, or stepping onto a large balance cushion or Bosu (on the spot).

(a)

(b)

STANDING SINGLE-ARM, SINGLE-LEG CABLE ROW

Benefits: This exercise is good for postural control, and it involves the back, shoulders, and biceps muscles. Any action that compresses the rib cage creates a challenge to breathing, and that's precisely what any pulling movement imposes. As with the bench and shoulder press, undertaking the rowing movement in an unstable, upright position transforms this exercise into a functional core activity, and the benefits will transfer into a seated row exercise. The single-arm nature of the exercise also adds a rotational challenge that will train the trunk rotators.

IMT loading level: light to moderate

External resistance: cable pulley machine (20RM load)

Duration: 10 to 15 repetitions

Sets: 2 sets (1 on each side) separated by 30 to 60 seconds of rest

Procedure: Stand on one leg in front of the cable machine, with your knee bent slightly, your BMT in your mouth, your opposite arm outstretched, and the cable in your hand (a). Once you are in position, brace the abdominal corset muscles (moderately), and ensure that your spine is in a neutral position. As you pull the cable handle toward you (b), inhale forcefully through your BMT throughout the movement (exhale as you extend your arm). Swap breathing phases halfway through the set so that you exhale as you pull the cable; swap sides between sets. Concentrate on not allowing the brace to release during either phase of breathing. Also focus on maintaining good form and a neutral spine. Don't swing your body back or forward; maintain a strict upright position.

Variations: You can add difficulty to this exercise by adding weight and adopting a single-leg one-quarter squat position.

GENERIC FUNCTIONAL EXERCISES

AB CRUSH

Benefits: This is a unique exercise with a very specific objective. The body positions of some sports restrict abdominal movements (e.g., the aero position in cycling and the catch in rowing), which can impede breathing. This exercise is a perfect way to train for this challenge, and it will help to make breathing more comfortable. The emphasis here is on developing strength, so really work hard to inhale against the resistance to abdominal movement.

IMT loading level: moderate to high

Duration: 30 breaths

Sets: 1 set

Procedure: Do your normal 30-breath training in the standing position, bent forward so that your thighs compress your abdomen. Bend forward from a standing position and grasp your ankles, with your knees bent slightly and with your BMT in your mouth. This exercise is very tough, and you may need to step down the load setting on your BMT when you commence. You should concentrate on maintaining the volume of each breath and inhaling the breath as quickly as possible. Focus on the diaphragm to get maximum benefit.

JUMP TO IT

Benefits: A number of sports involve movements where both feet leave the ground during play (e.g., passing and shooting in basketball or netball, the line-out in rugby, and the serve in tennis). When both your feet leave the ground, you only have the internal stability imparted by the core to provide a platform for movements, including breathing movements. This exercise helps you develop the ability to inhale forcefully when there is nothing but the core to "work against."

IMT loading level: moderate to heavy

Duration: 30 repetitions

Sets: 2 sets

Procedure: Stand with your feet shoulder-width apart and with your BMT in your mouth (a); ensure that you have a neutral spine, and brace your abdominal corset muscles (moderately). Jump in the air, and as soon as you are in flight, inhale forcefully through the BMT (b). Exhale as you return to the ground. Repeat at a comfortable but challenging pace, and swap breathing phases between sets so that you exhale as you leave the ground and inhale as you descend. Remember, you are training your ability to breathe in flight, not your jumping ability.

Variations: Add difficulty by holding a medicine ball and ripping the ball to one side while in flight.

a

b

GENERIC FUNCTIONAL EXERCISES

UPRIGHT CRUNCH

Benefits: This exercise is good for postural control, and it involves the rectus abdominis, transversus abdominis, and obliques. The exercise simulates and exaggerates the rotational movements of running. Balancing on one leg challenges the muscles that respond to the instability that is present during running (when running, you only have one foot on the ground at a time). The crunch itself also compresses the trunk and makes inhaling more challenging.

IMT loading level: light to moderate

Duration: 30 repetitions

Sets: 2 sets

Procedure: Stand upright with your BMT in your mouth, your right hand behind your head (elbow in line with your shoulder), and your left hand resting on your hip (*a*). Rotate and crunch your body to bring your right elbow toward your left knee (don't flex your elbow forward to meet your knee; keep your elbows level with your shoulders) (*b*). As you crunch, inhale forcefully through your BMT, exhaling as you return to upright. Then swap sides, bringing your left elbow toward your right knee.

Variations: You can add difficulty by standing on balance cushions or a Bosu.

DUMBBELL RUNNING ON BALANCE CUSHION

Benefits: This exercise is good for postural stability and control, and it involves the biceps, deltoid, rectus abdominis, transversus abdominis, obliques, and back muscles. When sprinting, people have a strong tendency to allow breathing to become locked into the rhythm of their arm movements. This makes breathing shallow and inefficient. Runners also have a tendency to allow the arm movements to cause overrotation of the shoulders. When weights are added to the hands, the tendency to slip into these bad habits is accentuated; therefore, this exercise will help you develop the muscles that control trunk rotation and promote the ability to control breathing cadence no matter how strong the drive is to lock into the rhythm of your arm movements.

IMT loading level: light to moderate

External resistance: dumbbells—light

Duration: 60 seconds

Sets: 2 sets (1 on each leg)

Procedure: Stand upright on one leg on a balance cushion, with your BMT in your mouth and a dumbbell in each hand. Pump your arms back and forth as you would if you were sprinting—and with a cadence that you find challenging (enough to throw you slightly off balance). At the same time, inhale forcefully through your BMT so that you complete 10 to 12 deep breaths in 60 seconds.

Variations: To add difficulty, use heavier dumbbells and more exaggerated arm movements. You can also use a Bosu.

AEROBARS

Benefits: This exercise is perfect for overcoming the mechanical restriction of abdominal and thoracic movements imposed by being crouched over the bars, or aerobars. The exercise also helps you develop the balance and coordination that is needed when you are stretched forward on the bike.

IMT loading level: moderate to high

Duration: 30 breaths

Sets: 2 or 3

Procedure: Do your normal 30-breath training session while seated on your bike (in the aero position), with your BMT in your mouth. If you don't have access to your bike, simulate the position while seated on a stool. Ensure that you maintain a neutral spine position throughout. You should concentrate on activating your diaphragm to ensure that you get maximum benefit.

Variations: Add difficulty by *not* taking your weight on your arms while in the crouch (engage your core to keep yourself in position); holding your arms out in front of you while in the crouch (with or without a small weight in your hands); or turning the pedals slowly in the lowest gear, concentrating on keeping your breathing steady and your pelvis level.

STANDING ONE-LEG CYCLE

Benefits: This exercise is good for postural control, and it involves the deep lumbo-pelvic stabilizing muscles, hip flexors, and back muscles. The exercise will help you develop the ability to keep your hips level and your spine neutral. The emphasis of this exercise is the development of efficient, coordinated muscle activation patterns, which are vital components of the stable platform you need to optimize force transfer.

IMT loading level: moderate

Duration: 60 seconds

Sets: 2 sets (1 per leg)

Procedure: Stand in a forward-flexed position, with a neutral spine and with your BMT in your mouth. Brace your abdominal corset muscles (moderately), lift one foot off the ground, and move it through the air in an exaggerated cycling action. As you rotate your leg, inhale forcefully through the BMT before exhaling slowly and fully for about 4 seconds (breathing rate should be around 12 per minute). Concentrate on maintaining a neutral spine, a level pelvis, and a smooth breathing rhythm that is *not* synchronized to your leg movements. Swap legs between sets.

Variations: Add difficulty by standing on a balance cushion or adding ankle weights.

RIDE 'EM COWBOY

Benefits: This exercise is good for postural control using primarily the muscles of the pelvis; it involves the lumbopelvic stabilizers and the adductors. The exercise will help you develop the fine control of pelvic stability that is needed when you are cycling in the saddle.

IMT loading level: moderate

Duration: 60 seconds

Sets: 2 sets

Procedure: Sit on top of a Swiss ball with your feet on the floor and with your pelvis level. Using external assistance if necessary, lift both feet off the floor and clasp the sides of the ball with your knees and ankles. This will take some practice, but the goal is to stay upright, with your pelvis level, and to control movement of the ball using your pelvic stabilizing muscles, not your arms. Initially, concentrate on keeping your breathing deep, slow, and controlled. Once you can do this and can sustain the exercise for 60 seconds, add the BMT, inhaling forcefully through the BMT before exhaling slowly and fully for about 4 seconds (breathing rate should be around 12 per minute).

Variations: To add difficulty, use a more inflated ball on a hard surface. You can also ask a training partner to give you *gentle* prods to destabilize you.

BIG GEAR CLIMB

Benefits: This is a good exercise for challenging the trunk muscles and for improving postural stability. The idea is to simulate climbing, and the exercise can be practiced in and out of the saddle. Climbing is one of the few situations where pedal forces are high, and synchronizing breathing with the pedal downstroke can be advantageous. This exercise is the only situation in which I recommend using a BMT *during* a whole-body aerobic exercise, and it should be undertaken for no more than one minute at a time.

IMT loading level: moderate

Duration: 60 seconds

Sets: 2 sets

Procedure: This exercise requires a bike and a turbo trainer or a gym bike that can be set up to provide a high pedal resistance. Adopt your normal climbing stance and brace your abdominal corset muscles (moderately), taking care to maintain a neutral spine position. Begin pedaling and settle at about 40 to 50 rpm; place your BMT in your mouth. As you drive the right pedal down, exhale forcefully; as you drive the left pedal down, inhale forcefully through your BMT, concentrating on maintaining the abdominal brace. Sustain this for about a minute. On the second set, swap breathing phases, exhaling on the left-pedal downstroke and inhaling on the right pedal (again sustaining this for a minute).

Exhale as you drive the right pedal down.

TRICKLE AND BLAST

Benefits: This is a good exercise for developing breathing control, the ability to maintain a high lung volume (which is good for buoyancy), and the ability to fill the lungs rapidly. The exercise was inspired directly by Coach Dan Bullock.

IMT loading level: low

External resistance: wide elastic resistance band

Duration: 60 to 120 seconds

Sets: 2 sets

Procedure: You can practice this exercise in or out of the pool. If on dry land, you should tension the elastic resistance band around your lower ribs, just below the sternum (see figure 8.2 on page 133), while in a standing or sitting position. Inhale as deeply and rapidly as you can, focusing on expanding your rib cage and activating your diaphragm, but keep your shoulders relaxed. Hold your breath for 3 to 5 seconds with your lungs full and your mouth open (don't close your glottis—use your inspiratory muscles to maintain the high lung volume). Then allow the air to trickle *slowly* out of your lungs through pursed lips for 3 to 5 seconds before finally "blasting" the remaining air out of the lungs. Immediately after the exhalation is complete, inhale again as rapidly as possible. You can modify the duration of the exhalation phase to coincide with your normal breathing rate during swimming. In the pool, simply replicate your normal breathing pattern, but for the exhalation phase, allow the air to trickle *slowly* out of your lungs through pursed lips for 3 to 5 seconds before finally blasting the remaining air out of the lungs.

Variations: On land, you can add difficulty by using a BMT or adding tension to the resistance band. You can also practice this exercise facedown with your hips resting on a Swiss ball. In the pool, you can make the exercise more difficult by adding the resistance band.

SWISS BALL HYPEREXTENSION

Benefits: This exercise involves the gluteals, trunk musculature, and, in particular, the back extensors; it is a good way to improve postural control and the ability to coordinate breathing and trunk movements. The exercise confines the overload of the inspiratory muscles to points during the swimming stroke when breathing takes place.

IMT loading level: light to moderate

External resistance: wide elastic resistance band

Duration: 30 repetitions

Sets: 2 sets

Procedure: Tension the elastic resistance band around your lower ribs, just below the sternum. Rest your hips on a Swiss ball, with your feet on the ground slightly more than shoulder-width apart; at first, you may need to anchor your feet against a wall. Relax over the ball with your BMT in your mouth (a). Extend at the hips as far as you can, and as you do so, inhale forcefully through the BMT (b). Hold the extended position for 2 seconds and then lower yourself to the start position, exhaling as you do so. When you exhale, use the "trickle and blast" technique described for the previous exercise. You can vary this exercise by leading with your shoulder (alternate shoulders between reps). Anchoring your feet makes the exercise easier, but it compromises the benefits to the development of core stability and postural control—after all, your feet aren't anchored in the pool!

SPORT- AND ACTIVITY-SPECIFIC EXERCISES

SWISS BALL CRAWL

Benefits: This exercise is very challenging to postural control; it involves the entire trunk musculature, and it helps improve postural control and the ability to coordinate breathing and trunk movements. As with the Swiss Ball Hyperextension exercise, this exercise focuses the overload of the inspiratory muscles during movements that are associated with breathing during the swimming stroke.

IMT loading level: light to moderate, if used

External resistance: wide elastic resistance band

Duration: 60 seconds

Sets: 2 sets

Procedure: Tension the elastic resistance band around your lower ribs, just below the sternum. Rest your hips on a Swiss ball, with your feet resting on a bench at roughly the same level as your hips; your feet should be shoulder-width apart. Start with your arms at your sides to establish your balance and then move them out in front of you at shoulder height (a). When comfortable, slowly simulate the front-crawl stroke and breathing movements (b). As you turn your head to inhale, do so as rapidly as possible, filling your lungs as far as you can. When you exhale, use the "trickle and blast" technique described earlier. The postural control element of this exercise is quite challenging, so it may help to have an assistant stabilize the ball initially.

Variations: Add difficulty by using a BMT or by adding tension to the elastic resistance band.

PLANK WITH ARM EXTENSION

Benefits: This exercise involves the lumbopelvic stabilizers and trunk musculature—in particular, the antirotation muscles. It helps improve postural control and requires strong stabilizing and antirotation activity. The exercise will help ensure that breathing is not compromised by the requirement to maintain a stiff, extended trunk during arm movements.

IMT loading level: moderate

External resistance: wide elastic resistance band

Duration: 30 to 60 seconds

Sets: 2 or 3 sets per side

Procedure: Tension the elastic resistance band around your lower ribs, just below the sternum. Facing the floor with your BMT in your mouth, rest on your elbows (or hands) and toes (shoulder-width apart), maintaining a straight body line and a neutral spine position. Once you are in position, brace the abdominal corset muscles (maximally) and extend the non-weight-bearing arm in front of you (as though reaching for a catch); hold for 5 seconds and then swap arms. Inhale in time with arm movements. Concentrate on keeping your body level, especially your shoulders and hips (control rotational movement using your core muscles).

Variations: To add difficulty, move your feet closer together or hold a small hand weight or dumbbell in the extended hand. You can also move your arm through the normal range of motion for your stroke.

SWISS BALL HIP EXTENSION

Benefits: This exercise helps improve postural stability, and it involves the rectus abdominis, transversus abdominis, hip flexors, and quadriceps. The exercise simulates the dual activity requirements of the breathing muscles at the finish of the rowing stroke. This exercise will develop your ability to breathe comfortably and freely at the finish.

IMT loading level: moderate to high

External resistance: disk weight or dumbbell on chest to add difficulty

Duration: 30 repetitions

Sets: 1 set

Procedure: Sit upright on the ball and extend at the hips as far as is comfortable, so that your shoulders are behind your hips. Your abdominal corset muscles should be braced (moderately). With your BMT in your mouth, rest your hands on your thighs or fold your arms across your chest. Once in position, inhale forcefully through your BMT, completing the 30 repetitions continuously.

Variations: To add difficulty, clasp a small disk weight or dumbbell to your chest, or extend alternate legs at the knee to generate a postural challenge. This exercise can also be undertaken in the finish position on a rowing ergometer.

SWISS BALL LATERAL ROTATION

Benefits: This exercise involves the rectus abdominis, transversus abdominis, and obliques. During sweep rowing, the trunk must be rotated and flexed in the seated position. The trunk muscles that bring about rotation (the obliques) need to be strong and well coordinated, especially as you approach the catch. When a rower is breathing heavily, conflict between the breathing and postural stabilizing roles of the trunk muscles can leave the spine vulnerable to injury. This exercise will help you develop the ability to control trunk movement, even when breathing demand is high. It is done in the seated position, because this exercise is specific to rowing.

IMT loading level: moderate

External resistance: cable pulley machine, resistance band or cord

Duration: 15 to 20 repetitions

Sets: 2 sets (1 on each side)

Procedure: Sit on the Swiss ball with your BMT in your mouth, your spine in a neutral position, and your abdominal corset muscles braced (moderately), facing sideways to the anchor point of the resistance, but with your trunk rotated toward the anchor point (*a*). Your hips should remain facing forward. Rotate your trunk away from the anchor point, inhaling forcefully through your BMT as you do so (*b*). Halfway through the set, swap breathing phases so that you exhale as you rotate away from the anchor point. On the second set, place the resistance on the opposite side of your body and repeat.

SPORT- AND ACTIVITY-SPECIFIC EXERCISES

SCULLING SIT-UP

Benefits: This exercise involves the rectus abdominis, transversus abdominis, hip flexors, and back muscles. It helps develop postural stability, balance, and the coordination of core muscles. The exercise also promotes the ability to breathe freely at the finish of the rowing stroke.

IMT loading level: moderate

External resistance: resistance band or cord or dumbbells

Duration: 30 to 60 seconds

Sets: 2 sets

Procedure: Sit on the floor with your hips flexed, your knees bent, your feet off the floor, your arms folded gently around your knees, and your BMT in your mouth (a). Brace your abdominal corset muscles (moderately), ensuring that your spine is in a neutral position, then extend your legs, lean back, and open your arms away from your body, inhaling forcefully through the BMT (b). Once you have extended as far as you can without losing control, return to the start position, exhaling as you do so (swap breathing phases between sets).

Variations: To add difficulty, hold dumbbells in your hands, or stretch a resistance band or cord between them.

SEATED ROW

Benefits: The action of the trunk muscles during rowing movements will compress the rib cage, which acts to oppose inhalation. Although inhalation during the drive is not recommended, this exercise is good for developing the ability to inhale during a movement that compresses the rib cage. In addition, performing this exercise with one arm helps develop the ability to control rotational movements of the trunk.

IMT loading level: moderate to heavy

External resistance: cable pulley, resistance band or cord, or rowing ergometer

Duration: 30 repetitions

Sets: 1 set

Procedure: Sit on the floor with your legs extended and your hands outstretched. Grasp the ends of the resistance (with one or two hands) (*a*). If this is a band, it should be anchored to your feet. If you are doing this exercise with one hand, the band or cord should be anchored to the opposite foot. With your BMT in your mouth, brace your abdominal corset muscles (moderately) and then pull your hand (or hands) toward the blade handle finish position of the rowing stroke, inhaling forcefully through the BMT (*b*). Return your hands to the start position, exhaling as you do so.

Variations: To add difficulty, tension the band or cord, or use a heavier machine weight. This exercise can also be done with one arm, as well as undertaken on a rowing ergometer.

BALANCE SQUATS

Benefits: This exercise involves the rectus abdominis, transversus abdominis, quadriceps, and gluteals. This is a great exercise for challenging postural control during flexion and extension at the hip, knee, and ankle. All sliding sports require this movement, which creates a state of dynamic instability that can result in loss of postural control if a person is unable to control and stabilize the trunk at the same time as meeting an elevated demand for breathing.

IMT loading level: moderate

Duration: 60 seconds

Sets: 2 to 4 sets

Procedure: Stand on a balance cushion with your spine in a neutral position and with your BMT in your mouth. Cross your arms over your chest so that you cannot use them to help you balance (*a*). Once you are in position, brace the abdominal corset muscles (moderately) and move into the squat position (*b*); as you do so, inhale forcefully through your BMT before standing and exhaling slowly and fully for about 3 seconds (breathing rate should be around 15 per minute). Your movements should be slow and controlled. On the next set, swap breathing phases so that you exhale during the downward movement and inhale as you stand.

Variations: To add difficulty, place your hands above your head with both palms facing forward, one on top of the other, and press your hands together (this fully engages your core musculature). You can also try this on one leg or while holding a weight.

BALANCE SQUATS WITH A TWIST

Benefits: This exercise involves the rectus abdominis, transversus abdominis, obliques, quadriceps, and gluteals. This is another great exercise for challenging postural control, but this one also works the obliques and forces the center of gravity off center, as may occur during alpine skiing.

IMT loading level: moderate

Duration: 60 seconds

Sets: 2 to 4 sets

Procedure: Stand on a balance cushion with your spine in a neutral position, your BMT in your mouth, and your arms crossed over your chest (so that you cannot use them to help you balance). Once you are in position, brace the abdominal corset muscles (moderately) and move into the squat position; as you do so, twist to one side and inhale forcefully through your BMT before standing and exhaling slowly and fully for about 3 seconds (breathing rate should be around 15 per minute). On the next repetition, twist in the opposite direction. Your movements should be slow and controlled. On the next set, swap breathing phases so that you exhale during the downward movement and inhale as you stand.

Variations: To add difficulty, place your hands above your head with both palms facing forward, one on top of the other, and press your hands together (this fully engages your core musculature). You can also try this on one leg or while holding a weight.

SKATER LEG DRIVES

Benefits: This exercise involves the rectus abdominis, transversus abdominis, obliques, quadriceps, gluteals, and back extensors. The exercise challenges postural control during a movement that simulates the drive ("mule kick") phase of the skating stroke. Adding the breathing challenge helps ensure that forceful breathing neither causes loss of postural control, nor threatens pelvic stability.

IMT loading level: moderate

External resistance: elastic resistance band or cord or ankle weights

Duration: 60 seconds

Sets: 2 to 4 sets (1 or 2 on each leg)

Procedure: Tether the resistance band around one ankle and stand on the opposite end with the other foot (ensure that there is a moderate resistance to backward and lateral movement of the tethered ankle). Start with your feet together, your BMT in your mouth, and your spine in a neutral position. Flex forward into the "skater position" (*a*). Once you are in position, brace the abdominal corset muscles (moderately) and move your leg backward and to one side (simulating the mule kick movement during skating) (*b*); as you do so, inhale forcefully through your BMT before returning to the start position and exhaling slowly and fully for about 3 seconds (breathing rate should be around 15 per minute). Repeat for 60 seconds, swapping breathing phases halfway through the set so that you exhale during the drive. Your movements should be slow and controlled. On the next set, swap legs. Don't forget to swap legs between sets and to swap breathing phases within a set.

Variations: To add difficulty, increase the external resistance or stand on a balance cushion.

SINGLE-LEG BALANCE
WITH OPPOSING ARM AND LEG RESISTANCE

Benefits: This exercise involves the rectus abdominis, transversus abdominis, obliques, gluteals, hamstrings, and deltoids. The exercise helps to coordinate the counter-rotational activation of the pelvic stabilizers and trunk antirotators by imposing resistance on opposite sides of the body simultaneously during a postural challenge. Adding the breathing challenge helps ensure that forceful breathing neither causes loss of postural control, nor threatens pelvic stability.

IMT loading level: moderate to heavy

External resistance: resistance band or cord

Duration: 30 to 60 seconds

Sets: 2 sets (1 on each leg)

Procedure: Stand on one foot and anchor the middle of the band under the standing foot. One end should be tied to your ankle, and the other should be held in the opposite hand (*a*). With your BMT in your mouth, bend at the hip until your body is parallel to the floor. Once in position, make sure your spine is in a neutral position and brace the abdominal corset muscles (moderately); then raise your tethered leg behind you (keeping your knee straight), and lift the opposite arm, extending at the shoulder (keep your elbow straight). Raise your foot and hand simultaneously until level with your body (*b*), and at the same time, inhale forcefully through your BMT. Hold momentarily before lowering your limbs (under control), exhaling as you do so. Repeat for 30 to 60 seconds, swapping breathing phases halfway through the set (so that you inhale as your limbs are lowered). Swap sides between sets.

Variations: To add difficulty, stand on a balance cushion, use a stronger band or cord, or use the band or cord under greater tension.

BACKPACK SHRUG AND BREATHE

Benefits: This exercise involves the rectus abdominis, transversus abdominis, and the muscles that lift the shoulders (trapezius and deltoids). The exercise helps develop the muscles that lift the shoulders and upper chest, enabling them to overcome the restrictions imposed by carrying a backpack. By adding a wide elastic resistance band around the abdomen (at the same level as the hip belt on your backpack), you can also accentuate the effects of the hip belt on diaphragm-induced abdominal movements.

IMT loading level: moderate to heavy

External resistance: backpack (loaded to a typical weight for you), wide elastic resistance band

Duration: 30 breaths

Sets: 1 set

Procedure: With your backpack in place (the pack should be loaded to a typical weight) and your BMT in your mouth, ensure that your spine is in a neutral position, and brace the abdominal corset muscles (moderately). You will probably notice that you have moved your center of gravity forward slightly to counteract the weight of the backpack. Now inhale forcefully through your BMT, lifting your shoulders and chest against the weight of the backpack; hold for 3 to 5 seconds before relaxing and exhaling slowly and fully for about 3 seconds.

Variations: To add difficulty, increase the weight of the backpack, or stand on a balance cushion or Bosu. Also add the elastic resistance band to the abdomen.

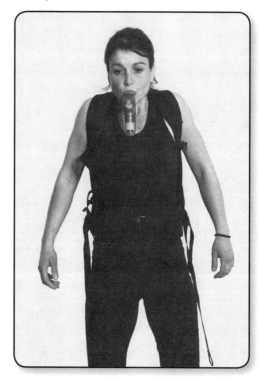

STEP-DOWN

Benefits: This exercise is good for postural control, and it involves the lumbopelvic stabilizers, quadriceps, gluteals, and calf muscles. Descending steep slopes is even more challenging posturally than ascending them, especially if you are wearing a backpack. A slight loss in control of your center of gravity can lead to a fall, especially when fatigued. This exercise will help develop your ability to cope with challenging descents.

IMT loading level: moderate

Step height: 12 to 24 inches (30 to 60 cm)

Duration: 60 seconds

Sets: 2 to 4 sets separated by 30 to 60 seconds of rest

Procedure: Stand upright with your hands by your sides or crossed on your chest (try not to use your arms to assist your balance). With your BMT in your mouth, make sure that your spine is in a neutral position, brace the abdominal corset muscles (moderately), then begin stepping. Step up with your right leg (a) and stand briefly on both feet before stepping down on the opposite side of the step, leading with your right leg (b). Stand briefly on both feet before turning and stepping up again, this time with the left leg. Alternate the lead stepping leg with each repetition, and step at a comfortable but challenging pace. Inhale forcefully through your BMT as you step up (swap breathing phases between sets so you are inhaling as you step down).

Variations: In addition to increasing duration or step height, you can make the exercise more challenging by increasing cadence, using hand weights, using a balance cushion (only if you are confident that you will not fall), or adding a weighted backpack.

COMPRESSED SHRUG AND BREATHE

Benefits: This exercise expands the lower rib cage and helps develop the muscles that lift the shoulders (trapezius and deltoids) and the upper chest, enabling them to overcome the restrictions imposed by protective equipment. The exercise can be performed while wearing equipment or by binding the trunk with a wide elastic resistance band.

IMT loading level: moderate to heavy

External resistance: protective equipment or an elastic resistance band

Duration: 30 breaths

Sets: 1 set

Procedure: With your protective equipment strapped in place tightly (or with your ribs and shoulders strapped with a resistance band) and with your BMT in your mouth, ensure that your spine is in a neutral position, and brace the abdominal corset muscles (moderately). Now inhale forcefully through your BMT, expanding your rib cage and lifting your shoulders and upper chest against the resistance around your trunk; hold for 3 to 5 seconds before relaxing and exhaling slowly and fully for about 3 seconds.

Variations: To add difficulty, increase the resistance around your trunk, or stand on a balance cushion or Bosu.

LINEMAN STANCE

Benefits: When you are in a three- or four-point lineman stance, your breathing will be challenged by the abdominal compression created by hip flexion. At the same time, you must maintain balance, and you must be braced and ready for whatever the game throws at you. Some coaches recommend that players put very little weight on the hands in this stance (despite often having their hips higher than their shoulders), which adds to the postural and breathing challenge. This exercise will help you develop the ability to breathe effectively during the lineman stance.

IMT loading level: moderate to heavy

Duration: 15 repetitions

Sets: 2 sets

Procedure: Assume your preferred lineman stance (with no weight on your hands), with your BMT in your mouth, your spine in a neutral position, and your abdominal corset muscles braced (moderately). Inhale forcefully through your BMT, inhaling as deeply as possible; hold for 3 to 5 seconds before relaxing and exhaling slowly and fully for about 3 seconds.

Variations: To add difficulty, increase instability by standing on two balance cushions.

SINGLE-LEG RESISTED KNEE RAISE AND TWIST

Benefits: During most of the critical moments in a soccer game, you will be performing the required actions while on one foot (shooting, passing, controlling the ball, and tackling). Because breathing disrupts the coordinated action of the trunk muscles in maintaining balance, the added challenge of breathing during key moments of the game can be sufficient to throw you off balance. This is a great exercise for challenging balance and coordination in a single-leg posture.

IMT loading level: moderate

External resistance: wide elastic resistance band

Duration: 15 to 20 repetitions

Sets: 2 sets (1 on each side)

Procedure: Stand with your feet slightly less than shoulder-width apart; one end of the elastic resistance band should be secured just above your ankle, and the other end should be secured underneath the opposite foot. Your arms should be folded across your chest, and your BMT should be in your mouth (a). With your spine in a neutral position and your abdominal corset muscles braced (moderately), bring your knee toward your opposite elbow, rotating your shoulders and crunching forward slightly as you do (this tips your center of gravity and challenges your balance a little more) (b). As you lift your knee, inhale forcefully through your BMT, exhaling as you bring your foot back to tap the ground next to your other foot. Without pausing, repeat the maneuver, swapping breathing phases halfway through the set so that you exhale as you lift your knee toward your elbow.

Variations: To add difficulty, increase the tension in the band, or increase instability by standing on a balance cushion.

SINGLE-LEG HIP TO SHOULDER LIFT

Benefits: Basketball and netball require you to be well balanced at all times, especially when you're on one foot, as occurs during jumping and landing. This exercise requires balance and coordination, and it helps you develop the ability to breathe effectively in a posturally challenging sport-specific position (lifting and reaching overhead toward the basket, on one leg).

IMT loading level: moderate

External resistance: small medicine ball

Duration: 12 to 15 repetitions

Sets: 2 sets (1 on each side)

Procedure: Assume a single-leg one-quarter squat position on the left foot. Hold the ball in both hands just outside or on the left hip (*a*). With your BMT in your mouth, your spine in a neutral position, and your abdominal corset muscles braced (moderately), bring the ball across your body, up past your right ear (*b*), and then lift it to full extension above your head. As you do so, inhale forcefully through your BMT, exhaling as you bring the ball back down toward your left hip. Without pausing, repeat the maneuver, swapping breathing phases halfway through the set so that you exhale as you lift the ball. Swap standing legs between sets.

Variations: To add difficulty, lower the start position of the ball from your hip to either your knee or just above your ankle. Stand on a balance cushion or Bosu.

KNEELING DIAGONAL LIFT

Benefits: Basketball and netball require you to be very strong through the shoulders and core, especially when you're attempting to complete a layup or contested shot. This exercise requires strength within the trunk musculature integrated with the shoulders. The exercise will help you develop the ability to breathe effectively in a posturally challenging sport-specific position.

IMT loading level: moderate

External resistance: cable pulley machine with rope attachment

Duration: 12 to 15 repetitions

Sets: 2 sets (1 on each side)

Procedure: Assume a kneeling lunge position with your left side toward the cable machine, your left knee down (use a low cable position), and your hands by your left hip. With your BMT in your mouth and your spine in a neutral position, ensure that your abdominal corset muscles are braced (moderately) and that your left gluteal is contracted (a). Once in position, bring the rope up and across your body, past your right ear, and to full extension (b). As you do so, inhale forcefully through your BMT, exhaling as you bring the ropes back down toward your left hip. Without pausing, repeat the maneuver, swapping breathing phases halfway through the set so that you exhale as you lift the ropes. Swap sides between sets by turning though 180 degrees.

Variation: Use a bilateral one-quarter squat position, or add difficulty by increasing the resistance.

STANDING PARTNER ANTIROTATION

Benefits: This is another great exercise for developing your ability to resist opposing players who are attempting to dislodge you from the post position. This exercise requires you to resist a rotational force, and it helps you develop the ability to breathe effectively in a posturally challenging sport-specific position. (Although players at all positions need to have this ability, this particular exercise is most beneficial for post players.)

IMT loading level: moderate to heavy

External resistance: partner and a pole or broomstick

Duration: 10 to 15 seconds per position

Sets: 1 set

Procedure: The exercise has three start positions (positions b and c are more difficult and simulate catching the ball to the side in the post position).

a. Neutral spine, with no trunk rotation and with hands straight ahead and at shoulder height

b. Thoracic spine rotated to the right, independent of the lumbar spine, which stays at neutral position, with hands at shoulder height but slightly to the right

c. Thoracic spine rotated to the left, independent of the lumbar spine, which stays at neutral position, with hands at shoulder height but slightly to the left

In each case, assume a bilateral one-quarter squat position with your hands directly in front of you, at shoulder height, holding a pole or broomstick (a). With your BMT in your mouth, ensure that your spine is in a neutral position and that your abdominal corset muscles are braced (moderately). Once you are in position, your partner should apply a rotational force to the end of the pole, gently pulling and pushing for 10 to 15 seconds. Resist the force, trying to maintain the designated position using your trunk muscles (b). As you do so, breathe forcefully but steadily through your BMT about four times (2-second inhale and 2-second exhale). Initially, you may be unable to breathe and hold a moderately braced position simultaneously; if this is the case, do not add the BMT until you can.

MEDICINE BALL PIVOT SERIES

Benefits: For guards or primary ball handlers, there will be many times that they are forced to pivot under heavy defense, while simultaneously protecting the ball from opposing players who are seeking to dislodge it from their grip. This exercise requires you to perform a traditional pivot multiple times in each of the three planes while ripping the ball (in this case, a medicine ball) through to mimic protecting the ball. Although players at all positions need to have this ability to pivot under duress, this particular exercise is most beneficial for guards (post players are encouraged to hold the ball high, or "chin" the ball, while guards should pull or rip the ball through in a lower position). This is a very challenging exercise, and you may initially be unable to hold a moderately braced position independent of breathing. Master this before adding the BMT.

IMT loading level: moderate to heavy

External resistance: medicine ball

Duration: 3 repetitions per pivot plane (9 in total)

Sets: 2 sets

Procedure: This exercise is undertaken in three planes.

a. Front-to-back plane: Maintain the left foot as the pivot while lunging forward and backward. With the forward lunge of the right foot, rotate the ball from inside your pivot thigh to outside, right to left (a and b); with the reverse lunge of the right foot, rotate the ball left to right so you finish inside the right thigh. You can vary this exercise by starting with the ball outside your pivot thigh, moving it inside your thigh as you pivot.

b. Lateral plane: Maintain the left foot as the pivot while lunging laterally to the right and rotating the ball to the right; pivot back through the frontal plane, ending in a reverse lateral lunge or "bowler" squat position with the ball finishing in a protected position to the left of your right thigh (c and d).

c. Diagonal plane: Maintain the left foot as the pivot (start the left foot at the 12 o'clock position) while lunging with the right foot to the 3 o'clock position, holding the ball over the right thigh (e). Complete the pivot position by stepping over your left foot while protecting the ball (f).

In each case, assume a bilateral one-quarter squat position with your hands directly in front of you and both hands gripping the ball firmly. With your BMT in your mouth, your spine in a neutral position, and your abdominal corset muscles braced (moderately), complete three repetitions of each pivot series in succession (a, b, c) for a total of nine pivot reps. When you complete these nine reps, switch pivot feet and repeat (this is one set). As you perform the first movement of each repetition, inhale forcefully through your BMT, and exhale as you pivot opposite to your start position. Switch breathing phases during your second set.

Front-to-back plane.

Lateral plane.

Diagonal plane.

SKI SQUATS WITH ALTERNATE LEG RAISE AND MEDICINE BALL RIP

Benefits: In basketball and netball, you need to maintain a balanced, strong platform at all times, and this can be difficult when you are trying to protect the ball by ripping it quickly away from an opponent. This exercise will help you develop the ability to keep your hips level during vigorous arm movements that challenge trunk control. The exercise also puts emphasis on the development of strength in the pelvic stabilizers, as well as increases the endurance of these muscles.

IMT loading level: moderate

External resistance: medicine ball

Duration: 10 to 15 repetitions

Sets: 2 sets (1 on each side)

Procedure: Assume the ski squat position with your back resting against a wall and with your thighs as close to horizontal as you can manage. With your BMT in your mouth and a medicine ball in your hands (resting beside your right thigh), adopt a neutral spine alignment (*a*). Once you are in position, brace the abdominal corset muscles (moderately) and extend your left leg so that your weight is on your right leg; as you do so, inhale forcefully through your BMT and "rip" the ball swiftly to rest beside your left thigh (*b*). Exhale slowly and fully as you return your foot to the floor. Repeat the maneuver, extending your left leg and moving the ball swiftly to your right side. Be careful not to allow your hip to drop to the unsupported side. Swap breathing phases between sets so that you exhale as you raise your leg and inhale as you lower it.

Variations: To add difficulty, deepen the squat, place a Swiss ball between your back and the wall, or stand on a balance cushion.

BOUNCE AND BREATHE

Benefits: In basketball, running, controlling the ball, and protecting the ball simultaneously ask a lot of your trunk muscles; add the high breathing demand of repeated
short sprints up and down the court, and you have a recipe for loss of postural
control (or for injury). This exercise is designed to simulate a specific postural and
breathing challenge created by the game.

IMT loading level: moderate

External resistance: basketball

Duration: 60 to 90 seconds

Sets: 2 sets

Procedure: With your BMT in your mouth, your spine in a neutral position, and your
abdominal corset muscles braced (moderately), begin bouncing the ball at a steady
rate; as you do so, inhale forcefully through the BMT before exhaling slowly and
fully for about 4 seconds (breathing rate should be around 12 per minute). Swap
the hand that is controlling the ball periodically during each set.

Variations: To add difficulty, stand on a Bosu, or stand on one leg.

POINT PLANK

Benefits: This exercise simulates the demands of shooting, passing, or stickhandling in hockey. It will help you develop the ability to breathe effectively in situations where the need for postural control and stabilization is high.

IMT loading level: light

Duration: 8 to 12 repetitions

Sets: 1 or 2 sets

Procedure: Assume a prone push-up position, with your hands and feet both shoulder-width apart and with your BMT in your mouth. Brace the abdominal corset muscles (moderately) and touch your right hand to your left shoulder; hold momentarily, inhaling forcefully through your BMT. Return to the start position, exhaling as you do so. Alternate the lifted hand between repetitions, and switch breathing phases halfway through the set. Be careful not to compensate for a weak core by elevating the hips. A length of PVC pipe or a broomstick can be placed on your back to ensure strict form.

Variations: To add difficulty, place your hands or feet closer together, or use a balance cushion or Bosu.

SINGLE-LEG RUSSIAN DEADLIFT WITH PRESS

Benefits: This exercise challenges core stabilization in all three planes of movement. Along with the shoulder muscles, it also engages the gluteals and hamstrings, as well as encourages full hip extension. The latter is often neglected in hockey players whose sport is dominated by forward flexion at the hip.

IMT loading level: light

External resistance: dumbbell (22 to 44 pounds [10 to 20 kg])

Duration: 8 to 12 repetitions

Sets: 2 sets (1 on each side)

Procedure: Stand on one foot with a dumbbell in the opposite hand and your BMT in your mouth. Ensure that you have a neutral spine alignment, and brace the abdominal corset muscles (moderately). Lower the dumbbell toward your standing foot, so that your trunk is parallel to the floor and your free leg is extended behind you (a). As you lower the weight, inhale forcefully through your BMT. Next, extend at the hip until you are in the upright position, cleaning the dumbbell to the shoulder and pressing it overhead (b); exhale as you do this (concentrate on achieving full hip extension and engaging the gluteal). Swap breathing phases halfway through the set, and swap sides between sets. You may find the postural challenge of the full sequence too much to begin with, so build the exercise in stages (deadlift, then clean, then press).

Variations: To add difficulty, stand on a balance cushion or Bosu.

STRIDE GRID

Benefits: This exercise helps to maximize stride length and reinforce stride mechanics during skating. Skaters typically reduce stride length as they fatigue, compensating by increasing frequency, which makes them slower. The addition of a breathing challenge to this exercise helps to reinforce appropriate breathing while in the skating position. Posture and range of movement are the points of emphasis for this exercise.

IMT loading level: moderate to high

External resistance: dumbbells or a weighted vest

Duration: 10 to 15 repetitions

Sets: 1 or 2 sets

Procedure: See the description of the stride grid pattern below. The objective is to simulate the skating position with knees bent and trunk slightly flexed. With your BMT in your mouth, ensure that you have a neutral spine alignment, and brace the abdominal corset muscles (moderately). Begin in the skating position and take a lateral striding lunge, then reset with your feet together. Next, externally rotate the inside leg and take a diagonal step adjacent to the original position, facing the opposite direction, and repeat in the opposite direction. Inhale forcefully through your BMT as you stride, exhaling as you reset (swap breathing phases halfway through the set). Concentrate on maintaining proper posture throughout the movement, as well as on maximizing the length of each stride. Resist the tendency to raise the hips when your legs become fatigued.

Variations: To add difficulty, use dumbbells (holding these at your shoulder facilitates the use of heavier weights). Additional resistance can also be added to the trunk in the form of a weighted vest, which simulates the resistance of equipment.

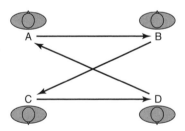

Stride grid pattern: Start at point A and take a lateral striding lunge toward point B. Maximize stride length and maintain skating position. Once at point B, reset, externally rotate the inside hip, and take a rotational lunge stride toward point C. Reset your position at point C, facing the opposite direction to the initial position at point A. Repeat C-D-A. One rep is A-B-C-D-A.

SINGLE-LEG BOX SQUAT

Benefits: Field hockey players are almost continuously in a semisquat position, leaning forward. This exercise involves the lumbopelvic stabilizers, gluteals, and quadriceps, as well as the hip flexors of the opposite leg. Not only does this exercise challenge the strength of these major muscle groups, but it also challenges your balance and coordination.

IMT loading level: moderate to heavy

External resistance: hockey stick, medicine ball, or other weight

Duration: 8 to 10 repetitions

Sets: 2 sets on each leg

Procedure: Stand on one foot on a box or deep step. With your BMT in your mouth and with your spine in a neutral position, brace the abdominal corset muscles (moderately). Once you are balanced, perform a controlled squat, extending your free leg and your arms in front of you. Squat as deeply as possible. Concentrate on not allowing the unsupported hip to drop. As you descend, inhale forcefully through your BMT; exhale as you rise to a standing position. Halfway through the set, swap breathing phases so that you exhale as you descend into the squat. On the second set, swap legs.

Variations: To add difficulty, increase the depth of the squat, stand on a balance cushion, or hold small weights or a medicine ball in your hands. You can also do this exercise holding a hockey stick. Move the weight between your hands during the exercise.

ALTERNATE ARM CABLE FLY

Benefits: In rugby, the objective of opposing players is to wrestle the ball from your grip. Whether you are on your feet or on the ground, the better your ability to resist being turned to face these opponents, the more likely you are to retain possession. This exercise targets the pectorals, thoracic rotators, and obliques, while also emphasizing stability and control of the lumbar spine, which should not rotate. Controlling trunk rotation under a turning force is the perfect training stimulus for improving resistance to being turned by an opponent.

IMT loading level: moderate

External resistance: double cable pulley machine

Duration: 15 to 20 repetitions

Sets: 2 or 4 sets

Procedure: Assume a normal cable fly position, with a wide stance, a cable in each hand, and your arms outstretched (elbows bent slightly) (a). Brace the abdominal corset muscles (moderately) and move one hand toward the midline (b), keeping the hips and lumbar spine in line; do not allow your trunk to rotate. As you move your arm forward, inhale forcefully through your BMT; then return (under control) to the start position, exhaling as you do so. Repeat for the other arm, inhaling through your BMT as you move your arm forward. On the second set, swap breathing phases so that you exhale as you move your arm forward. Emphasis should be placed on maintaining the brace and sustaining trunk alignment (do not rotate in the lumbar or thoracic region).

Variations: This exercise can also be undertaken with a single pulley (with the free hand held in the small of your back) or in an upright stance with knees slightly bent. To add difficulty, increase the weight lifted, or stand on one leg (opposite leg to loaded hand), a balance cushion, or a Bosu.

SINGLE-ARM STANDING CABLE PRESS

Benefits: This is another exercise that challenges the thoracic rotators and obliques, as well as the lats and pectorals. As with the Alternate Arm Cable Fly, this exercise improves your resistance to being turned by an opponent.

IMT loading level: moderate

External resistance: cable pulley machine or resistance band or cord

Duration: 15 to 20 repetitions

Sets: 2 sets on each side

Procedure: Assume a split stance with feet shoulder-width apart, the resistance in one hand, and your arm in the start position for a chest press (a). Brace the abdominal corset muscles (moderately) and press the resistance until your arm is fully extended; do not allow your trunk to rotate (b). As you press the resistance, inhale forcefully through your BMT; then return (under control) to the start position, exhaling as you do so. Swap breathing phases halfway through the set so that you are exhaling as you press. Swap arms on the second set. Emphasis should be placed on maintaining the brace and sustaining trunk alignment (do not rotate in the lumbar or thoracic region).

Variations: To add difficulty, increase the weight lifted, or stand on a Bosu.

BALL SNATCH

Benefits: Retaining possession is the name of any team sport, which means being able to move the ball away from an opponent quickly without losing balance or control. This exercise requires you to perform a series of multidirectional lunges while snatching a medicine ball or weight bag from one side of the body to the other. This exercise mimics the act of protecting the ball from an opposing player, and it challenges your ability to breathe while maintaining a strong core during a postural challenge. This is a very challenging exercise, and you may initially be unable to hold a moderately braced position independent of breathing. Master this before adding the BMT.

IMT loading level: moderate to heavy

External resistance: medicine ball or weight bag

Duration: 30 to 60 seconds

Sets: 3 sets

Procedure: Assume a half-squat position and grip the ball or bag firmly with both hands. With your BMT in your mouth, your spine in a neutral position, and your abdominal corset muscles braced (moderately), begin stepping (a). Each step should start with a lunge position in a different direction (including backward) and finish in a deep, forward-flexed position. As you step, move the ball or bag from one side of your body to the other, so your hands finish to the side of the forward thigh (b); inhale forcefully through your BMT on one step, and exhale on the next. Don't allow the abdominal brace to relax as you get tired.

CLOCKWISE WEIGHTED LUNGE

Benefits: Lunging is an integral part of all racket sports. This exercise involves the lumbopelvic stabilizers, gluteals, and quadriceps; it will prepare you for this fundamental challenge and the demands it places on your breathing, stabilizing, and postural control systems.

IMT loading level: moderate to heavy

External resistance: dumbbells

Duration: 30 to 60 seconds

Sets: 2 sets (1 on each side)

Procedure: Stand with your feet shoulder-width apart and with your BMT in your mouth (*a*); ensure that you have a neutral spine, and brace your abdominal corset muscles (moderately). Step forward into a deep lunge at the 12 o'clock position while inhaling forcefully through the BMT (*b*). Return to the start position, exhaling as you do so; lunge again, but this time to the 1 o'clock position. Repeat at "1-hour intervals" (*c*; 3 o'clock) until you have reached the 6 o'clock position, pivoting on your stationary foot. Repeat the sequence until the time is up. Swap breathing phases halfway through the set, and swap legs between sets.

Variations: You can add difficulty by increasing the depth of the lunge or by carrying dumbbells (holding these at the shoulder facilitates the use of heavier weights).

a b c

SLIDE BOARD LUNGE

Benefits: During a match, you will change direction hundreds of times. Because this exercise requires you to control and return the sliding leg, it challenges the hamstrings, as well as the muscles involved in a conventional lunge (the lumbo-pelvic stabilizers, gluteals, and quadriceps). This exercise will develop your ability to maintain breath control and a balanced, stable core.

IMT loading level: moderate to heavy

Duration: 30 to 60 seconds

Sets: 2 sets (1 on each side)

Procedure: This exercise requires a carpeted or slippery floor and a slide board or similar item (a large shiny Frisbee will do the job). Stand with one foot on the slide board, with your feet shoulder-width apart and your BMT in your mouth; ensure that you have a neutral spine, and brace your abdominal corset muscles (moderately). Slide your foot away from you into a lunge while inhaling forcefully through the BMT. Return to the start position by pulling your foot toward you, exhaling as you do so; then lunge again, but in a different direction. Swap breathing phases halfway through the set, and swap legs between sets.

Variations: To add difficulty, carry dumbbells (holding these at the shoulder facilitates the use of heavier weights), increase the depth of the lunge, or place a weight or racket in your hand and reach forward as you lunge (be sure to use the added weight on both sides to maintain balance).

RACKET LUNGE

Benefits: If you have to lunge and reach for a ball, chances are you will have to do so after a flurry of sprints and direction changes that will have you breathing heavily. The addition of an outstretched arm to this exercise is not only sport-specific, but it will also trigger the automatic contribution of the transversus abdominis and diaphragm in their postural control roles. This exercise places you in a potentially unstable posture that requires good core stability and postural control. It will help you develop breath and trunk control in the lunge position.

IMT loading level: moderate

External resistance: dumbbell, resistance band or cord, or racket

Duration: 60 seconds

Sets: 2 sets (1 on each side)

Procedure: Standing upright with your feet together and your BMT in your mouth, hold a dumbbell or racket in your dominant hand (if using a band or cord, anchor this under your stationary foot); ensure that you have a neutral spine, and brace your abdominal corset muscles (moderately) (a). Once in position, step forward with your dominant foot into a lunge, extending your arm in front of you (as if holding a racket) (b). As you lunge forward, inhale forcefully against your BMT; exhale as you return to the start position with your feet together and your arm at your side. Use a challenging but well-controlled stepping frequency, and swap breathing phases halfway through the set so that you exhale as you lunge forward. To avoid muscle imbalance, you should lead with your nondominant hand in the second set (imbalance equals injury risk).

Variations: To add difficulty, increase the magnitude of the resistance, step onto or from a balance cushion, or use lateral lunging at different angles.

STANDING RACKET SWING

Benefits: Swinging a racket disrupts postural control and can leave you off balance if you're not "set up" for it. This exercise involves the trunk rotator muscles and pectorals, and challenges your ability to rotate the trunk and arm while maintaining pelvic stability under a breathing challenge.

IMT loading level: moderate

External resistance: cable machine or resistance band or cord

Duration: 15 repetitions

Sets: 2 sets (1 on each side)

Procedure: Stand sideways to the cable column, with your feet shoulder-width apart and with your BMT in your mouth (*a*). Hold the resistance in your dominant hand (if using a band or cord, this can be anchored under your foot or tied to an immovable object); ensure that you have a neutral spine, and brace your abdominal corset muscles (moderately). Once in position, move your dominant hand through an arc in front of you and rotate your trunk as your arm reaches the end of the movements (*b*). Inhale forcefully against your BMT as you rotate; exhale as you return your arm to its start position. Concentrate on rotating your trunk and keeping your hips facing forward in order to emphasize thoracic rotation. Repeat the maneuver for the defined number of repetitions, swapping breathing phases halfway through the set so that you exhale as you bring your arm across in front of you. To maintain balance, you should use your nondominant side in the second set (imbalance equals injury risk).

Variations: To add difficulty, increase the magnitude of the resistance, or stand on a balance cushion or Bosu. By placing the resistance on the opposite side, you can simulate a backhand movement.

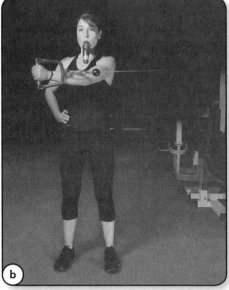

SPLIT SQUAT WITH RACKET SWING

Benefits: This exercise combines many of the challenges of the two previous exercises. It is an excellent way to develop your ability to produce a controlled stroke during a lunge, while also maintaining breath control.

IMT loading level: moderate

External resistance: cable machine or resistance band or cord

Duration: 15 repetitions

Sets: 2 sets (1 on each side)

Procedure: Assume a split-squat position (nondominant leg in front) sideways to the cable column with your BMT in your mouth (a). Hold the resistance in your outstretched dominant hand (if using a band or cord, this can be anchored under your front foot or tied to an immovable object at waist height on your dominant side); ensure that you have a neutral spine, and brace your abdominal corset muscles (moderately). Once balanced, move your dominant hand through an arc in front of you (b), inhaling forcefully against your BMT as you do so; exhale as you return your arm to its start position. Maintaining the split-squat position, repeat the maneuver for the defined number of repetitions, swapping breathing phases halfway through the set so that you exhale as you bring your arm across in front of you. To maintain balance, you should use your nondominant hand in the second set (imbalance equals injury risk).

Variations: To add difficulty, increase the magnitude of the resistance, or stand on a balance cushion.

OVERHEAD RACKET SWING

Benefits: This exercise produces a postural challenge that is similar to that created during an overhead shot. This type of challenge requires the anticipatory activation of a number of postural control muscles, including the transversus abdominis and diaphragm. The addition of a crunch and rotation at the end of the arm movement also involves the trunk flexor and rotator muscles. The exercise creates a posterior (backward) destabilizing force that must be counteracted by your core and diaphragm.

IMT loading level: moderate to heavy

External resistance: cable machine or resistance band or cord

Duration: 15 repetitions

Sets: 2 sets (1 on each side)

Procedure: Stand with your back to the cable column, your feet shoulder-width apart, and your BMT in your mouth. Hold the resistance in your dominant hand above your head (if using a band or cord, anchor this under your heel or tie it to an immovable object) (a); ensure that you have a neutral spine, and brace your abdominal corset muscles (moderately). Once in position, move your arm forward (b), finishing the movement with a twisting crunch forward, rotating your shoulder toward your midline slightly using your rib cage muscles (but keep your hips facing forward) (c). Inhale during the forward rotation of your arm, then exhale as you return to the start position. Repeat the maneuver for the defined number of repetitions, swapping breathing phases halfway through the set so that you exhale as you bring your arm forward. To avoid imbalance, hold the resistance in your nondominant hand for the second set (imbalance equals injury risk).

Variations: To add difficulty, increase the magnitude of the resistance, or stand on a Bosu or balance cushion.

a   b   c

RESISTED LATERAL RAISE

Benefits: Lifting your racket into position creates a postural challenge that requires the anticipatory activation of a number of postural control muscles, including the transversus abdominis and diaphragm. This exercise creates a lateral destabilizing force across your hips that must be counteracted by your core and diaphragm.

IMT loading level: moderate to heavy

External resistance: cable machine or resistance band or cord

Duration: 15 repetitions

Sets: 2 sets (1 on each side)

Procedure: With your BMT in your mouth, stand with your nondominant side to the cable column on your dominant foot (if using a band or cord, anchor this under the standing foot or tie it to an immovable object), holding the cable in your dominant hand (a); ensure that you have a neutral spine, and brace your abdominal corset muscles (moderately). Raise the hand swiftly to head height (b), keeping the cable close to and in line with your body (don't allow your hand to move forward or backward); as you raise your arm, inhale forcefully through the BMT. Concentrate on keeping your hips level at all times. Immediately lower your hand (under control) to your side, exhaling as you do so. Repeat for the defined number of repetitions, swapping breathing phases halfway through the set so that you inhale as your arm is lowered. To avoid imbalance, turn through 180 degrees and hold the resistance in your nondominant hand during the second set (imbalance equals injury risk).

Variations: To add difficulty, use a stronger band or cord (or use the cord under greater tension). You can also stand on a Bosu or balance cushion.

SINGLE-LEG BALANCE WITH RESISTED SHOULDER FLEXION

Benefits: This exercise accentuates the postural and breathing challenges that arise if you are reaching for a ball during a cross-court run. The exercise can be done with both hands, or it may be done with one hand (the opposite hand to your standing foot) to create a rotational challenge across the trunk and pelvis.

IMT loading level: moderate to heavy

External resistance: resistance band or cord

Duration: 15 repetitions

Sets: 2 sets (1 on each leg)

Procedure: Stand on one foot and anchor the middle of the band or cord under the standing foot, with one end in each hand (or in the opposite hand to your standing foot if doing this one handed); ensure that you have a neutral spine, and brace your abdominal corset muscles (moderately). With your BMT in your mouth, bend at the hip and extend your free leg behind you (a). Once in position, raise your hands in front of you as far as you can until level with your body (b); at the same time, inhale forcefully through your BMT. Hold the position momentarily before lowering your hands (under control), exhaling as you do so. Repeat the arm movement for the defined number of repetitions, swapping breathing phases halfway through the set so that you inhale as your arms are lowered. Swap standing legs between sets.

Variations: To add difficulty, use a stronger band or cord (or use the cord under greater tension). You can also stand on a Bosu or balance cushion.

FRONT ARM EXTENSION

Benefits: Opposing trunk rotation during an exercise is just as effective for developing the ability to produce rotational movements as actually rotating your trunk. This exercise creates a posterior (backward) rotational force that must be controlled during arm extension (as occurs when you swing your bat or club toward the ball).

IMT loading level: moderate to heavy

External resistance: cable machine or resistance band or cord

Duration: 15 to 20 repetitions

Sets: 2 sets (1 on each side)

Procedure: Stand with your back to the resistance, with your feet shoulder-width apart (*a*). Hold the resistance with both hands next to your shoulder (if using a band or cord, tie it to an immovable object above shoulder height). With your BMT in your mouth, ensure that you have a neutral spine, and brace your abdominal corset muscles (moderately). Keeping your trunk facing forward, extend your arms in front of you and to the center (a chopping action), inhaling forcefully through the BMT as you do so (*b*). Concentrate on keeping your entire body facing forward at all times. Swap breathing phases halfway through the set (exhale as you extend your arms), and swap sides between sets to avoid imbalance (imbalance equals injury).

Variations: To add difficulty, use a stronger band or cord (or use the cord under greater tension). You can also stand on a Bosu or balance cushion as well as on one leg (the opposite leg of the side on which the cable is held).

a

b

SPORT- AND ACTIVITY-SPECIFIC EXERCISES

LUNGE AND SWING

Benefits: Swinging a bat usually involves moving the body toward the ball while rotating your shoulders and arms to transfer as much rotational speed to the bat as possible. This exercise involves the gluteals, quadriceps, and trunk rotator muscles, requiring a sequential recruitment of the kinetic chain involved in generating bat speed.

IMT loading level: moderate to heavy

External resistance: cable machine with rope attachment or a resistance band or cord

Duration: 15 to 20 repetitions

Sets: 2 sets (1 on each side)

Procedure: Stand with your back to the resistance; your feet should be in a wide stance similar to one you'd use when striking the ball. Hold the rope firmly with a wide grip and with your arms behind you, but facing forward (if using a band or cord, tie it to an immovable object at shoulder height) (*a*). With your BMT in your mouth, ensure that you have a neutral spine, and brace your abdominal corset muscles (moderately). Step forward and simultaneously swing your arms in a wide arc, finishing in a lunge position (*b*). Then reverse the movement, returning to the start position. Inhale forcefully through the BMT as you swing your arms forward, and exhale during the return to the start position. Swap breathing phases halfway through the set (exhale as you swing forward), and swap sides between sets to avoid imbalance (imbalance equals injury).

ONE-LEG OVERHEAD CABLE PULLS

Benefits: Throwing requires the coordinated action of the anterior (front) chain of muscles. This exercise builds coordination (not strength) of these muscles. It involves the trunk muscles, lumbopelvic stabilizers, and hip flexors, emphasizing flexion at the hip while maintaining a stiff, strong trunk.

IMT loading level: moderate

External resistance: resistance band or cord, cable machine

Duration: 15 repetitions

Sets: 2 sets

Procedure: Stand on one leg, with your BMT in your mouth and with your arms extended above you holding the resistance (if using a band or cord, tie it to an immovable object above shoulder height) (*a*). Ensure that you have a straight body line between your ankle and shoulders, that you have a neutral spine, and that your abdominal corset muscles are braced (lightly). Flex forward, rotating at the hip (*b*), and inhale forcefully through your BMT as you do so. Exhale as you return to the upright start position. Swap breathing phases between sets so that you exhale as you flex forward.

Variations: This exercise can also be performed one-handed to create a rotational challenge across the trunk and pelvis (the resistance should be held in the opposite hand to the supporting foot). To add difficulty, increase the size of the resistance, or stand on a balance cushion.

SPORT- AND ACTIVITY-SPECIFIC EXERCISES

STANDING CABLE CHEST PRESS WITH LUNGE

Benefits: This exercise addresses the anterior (front) and rotational musculature by applying the load via one hand in a way that creates a rotational force. As a result, the exercise helps develop rotational as well as anterior control. The exercise involves the gluteals, quadriceps, and lumbopelvic stabilizers, as well as the trunk muscles (including the obliques) and pectorals. The addition of the lunge provides added instability and promotes a drive from one foot.

IMT loading level: moderate

External resistance: resistance band or cord, cable machine

Duration: 15 repetitions

Sets: 2 sets (1 on each side)

Procedure: Begin with your feet shoulder-width apart and with your BMT in your mouth. Hold the resistance in one hand, with your hand near your shoulder (if using a band or cord, tie it to an immovable object above shoulder height) (a). Ensure that you have a neutral spine, and brace your abdominal corset muscles (lightly). Press the handle of the cable away from you, lunging forward as you do so (b). As you move forward, inhale forcefully through your BMT. Exhale as you return to the upright start position. Swap breathing phases halfway through the set so that you exhale as you move forward. Swap sides between sets.

Variations: To add difficulty, increase the size of the resistance, or step off or onto a balance cushion.

ROTATING CHEST PRESS

Benefits: Forceful trunk rotation is an integral part of all racket, striking, and throwing sports. The exercise involves the trunk rotator muscles and pectorals, and combines stabilization with controlled, full-range trunk rotation. In contrast to some preceding exercises, this exercise adds hip rotation to trunk rotation to involve the hip rotators in the kinetic chain of the movement. The strong rotational element compresses and stiffens the rib cage and abdomen, making inhalation more challenging.

IMT loading level: moderate

External resistance: cable pulley machine or resistance cord or band

Duration: 15 to 20 repetitions

Sets: 2 sets (1 on each side)

Procedure: Stand with your back to the resistance, holding the handle with one hand at shoulder height (if using a band or cord, tie it to an immovable object at shoulder height). Adopt a split stance, with your opposite foot in front (*a*). With your BMT in your mouth, your spine in a neutral position, and your abdominal corset muscles braced (moderately), rotate your shoulders, trunk, and hips away from the resistance and press the cable away from you (*b*); concentrate on maximizing trunk rotation range of movement. Reverse the movement to return to the start position. Inhale forcefully through your BMT as you rotate and press, and exhale during the return to the start position; swap breathing phases halfway through the set so that you exhale as you rotate and press. Swap sides between sets.

ASSISTED CROSSOVER LUNGE

Benefits: Remaining balanced and poised at all times is an essential skill in sports that necessitate weight transfer and trunk rotation. This exercise involves the lumbopelvic stabilizers, gluteals, and quadriceps, and challenges postural control during a rotating lunge that is assisted by an external pulling force.

IMT loading level: moderate

External resistance: cable pulley machine or resistance cord or band

Duration: 15 to 20 repetitions

Sets: 2 sets (1 on each side)

Procedure: Stand sideways to the resistance, which should be attached to your waist via a belt or similar device (if using a band or cord, tie it to an immovable object at waist height). Stand with your feet slightly more than shoulder-width apart, your BMT in your mouth, your spine in a neutral position, and your abdominal corset muscles braced (moderately) (a). Commence by pivoting on the foot closest to the resistance, rotating your body so that you are facing the resistance, and lunge down (b). Concentrate on maintaining vertical alignment of the head, shoulders, and hips in a strict lunge. Then push back firmly to return to the start position. Inhale forcefully through your BMT as you rotate and lunge, and exhale during the return to the start position; swap breathing phases halfway through the set so that you exhale as you rotate and lunge. Swap sides between sets.

Variations: To add difficulty, carry dumbbells during the exercise.

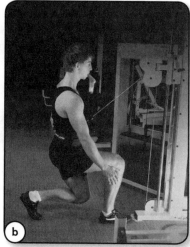

RESISTED CROSSOVER LUNGE

Benefits: This exercise is paired with the previous exercise (Assisted Crossover Lunge) and also involves the lumbopelvic stabilizers, gluteals, and quadriceps. It challenges postural control during a rotating lunge, but this time, the pulling force opposes the rotational movement.

IMT loading level: moderate

External resistance: cable pulley machine or resistance cord or band

Duration: 15 to 20 repetitions

Sets: 2 sets (1 on each side)

Procedure: Stand sideways to the resistance, which should be attached to your waist via a belt or similar device (if using a band or cord, tie it to an immovable object at waist height) (a). Stand with your feet slightly wider than shoulder-width apart, your BMT in your mouth, your spine in a neutral position, and your abdominal corset muscles braced (moderately). Pivot on the foot farthest from the resistance, rotating your body so that you are facing away from the resistance, and lunge down (b). Concentrate on maintaining vertical alignment of the head, shoulders, and hips in a strict lunge. Then push back firmly to return to the start position. Inhale forcefully through your BMT as you rotate and lunge, and exhale during the return to the start position; swap breathing phases halfway through the set so that you exhale as you rotate and lunge. Swap sides between sets.

Variations: To add difficulty, carry dumbbells during the exercise.

References

Armour, J., Donnelly, P.M., & Bye, P.T. (1993). The large lungs of elite swimmers: An increased alveolar number? *European Respiratory Journal, 6,* 237-247.

Boyle, M.J. (2010). *Advances in functional training.* Aptos, CA: On Target Publications.

Caine, M.P., & McConnell, A.K. (1998). Pressure threshold inspiratory muscle training improves submaximal cycling performance. In A.J. Sargeant & H. Siddons (Eds.), *Third Annual Conference of the European College of Sport Science* (p. 101). Manchester, UK: The Centre for Health Care Development.

Caine, M.P., & McConnell, A.K. (1998). The inspiratory muscles can be trained differentially to increase strength or endurance using a pressure threshold, inspiratory muscle training device. *European Respiratory Journal, 12,* 58-59.

Caine, M.P., & McConnell, A.K. (2000). Development and evaluation of a pressure threshold inspiratory muscle trainer for use in the context of sports performance. *Journal of Sports Engineering, 3,* 149-159.

Chatham, K., Conway, J., Enright, S., Oliver, W., Trott, J., & Campbell, I.A. (1995). A new test of incremental respiratory endurance (TIRE). *American Journal of Respiratory and Critical Care Medicine, 151,* A416.

Cook, G. (2003). *Athletic body in balance: Optimal movement skills and conditioning for performance.* Champaign, IL: Human Kinetics.

DePalo, V.A., Parker, A.L., Al-Bilbeisi, F., & McCool, F.D. (2004). Respiratory muscle strength training with nonrespiratory maneuvers. *Journal of Applied Physiology, 96,* 731-734.

Dickinson, J.W., Whyte, G.P., McConnell, A.K., & Harries, M.G. (2005). Impact of changes in the IOC-MC asthma criteria: A British perspective. *Thorax, 60,* 629-632.

Donnelly, J.E., Blair, S.N., Jakicic, J.M., Manore, M.M., Rankin, J.W., & Smith, B.K. (2009). American College of Sports Medicine position stand. Appropriate physical activity intervention strategies for weight loss and prevention of weight regain for adults. *Medicine & Science in Sports Exercise, 41,* 459-471.

Downey, A.E., Chenoweth, L.M., Townsend, D.K., Ranum, J.D., Ferguson, C.S., & Harms, C.A. (2007). Effects of inspiratory muscle training on exercise responses in normoxia and hypoxia. *Respiratory Physiology & Neurobiology, 156,* 137-146.

Edwards, A.M., & Cooke, C.B. (2004). Oxygen uptake kinetics and maximal aerobic power are unaffected by inspiratory muscle training in healthy subjects where time to exhaustion is extended. *European Journal of Applied Physiology, 93,* 139-144.

Edwards, A.M., Wells, C., & Butterly, R. (2008). Concurrent inspiratory muscle and cardiovascular training differentially improves both perceptions of effort and 5000 m running performance compared with cardiovascular training alone. *British Journal of Sports Medicine, 42,* 523-527.

Enright, S.J., Unnithan, V.B., Heward, C., Withnall, L., & Davies, D.H. (2006). Effect of high-intensity inspiratory muscle training on lung volumes, diaphragm thickness, and exercise capacity in subjects who are healthy. *Physical Therapy, 86,* 345-354.

Fredericson, M., & Moore, T. (2005). Core stabilization training for middle- and long-distance runners. *IAAF New Studies in Athletics, 1* (20), 25-37.

Fry, A.C. (2004). The role of resistance exercise intensity on muscle fibre adaptations. *Sports Medicine, 34,* 663-679.

Gamble, P. (2010). *Strength and conditioning for team sports: Sport-specific physical preparation for high performance.* Oxford: Routledge.

Gething, A.D., Williams, M., & Davies, B. (2004). Inspiratory resistive loading improves cycling capacity: A placebo controlled trial. *British Journal of Sports Medicine, 38,* 730-736.

Griffiths, L.A., & McConnell, A.K. (2007). The influence of inspiratory and expiratory muscle training upon rowing performance. *European Journal of Applied Physiology, 99,* 457-466.

Harms, C.A., Babcock, M.A., McClaran, S.R., Pegelow, D.F., Nickele, G.A., Nelson, W.B., & Dempsey, J.A. (1997). Respiratory muscle work compromises leg blood flow during maximal exercise. *Journal of Applied Physiology, 82*, 1573-1583.

Hodges, P.W., Eriksson, A.E., Shirley, D., & Gandevia, S.C. (2005). Intra-abdominal pressure increases stiffness of the lumbar spine. *Journal of Biomechanics, 38*, 1873-1880.

Hodges, P.W., Heijnen, I., & Gandevia, S.C. (2001). Postural activity of the diaphragm is reduced in humans when respiratory demand increases. *Journal of Physiology, 537*, 999-1008.

Holm, P., Sattler, A., & Fregosi, R.F. (2004). Endurance training of respiratory muscles improves cycling performance in fit young cyclists. *BioMed Central Physiology, 4*, 9.

Impellizzeri, F.M., Rampinini, E., Maffiuletti, N.A., Castagna, C., Bizzini, M., & Wisloff, U. (2008). Effects of aerobic training on the exercise-induced decline in short-passing ability in junior soccer players. *Applied Physiology, Nutrition & Metabolism, 33*, 1192-1198.

Isacowitz, R. (2006). *Pilates: Your complete guide to mat work and apparatus exercises*. Champaign, IL: Human Kinetics.

Jakovljevic, D.G., & McConnell, A.K. (2009). Influence of different breathing frequencies on the severity of inspiratory muscle fatigue induced by high-intensity front crawl swimming. *Journal of Strength & Conditioning Research, 23*, 1169-1174.

Janssens L., Brumagne, S., Polspoel, K., Troosters, T., & McConnell, A. (2010). The effect of inspiratory muscles fatigue on postural control in people with and without recurrent low back pain. *Spine (Phila Pa 1976), 35*, 1088-1094.

Johnson, M.A., Sharpe, G.R., & Brown, P.I. (2007). Inspiratory muscle training improves cycling time-trial performance and anaerobic work capacity but not critical power. *European Journal of Applied Physiology, 101*, 761-770.

Kaminoff, L. (2009). *Yoga anatomy*. Champaign, IL: Human Kinetics.

Kilding, A.E., Brown, S., & McConnell, A.K. (2009). Inspiratory muscle training improves 100 and 200 m swimming performance. *European Journal of Applied Physiology, 108*, 505-515.

Laursen, P.B., Shing, C.M., Peake, J.M., Coombes, J.S., & Jenkins, D.G. (2002). Interval training program optimization in highly trained endurance cyclists. *Medicine & Science in Sports Exercise, 34*, 1801-1807.

Leddy, J.J., Limprasertkul, A., Patel, S., Modlich, F., Buyea, C., Pendergast, D.R., & Lundgren, C.E. (2007). Isocapnic hyperpnea training improves performance in competitive male runners. *European Journal of Applied Physiology, 99*, 665-676.

Lin, H., Tong, T.K., Huang, C., Nie, J., Lu, K., & Quach, B. (2007). Specific inspiratory muscle warm-up enhances badminton footwork performance. *Applied Physiology, Nutrition & Metabolism, 32*, 1082-1088.

Lomax, M.E., & McConnell, A.K. (2003). Inspiratory muscle fatigue in swimmers after a single 200 m swim. *Journal of Sports Science, 21*, 659-664.

Markov, G., Spengler, C.M., Knopfli-Lenzin, C., Stuessi, C., & Boutellier, U. (2001). Respiratory muscle training increases cycling endurance without affecting cardiovascular responses to exercise. *European Journal of Applied Physiology, 85*, 233-239.

McConnell, A.K., & Griffiths, L.A. (2010). Acute cardiorespiratory responses to inspiratory pressure threshold loading. *Medicine & Science in Sports Exercise, 42*, 1696-1703.

McConnell, A.K., & Romer, L.M. (2004). Respiratory muscle training in healthy humans: Resolving the controversy. *International Journal of Sports Medicine, 25*, 284-293.

McGill, S. (2007). *Low back disorders: Evidence-based prevention and rehabilitation*. Champaign, IL: Human Kinetics.

McMahon, M.E., Boutellier, U., Smith, R.M., & Spengler, C.M. (2002). Hyperpnea training attenuates peripheral chemosensitivity and improves cycling endurance. *Journal of Experimental Biology, 205*, 3937-3943.

Nicks, C.R., Morgan, D.W., Fuller, D.K., & Caputo, J.L. (2009). The influence of respiratory muscle training upon intermittent exercise performance. *International Journal of Sports Medicine, 30*, 16-21.

Ranney, D. (2008). Breathing to improve your game. *Tennis Life,* March/April, 31.

Romer, L.M., & McConnell, A.K. (2003). Specificity and reversibility of inspiratory muscle training. *Medicine & Science in Sports Exercise,* 35, 237-244.

Romer, L.M., McConnell, A.K., & Jones, D.A. (2002a). Effects of inspiratory muscle training on time-trial performance in trained cyclists. *Journal of Sports Science,* 20, 547-562.

Romer, L.M., McConnell, A.K., & Jones, D.A. (2002b). Effects of inspiratory muscle training upon recovery time during high intensity, repetitive sprint activity. *International Journal of Sports Medicine,* 23, 353-360.

Rundell, K.W., & Jenkinson, D.M. (2002). Exercise-induced bronchospasm in the elite athlete. *Sports Medicine,* 32, 583-600.

Sheel, A.W., Derchak, P.A., Pegelow, D.F., & Dempsey, J.A. (2002). Threshold effects of respiratory muscle work on limb vascular resistance. *American Journal of Physiology: Heart & Circulatory Physiology,* 282, H1732-1738.

Sovndal, S. (2009). *Cycling anatomy.* Champaign, IL: Human Kinetics.

Stuessi, C., Spengler, C.M., Knopfli-Lenzin, C., Markov, G., & Boutellier, U. (2001). Respiratory muscle endurance training in humans increases cycling endurance without affecting blood gas concentrations. *European Journal of Applied Physiology,* 84, 582-586.

Tong, T.K., & Fu, F.H. (2006). Effect of specific inspiratory muscle warm-up on intense intermittent run to exhaustion. *European Journal of Applied Physiology,* 97, 673-680.

Tong, T.K., Fu, F.H., Chung, P.K., Eston, R., Lu, K., Quach, B., Nie, J., & So, R. (2008). The effect of inspiratory muscle training on high-intensity, intermittent running performance to exhaustion. *Applied Physiology, Nutrition & Metabolism,* 33, 671-681.

Tsatsouline, P. (2000). *Power to the people!: Russian strength training secrets for every American.* St. Paul, MN: Dragon Door Publications Inc.

Verges, S., Boutellier, U., & Spengler, C.M. (2008). Effect of respiratory muscle endurance training on respiratory sensations, respiratory control and exercise performance: A 15-year experience. *Respiratory Physiology & Neurobiology,* 161, 16-22.

Volianitis, S., McConnell, A.K., Koutedakis, Y., & Jones, D.A. (2001). Specific respiratory warm-up improves rowing performance and exertional dyspnea. *Medicine & Science in Sports Exercise,* 33, 1189-1193.

Volianitis, S., McConnell, A.K., Koutedakis, Y., McNaughton, L., Backx, K., & Jones, D.A. (2001). Inspiratory muscle training improves rowing performance. *Medicine & Science in Sports Exercise,* 33, 803-809.

Wagner, P.D. (2005). Why doesn't exercise grow the lungs when other factors do? *Exercise & Sport Science Reviews,* 33, 3-8.

Index

Note: The italicized *f* and *t* following page numbers refer to figures and tables, respectively.

About the Author

Alison McConnell holds a BSc in biological sciences from the University of Birmingham (UK) and an MSc in human physiology and a PhD in respiratory physiology from the University of London (UK). Alison is a professor of applied physiology at Brunel University in London. She is a fellow of both the American College of Sports Medicine and the British Association of Sport and Exercise Sciences (BASES) and is a BASES-accredited physiologist. McConnell is acknowledged as a leading authority on breathing muscle training and is the author of numerous scientific articles and book chapters. She is a regular presenter at international scientific and medical conferences.

McConnell is the inventor of POWERbreathe, a breathing muscle training system created in the early 1990s. She pioneered the introduction of breathing muscle training into athlete preparation and has worked with Olympic and world champions around the world to help them to optimize the use of POWERbreathe in their preparation for competition. She has also been influential in the acceptance of breathing muscle training as a treatment for breathlessness in patients with lung disease, and POWERbreathe is now a prescribed treatment within the UK National Health Service.

Alison remains an avid sportswoman with an active involvement in running, cycling, weight training, skiing, and windsurfing.

The evolution of POWERbreathe training

2009
ActiBreathe
Complete body conditioning programmes, DVDs and accessories that integrate POWERbreathe training to develop breathing strength ...st toning and sculpting ...ntire body.

2001 Classic
The result of intense research trials and development by sci...
at Birmingham and Loughborough Univ...

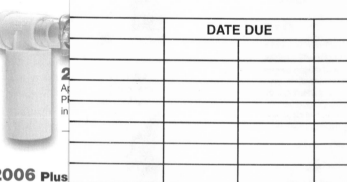

2...
Ap...
PF...
in...

2006 Plus
Improved features...
better airflow dyna...
antibacterial mout...
and ergonomic de...

	DATE DUE	

...ERbreathe®
...ic downloadable
...of the much
...POWERbreathe
...4 and K5 models
...grated PC interface
...wnloadability. Enables
...sable training, testing
...itoring.

...WER®
...eathe